The Making of Telecommunications Policy

Explorations in Public Policy

The Making of Telecommunications Policy

Dick W. Olufs III

BOULDER
LONDON

Published in the United States of America in 1999 by
Lynne Rienner Publishers, Inc.
1800 30th Street, Boulder, Colorado 80301

and in the United Kingdom by
Lynne Rienner Publishers, Inc.
3 Henrietta Street, Covent Garden, London WC2E 8LU

Library of Congress Cataloging-in-Publication Data
Olufs, Dick.
The making of telecommunications policy / Dick W. Olufs III.
p. cm. — (Explorations in public policy)
Includes bibliographical references and index.
ISBN 1-55587-707-9 (alk. paper)
1. Telecommunication policy—United States. I. Title.
II. Series.
HE7781.038 1998
384'.0973—dc21 98-7499
CIP

British Cataloguing in Publication Data
A Cataloguing in Publication record for this book
is available from the British Library.

Printed and bound in the United States of America

The paper used in this publication meets the requirements
of the American National Standard for Permanence of
Paper for Printed Library Materials Z39.48-1984.

5 4 3 2 1

Contents

Acknowledgments

Many people were helpful and encouraging to me in the preparation of this book. Ranjit Rakhra got the ball rolling, and I offer the book to him as a way of saying thank you. E. Wayne Carp, Robert J. Duffy, Barry Orton, Don Riesman, James Savage, David Schuman, and three anonymous reviewers helped in a variety of ways, ranging from friendly encouragement to long and detailed explanations of my errors. Their advice kept the project interesting and challenging, and I am grateful.

—Dick W. Olufs III

Acknowledgments

Acronyms

ACLU	American Civil Liberties Union
APA	Administrative Procedures Act
AT&T	American Telephone and Telegraph
CDA	Communications Decency Act
CFA	Consumer Federation of America
DBS	direct broadcasting satellite
DLC	Democratic Leadership Council
DOJ	Department of Justice
FCC	Federal Communications Commission
FTC	Federal Trade Commission
GTE	General Telephone and Electronics
HDTV	High Definition Television
ICC	Interstate Commerce Commission
ISDN	Integrated Services Digital Network
LEC	local exchange carrier
MCI	Microwave Communications, Inc.
MFJ	Modified Final Judgment
MSN	Microsoft Network
NARUC	National Association of Regulatory Utility Commissioners
NCSL	National Conference of State Legislatures
NII	National Information Infrastructure
NRC	National Research Council
OTA	Office of Technology Assessment
OVS	open video systems
PEG	public, educational, and governmental
PNB	Pacific Northwest Bell
RBOC	regional Bell operating company
USTA	United States Telephone Association
WIPO	World Intellectual Property Organization
WUTC	Washington Utilities and Transportation Commission

1 Introduction

It was spring 1993. An eleven-year-old boy, a bright boy, asked to use my telephone. I pointed him to the rotary telephone mounted on the wall. He picked up the receiver and looked at the rotary dialer for about ten seconds. Then he turned to me and said, "How do you work this thing?"

Telecommunications technologies are changing—so rapidly that an item like a rotary telephone can change from a common item in America's kitchens to a mysterious antique in ten short years.

Telecommunications—the transmission and reception of information over wires and through the electromagnetic spectrum—are important to us. Transmitters and receivers are found all around us and are part of everyday life for most citizens. The way most people work, play, consume, socialize, and learn about their world is organized around telecommunications. Drafts of this book took electronic form and traveled between authors, editors, and typesetters; without that transformation, production costs would have been far higher. Someone watches television in most households for, on average, more than a third of waking hours. The average person uses a telephone several times each day. It is a rare business that does not rely on dependable telecommunications that link them to customers and suppliers.

Governments in the United States have regulated telecommunications since the invention of the telephone in 1876. For a good portion of this period, government agencies were closely involved in telecommunications companies—deciding who could enter the business, what each company could and could not own, what services could and could not be offered, and what prices the companies could charge for those services. In the 1970s, national policymakers began to change the role of government in the regulation of telecommunications. Over the next two decades, they produced fundamental changes in policy, although telecommunications was, compared to other policy areas, slow to be added to the trend to deregulation.

In February 1996, President Bill Clinton signed the Telecommunications Act of 1996.[1] According to the claims of the bipartisan supporters of the act, the new law would create at least ten million new jobs, dramatically transform telecommunications industries, enable U.S. companies to lead the world in developing and selling new technologies, hasten and enlarge the spread of new technologies in the domestic market, and dramatically lower prices for consumers. Judging by such claims, the act was the single largest economic policy passed by either the 103rd or 104th Congress.

The bill's supporters claimed these alleged benefits would result from the variety of policies embodied in the bill. The new law permitted the regional Bell operating companies (RBOCs), over time and under specified conditions, to engage in long-distance service outside their areas, to manufacture equipment, and, in general, act like the old AT&T out of which the RBOCs were created in an earlier regulatory bargain. Rules about concentrated ownership of stations by media companies were virtually eliminated. Cable television regulations, again over time and under specified conditions, were relaxed, including those prohibiting telephone companies from entering the business. The bill applied stricter rules on obscenity and "indecency" in telecommunications, including computer services like the Internet and a rating system for television programming. Except for the obscenity and indecency provisions, the general direction of the bill was touted by the president and congressional leaders as an application of deregulation and competitive markets. Yet the bill contained contradictory language. Many of the staunchest supporters of competition were surprised that the legislation called for a continuing and vigorous role for federal regulators. The ideas underlying the consensus seemed to be more important than the actual content of rules.

During an interview, a lobbyist for one of the major regional telephone companies said that the "industry is happy" with the bill. Proponents of the bill included the major regional telephone companies, long-distance telephone companies, cable television companies, wireless communications companies, television broadcasters, and computer software companies. One obvious reason many were pleased with the act was that they would soon be allowed to enter businesses formerly closed to them: cable companies might be able to become telephone companies, and vice versa; and broadcasters might be able to become wireless communications companies. The blending of computer and communications technologies opened new opportunities for software companies. Some of the new opportunities might come at the expense of other proponents of the act, but the potential conflicts were hypothetical. The telecommunications industries generally agreed that deregulation was good policy.

Opponents of the bill included a host of small public-oriented interest groups that together warned of several dangers inherent in a policy so much desired by industry. Some argued that deregulation would enable companies to raise prices and gouge customers. Some argued that communications are similar to roads, an essential part of the infrastructure of everyday life, and as such should be closely regulated or even owned and operated by public agencies. Some argued that the bill would encourage industrial concentration, leading to an undesirable growth of corporate power. Others argued that the bill lacked adequate protection for the interests of the poor and others who might be left behind in a race to embrace new technologies. Lobbying by some of these groups did contribute to changes incorporated into the act, but for the most part these groups were small and relatively powerless.

What did the conflict show us about policy? This book describes how telecommunications legislation illustrates several things about policymaking in the United States.

• Highly technical policy issues are largely ignored by the general public. Organized interests with specific designs on the resources of government—whether economic, juridical, or symbolic—are virtually the sole voices heard by elected officials. In the case of the telecommunications bill, the large corporations that lead the affected industries were clearly the dominant voices, although significant differences divided potential corporate rivals. These interests conceived of citizens mainly as consumers, and policymakers for the most part adopted this view. Many small groups sought to speak for a larger public interest but did so in name only, without the participation, support, or understanding of the general citizenry.

• Power is divided in the U.S. federal system, but where national economic forces are involved, state sovereignty is limited. The legislation acknowledged a continuing role for state regulation of telecommunications, but implementation over a five-year period was to reduce this to a shadow of its former self. Federalism indirectly influenced the general direction of the legislation, in that the antitax and deregulation themes that had worked so powerfully in the states provided a conceptual framework shared by national and state elected officials and contributed to the lack of involvement of state officials in the legislative process.

• Ideas have consequences. The consensus underlying the legislation, and the general quiescence of those not directly jostling for preferred language in the bill, was a product of a consensus in national economic policy that had developed and then solidified over the previous forty years. Mainstream economists began to shift views regarding the desirability of direct government regulation as early as the late 1950s and were decidedly skeptical within a decade. Scholars of the policy process joined the shift by the late 1970s, which had fairly immediate effects on national policy debates. In the wake of these changes, policymakers and citizens who understood little or nothing about the legislation could make comfortable and quick judgments through code words like *deregulation* and *competition.*

• The shift in ideas underlying the legislation helps to illuminate the fortunes of the two major political parties. Democrats had in an earlier decade been the chief advocates of regulation of areas like telecommunications. Democratic leaders of the 103rd Congress and in the Clinton presidency agreed that less regulation would lead to faster economic growth, which on balance would provide more benefits than existing regulation. Republicans were in the majority in both houses of the 104th Congress, but views of economic policy changed only a little. The legislation that emerged from the Republican Congress differed in only minor ways from a bill that nearly passed under the Democrats the previous year.

• For students of U.S. politics who look for signs that democracy is alive and well, the telecommunications legislation can be interpreted as a sign that where consensus exists, government acts. In this sense, our government is not ineffective even when major institutions are led by rival political parties, as in the case of the Democratic president and the Republican 104th Congress. For students of U.S. politics who look for signs that the policy process ignores important dimensions of pressing problems, the legislation also contains a lesson. What appears as consensus may not be closely examined by the parties that form a policy coalition, and the public interest enacted in the policy system becomes, by definition, the sum of narrow private interests that capture the ear of elected officials. When consensus is the test of good policy, other ways of understanding policy are nudged aside.

The preceding list is a simplification of a complicated policy process. Various interests attempted to wield influence in an array of institutions that contribute to telecommunications policy. Biases in the policy process, tactics and resources brought to bear for applying pressure, leadership, and analysis are among the many relevant features. How can the story be told?

This analysis approaches the topic through two models of policymaking. The first focuses on the interplay of interest groups, events, and institutions—a variant of the "garbage can" model.[2] Here it is referred to as the *political model.* The second focuses on the knowledge requirements for reasoned policymaking, an application of the simple idea that actions are directed at achieving purposes, and direction is based on experience acquired in attempts to achieve desired ends. Here it is referred to as the *analytical model.*

The story is not a matter of showing one model is right and the other wrong. Both help us understand policymaking. We need both models because real life is complicated. In democratic policymaking, points of view are representations of real people, who see the world through many different perspectives, pursue conflicting interests, and have different experiences.

The policies enacted by government are the product of compromise—which might mean that no sane person would have chosen the same way. Yet we try to make sense of political life. We still ask, is this wise policy? The analytical model tries to make sense of the policy in light of knowledge acquired through experience. The two models are a way to make sense of the interplay between reason and collective action.

The double approach makes ontological sense as well. Each model provides a window into a blind spot of the other. Our thinking commonly involves a sharp dichotomy between analysis and affect. Humans use emotions to make sense of the world; they constitute intentional and intelligent judgments.[3] The logic within emotions is often not explicit, but it can be made so. The attachment we have to certain ideas or affect in politics reveals itself in the political model. In most treatments of policymaking, it is regarded as an exogenous force. This creates an inherent bias against understanding the importance of ideas in the policy process. The analytical model directs us to ask whether attachments to ideas survive the test of experience. Here ideas are endogenous. Unwillingness to subject ideas to reasoned scrutiny is a fact of life in politics, which the political model accepts; the analytical model examines its effects on choice.

A Political Model of Policymaking

Telecommunications policy is not made in a single institution of national government. Instead, several organs of the national government, as well as state governments, are involved in important decisions. Moreover, telecommunications technologies are embedded in the everyday lives of almost every citizen. And perhaps most important, the process leading to the themes embodied in the Telecommunications Act of 1996 culminated a more than twenty-year struggle among a wide variety of political actors. The story of telecommunications policy requires a model of policymaking that encompasses changes in officials, organizations, ideas, and decisions over a long period. The story requires a historical analysis.

John Kingdon produced an approach to policy that encompasses these factors and lends itself to historical analysis. To begin with, he pays closest attention to the agenda-setting portions of the policymaking process.[4]

- An *agenda* is the list of subjects or problems to which government officials and interested private parties pay some serious attention.
- Once a problem is on an agenda, *alternatives* are somehow considered by officials within their institutions.
- *Decisionmaking* and *implementation* are later stages, where government takes action and actually devotes resources to changing

> some part of the world. For those interested in the role of ideas in the policy process, the action lies in setting an agenda and posing a limited set of alternative approaches to policy.

With this focus, Kingdon embarked on a general study of trends in public policy. He asked officials and lobbyists what issues and problems they considered important and what kinds of alternatives they had in mind. He did this during the years 1976–1979, when deregulation became a trend in Washington.

Kingdon found that the most influential people in getting items on institutional agendas are—few surprises here—the administration (a president and political appointees), elected representatives, and congressional staffers. Interest groups are not far behind in getting ideas on agendas, although their main effect seems to come more in blocking items for consideration. Academics and researchers seem to affect the alternatives considered more than the agenda itself, and civil servants seem to be somewhat influential in selection of alternatives and very influential in implementation. The media did not seem to be very important in setting agendas and selecting alternatives.

Ideas seem to come to officials in different branches of government simultaneously. To use a metaphor, it seems that ideas become ripe for the picking. Kingdon instructs us to respect the power of an idea whose time has come. He explains the ripening of ideas with a variant of the garbage can model of policymaking. Policy is not the product of a clear or rational process, or even variations on previous policy. It is rather like a garbage can—lots of things produced by separate processes get thrown in, and in the rare instances where the separate processes converge on a similar idea, policy can be affected.

Figure 1.1 depicts the main concepts in Kingdon's model. It uses a metaphor of converging streams to suggest how several variables explain why an idea's time has come.

- The *problem stream* consists of government officials who routinely deal with indicators of problems; events such as disasters that focus attention on problems; and feedback on existing policies—always within the context of a limited budget. Telecommunications regulators monitored their industry through indicators such as mean time between request for new line service and installation or return on investment. Focusing events grab the attention of the public and public officials and prompt some kind of response, as in the case of the telephone system failure in Manhattan in 1966. Regulators and legislators have channels through which they receive feedback on existing policies, including annual budget hearings, meetings with constituents, and industry conferences. Budgets are a context for

Figure 1.1 A Political Model of the Policy Process

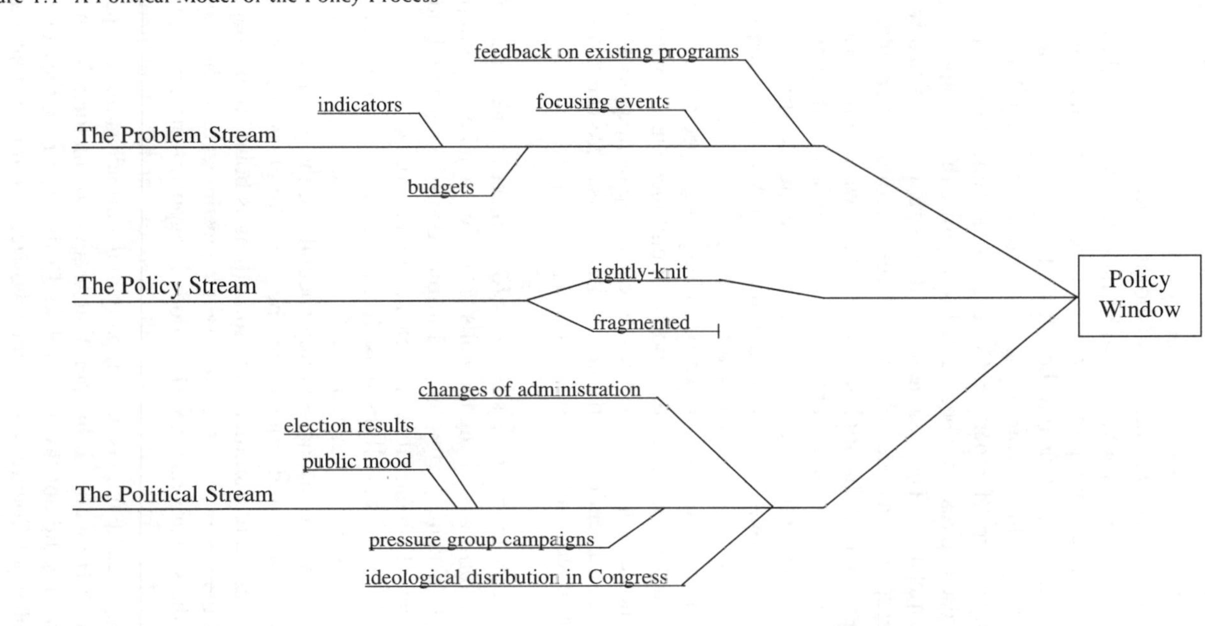

Source: This figure is adapted from John W. Kingdon, *Agendas, Alternatives, and Public Policies* (Boston: Little, Brown, 1984).

understanding problems. For example, as telecommunications legislation made its way through the 104th Congress, the Congress and president were locked in a series of budget duels that led to the temporary closing of many national government offices. A bill that promised to reduce the regulatory budget and deliver new nontax dollars to the treasury had an intrinsic appeal to these elected officials.

• The *policy stream* consists of communities of policy specialists. These are employees of a variety of organizations—what they share is a professional interest in a policy area. A policy community might be fairly tight-knit, such as in the field of health, or fairly fragmented, as in the case of transportation. In telecommunications policy, the regulators were just one of many centers of expertise. Congressional committee staffers and industry representatives were persuasive in arguing that the approach to regulation must change. The fragmented policy stream meant that widely accepted ideas, such as the relation between economic competition and growth, were more influential than would otherwise be the case.

• The *political stream* consists of the public mood, pressure group campaigns, election results, partisan and ideological distribution of members of Congress, and changes of administration. With the election of President Clinton in 1992, business interests knew they had a sympathetic president. An increasingly conservative Congress, especially after the 1994 elections, coupled with a public mood that embraced less government regulation of the economy, meant that interest group campaigns for deregulation met with a friendly reception. Similar ideas were raised prior to the Clinton presidency and went nowhere.

The routines of the three streams seldom meet in one place, but when they do they form what Kingdon calls a "policy window," an opportunity for an idea to become part of an institution's decision agenda. Under those circumstances, it appears that an idea's time has come.

At one level, this is all obvious. If a policy idea is not widely shared, the policy window does not open. If (to list the actors in the various streams) government officials, policy specialists, the general public, pressure groups, voters in elections, members of Congress, and the president and appointees share a similar idea, something is bound to happen. Yet the strength of the model is that it encourages questions about the ways actors in each of the streams change. How does it happen that members of Congress did not favor relaxed rules about cross-ownership (a telephone company owning a cable television company and a broadcasting company), but now they do? How does it happen that leaders of major telecommunications companies did not favor the relaxed rules, but now they do? Why is it that members of Congress were once worried about rules that guaranteed access for low-income families, but now they are not? The model steers analysis toward these loci of change.

Since each stream in the process consists of a wide variety of influences and components, the outcome of the entire system is largely unpredictable. It is an armchair sport to claim, after the fact, to know why something happened. The model does, in effect, give up on trying to make predictions of future directions in policy. Without some refinement, it offers no predictive advantage over a journalistic account of events. But the model does have its attractions.

One important finding from Kingdon's perspective is that an idea, once successful, spreads rapidly. Whereas prior to 1978 hardly anyone in Washington thought deregulation was an important idea or an answer to problems, with the enactment of airline deregulation the idea leapt to the top of many agendas. We can mark 1978 as the time deregulation arrived on the decision agenda for Congress.[5] The model suggests that we find out why this happened. Perhaps more important, we should ask what was special about telecommunications that it took nearly two more decades for policymakers to embrace legislation that invoked themes applied to other industries.

The focus in this model is on the early stages in policymaking. Once a bill is before a legislature with some chance of passage, it is probably time for political horse trading. The ideas have done most of their work, but the conceptual work has just begun. Some of the notions in the model are difficult to discuss (is there an unambiguous measure of "public mood"?), but we should not let that detract from the focus of the argument here: that ideas matter. Where do ideas get plugged into this policy process? Here is an opportunity for a refinement that deals with the problem of random elements in the model. Elaine Sharp[6] suggests that explanatory power can be added by distinguishing different ways items reach institutional agendas. First, ideas can emerge from grassroots politics, in which case we will see public officials responding to a broad public. She calls this *outside initiative*. For example, not long after their creation in the mid-1980s, the regional Bell telephone companies urged Congress to allow them to make and sell equipment. They were able to persuade the Senate to pass such a bill in 1991 but failed in the House.[7] Second, ideas can be, in essence, planted by people within government, educating and cajoling the public in order to build support for their agenda. Sharp calls this *mobilization*. For example, the Communications Decency Act (CDA) became part of the 1996 Telecommunications Act as the result of skillful persuasion by Senator James Exon (D-NE). He had an aide download pornographic photos from the Internet, which he kept in a blue file on his desk for viewing by his Senate peers. He announced that a vote against his bill was a vote to protect the pornographers who made such material available to children. Members of his own party later said the pressure was too much to resist, even though they later regretted voting for the bill.[8] Third, ideas can get on institutional agendas by insider influence, whether from within powerful interest groups or governmental bureaus. Widespread political support, a part of the first two options, is not necessary here. The inside-access route has the effect of limiting political participation. The story of the Telecommunications Act of 1996 shows that many of its central ideas entered the political stream through this route.

Here arises an important methodological issue. One must be careful to avoid mistaking the trees for the forest. For example, it is possible to identify the first time deregulation became the focus of congressional hearings, the first time the word *decentralization* was used in a presidential speech, or the first time a Brookings Institution Fellow who had authored a book on deregulation went to work for a national government institution. But such a search for roots can lead to an infinite regress—earlier events that can be said to have been critical might include a failed piece of regulatory legislation, attendance at a business and government conference by a White House aid, or a Ford Foundation grant to the Brookings Institution to encourage studies of regulatory policy.

A related issue concerns a historical use of the model. Figure 1.1 depicts three separate streams. At a given time, a snapshot may suggest separation of the streams, but this is misleading. Activities in one stream can, over time, influence activities in another.[9] Here are three examples that emphasize the crossover between streams.

1. Between 1970 and 1980, the ideas coming out of major Washington think tanks (such as the Brookings Institution) took a strongly conservative turn. Particularly in the area of industrial regulation, the policy arguments more often emphasized the importance of cooperative rather than adversarial relationships, and reliance on competition rather than planning. This shift within the policy stream contributed to a change in the political stream by shifting the expertise and views of those recruited to key staff positions in the Congress.[10]

2. The election results of 1980 introduced a conservative president and Senate to national politics. The Reagan administration's approach to running the national government included a heavy dose of deregulation. This shift in the political stream constrained the range of options possible within the problem stream, not the least through the greater pressure on budgets.[11]

3. The shift in regulatory politics during the late 1970s influenced the way business elites saw their relations with government. Experience under the new programs changed minds. In the mid-1970s, AT&T leaders saw themselves as protectors of the value of universal service, which required close regulation of prices and limitations on competitors entering AT&T lines of business. Continued regulation was, they asserted, the best way to serve the public. By the 1990s, AT&T leaders asserted that their mandate

was to bring the company into a more competitive era, and the best way to serve the public was to be an efficient competitor.

The political model emphasizes democratic politics—policies pursued because some people, somewhere, wanted them. Concepts from the model guide the narratives of telecommunications policy history presented chronologically in Chapters 2 and 3. Chapter 4 focuses on the role of ideas in the policy process and some of the issues raised by paying attention to ideas. The model does not lead us to seriously consider the justification for policies. Separated from its political supporters, does a policy remain a good idea? That is the focus of the analytical model.

An Analytical Model of Policymaking

In practice, the disciplines of political science and public administration do a poor job of approaching the question, What policy should be made? The question suggests that a particular policy be analyzed, and that calls for action in the field of policy analysis.

Sometimes policy analysis means describing general directions in government spending. Is defense spending increasing or decreasing? Are the poor getting more or less under this administration? So construed, it is not clear what one means by a "policy." It is a trend in spending, but it might also be a law that creates an agency empowered to do many activities, or it might be a change in a specific rule, such as an exemption from cable television service price controls for cable systems serving less than 15,000 customers. A loose concept of policy defies analytical precision.

The field itself often focuses on program evaluation.[12] A program is a collection of activities, usually within one governmental agency but not necessarily so, directed toward some set of similar goals. This mutation of the idea of policy analysis is unfortunate. It is essentially a bureaucratic classification, based on the need of government agencies to evaluate and justify annual budgets. This apparent concession to practicality endorses an approach to knowledge that guarantees frustration and leaves policy debate mainly in the hands of program advocates and detractors.

The distinction presents a challenge to an analytical perspective. A program is, in one sense, a collection of resources: money, legal authority, skilled people, buildings or offices, equipment, procedures, and the like. It is also a collection of outputs: procedures applied to cases produce changes in the world. In practice, program evaluation focuses on a wide range of attributes, such as efficiency measures (dollars per case), productivity measures (cases per worker), process or organizational measures (span of control, comparisons of case procedures), and benefit-cost analysis.

Program analysis is not one thing—programs are complicated and analysis is required by many authorities, such as executive budget offices, legislative committees, and top managers. This sense of evaluation is a "field" only because of academic departments and terminology within bureaucracies. There is no unifying approach to knowledge.

Even though political actors tend to sound sure of their claims, we should remain skeptical about cause-and-effect relationships. David Hume's lesson on the problem of knowledge lays out the challenge for us. We assert from experience that *x* leads to *y*. We further assert that the future will resemble the past, so that future *x*'s will lead to more *y*'s. Yet this is a fallacy: the principle that we can learn from experience is not prior to experience, although we use it as if it is.

Hume suggested a practical solution. We get in the habit of considering *x*'s in relation to *y*'s, because we care about achieving *y*'s. We are not indifferent toward outcomes. He wrote that "reason is, and ought only to be the slave of the passions, and can never pretend to any other office than to serve and obey them." A political discussion of our ends can be disciplined by analyzing experience we have had with earlier attempts to achieve similar ends.

The knowledge problem can be illustrated through an analogy to policies made in the fields of agriculture and medicine.[13] Knowledge is collected with clear goals in mind. A particular patient is ill, and the criterion for success is the patient's health. A farmer is growing tomatoes, and the criterion for success is yield per acre at a given quality standard. In these situations, the purpose for policymaking is clear, the farmer or physician focuses on an action taken to bring about a desirable change, and the action is evaluated in light of their purposes.

Is something like this possible in public policies? Can they be based on knowledge, as conceived here?[14] The farmer and the physician take action to produce a preferred outcome. They do applied science—taking into account the social situation, thus using both empirical and normative knowledge. What they are doing is complicated, but they use the same mental tools available to any healthy person.[15]

First, they have their priorities. This means they have come to conclusions about why they prefer one outcome to another. Farmers and physicians generally have these imposed from the outside (a tomato sauce maker pays by the pound for a stated quality, so greater yields per acre is the best outcome; patients want to return to normal health). In the world of policy this is more difficult, but in principle it is the same problem. What are the possible outcomes—that is, given the range of end states that are within our power to bring about, which do we prefer? Why? Once we have answered those questions, we can describe our priorities.

Second, the farmer and the physician have rules for action. The policy takes the form of a rule: In situation *m*, do *y*. The farmer knows enough about the state of his tomato field on a particular day so that his discovery of a certain insect elicits a response. The farmer has several options: spray with pesticides *a*, *b*, or *c* within a certain number of days; spray with bacillus *h* within a certain number of days; release predator bug *n* in certain numbers within a certain number of days; do nothing. Based on knowledge acquired from earlier personal experience and the acquired experience of others, the farmer arrives at a rule to apply in the specific situation, say, spray with bacillus *h*. The physician is similarly guided by knowledge of similar cases. A fifty-year-old Caucasian male, former smoker but otherwise in good health for his age, complains of a sore throat. There is some localized irritation below the left tonsil, and one lymph node on the left side is swollen. In a twenty-year-old nonsmoking patient, it is highly likely that the cause is a viral infection that will run its course in ten days. The physician would culture the irritated area to rule out a nasty strain of strep known to be in the area but would otherwise advise the patient to check in again if it has not cleared up in ten days. The fifty-year-old man presents a different story. A significant number of such cases are early tumors. While a $1,000 magnetic resonance imager (MRI) scan or a biopsy are too expensive or dangerous at this early stage, a more diligent watch is in order than for the twenty-year-old patient. The action is different because experience with similar cases is different.

In the world of public policy, this detailed and specific knowledge of cases is often difficult to acquire. This is not because the information is impossible to collect. It is usually because no one collected the relevant information and built experience that would inform an impending choice.[16] The lack of data is not surprising, given that policies often change for reasons unrelated to experience with actual cases. For example, legislators and executives with broad goals acquire power and enact different visions about the proper role of government. The cuts or additions in various areas of the state or national budget are not based on detailed knowledge of cases. Farmers and physicians know they cannot act that way.

Third, the farmer and the physician are able to test their policies. The rule must force an outcome. That is, the rule must bring about the desired state of affairs, the priority, in the situation where it was applied. If it does not, the policy is a failure. If the farmer is not able to apply bacillus *h* to the field within the given number of days, the policy does not pass the test. If the physician has a bad tracking system, so that the fifty-year-old patient feels a little better and ignores the frequent sore throats for six months—at which point an invasive cancer may have developed—the policy does not pass the test.

The entire procedure of using this view of policy is described by Eugene Meehan:

> Reasoned choice involves five basic stages or processes: (1) projection of a set of two or more outcomes on the future, using some selection of

> normative variables; (2) comparison of those outcomes, seeking reasons for preferring one to the others; (3) generalizing the preferred solution in that case to create a priority system; (4) application of the priority system to specific cases through appropriate policies; and (5) refining the structure in the light of experience with use.[17]

The analytical approach involves three kinds of claims. Empirical claims answer questions of the type, "Does evidence suggest the change to be introduced into the situation is likely to produce the desired outcome?"[18] These kinds of claims are inherently testable, given the focus on outcomes relating to individual lives. For example, a policymaker might claim that "allowing telephone and cable television companies to enter each other's businesses will reduce consumer prices." Is this true? For which customers? How soon? By specifying the conditions under which the claim will be tested for identifiable individuals, all that remains is collecting facts. Normative claims answer questions of the type, "Can reasons be found in our experience for maintaining that preference or priority?"[19] These can't be tested in the same way as empirical claims but must instead rely on arguments. There is no magic for generating consensus on priorities, although a focus on policies narrows the range of arguments that need to be considered.[20] For example, a policymaker might claim, We want the lowest possible prices for consumers. The question follows, Why? Average prices insufficiently clarify the effects on specific individuals, so the claim should be bolstered by arguments about different classes of customers (businesses and households, poor and well-off customers, urban and rural, basic service and high-end customers, etc.). The normative claims may be less precise, but they only need to be specific enough to assert that one outcome is preferable to another.[21] Methodological claims answer questions about whether the other types of claims are appropriately drawn. The process for evaluating policy claims is represented in Figure 1.2.

This approach leaves many grounds for criticizing policy. First, and perhaps most important, is how a policy affects humans. Individual human beings are the bearers of the costs and benefits of government action. Vigorous argument is possible over what constitutes an improvement in the lives of people affected by a policy and which improvements or costs are most important to emphasize.

Criticism of a policy involves comparison with some other policy. That is, if one disagrees with a rule, one proposes another rule to be applied in the same situation. The argument focuses on reasons for desiring the outcomes of one rule over the other.

This view of policy is a tough standard in that actual policymaking often fails to apply important parts of the procedure. It can be helpful to

Figure 1.2 An Analytical Model of Policymaking

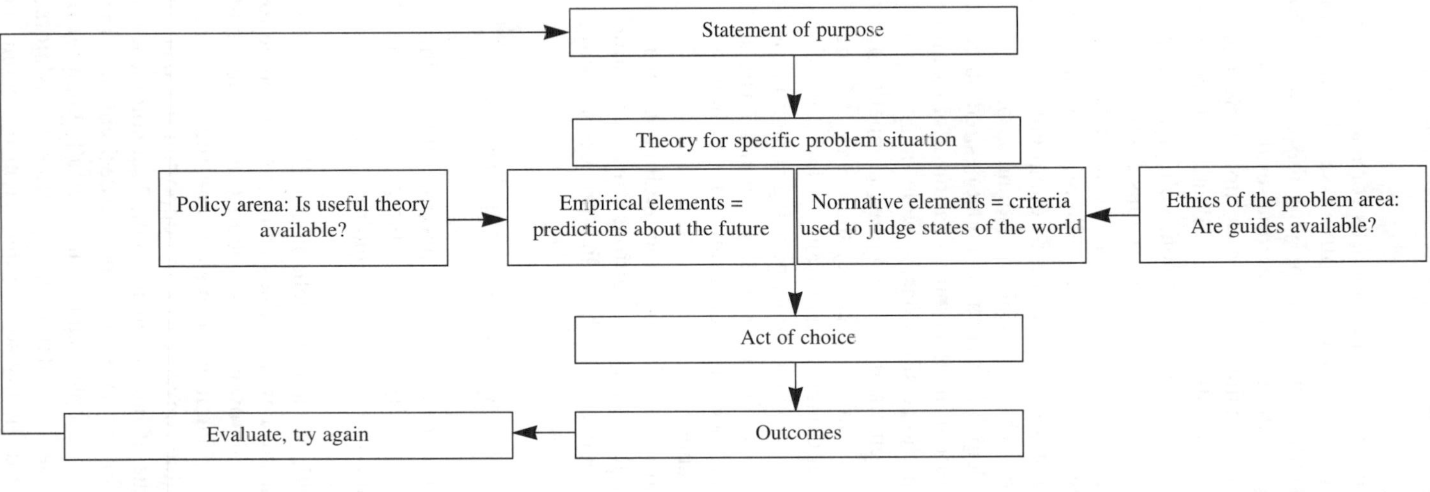

Source: This figure is adapted from Eugene J. Meehan, *Reasoned Argument in Social Science: Linking Research to Policy* (Westport, CT: Greenwood Press, 1981).

have an approach that sets benchmarks for learning from experience and clarifying both empirical and normative issues in policymaking.

The practical difficulties of applying this approach to policy are formidable. To begin with, priorities are the result of consensus on the nature of a good life. Our mainstream values, not to mention those of citizens who criticize the mainstream, are a collection of widely disparate propositions that fit together loosely.[22] In our policymaking institutions, the people who actually make important decisions are not the people with experience about relevant cases. The reasons for changes in legislation are typically quite broad—election campaign promises, a felt need to do something in the face of catastrophic events, compromise among contending interests, responses to broad social trends, and so on.[23]

In practice, legislation is vague about desired outcomes. A preference for more competition in telecommunications, for example, is not terribly helpful in actual choice situations. A wide range of policies may be consistent with the command "to encourage competition." Resorting to the hearings record is unlikely to clarify the intent of Congress in such situations. Members of Congress may want to "lower prices for consumers" or "create millions of new jobs" and pass legislation in the belief that a general change in rules will accomplish these ends. The analytical approach instructs us to ask whether supporters of a policy have any reasonable basis for their claims.

The model does not ask about the intelligence or motivations of policymakers. Rather, given the conditions for basing policy on knowledge, how do specific policies and the policy process measure up?

A Technological Context

An earlier section of this chapter contained this claim: Highly technical policy issues are largely ignored by the general public. Americans have strong beliefs and values about technology, and this shapes policy in important ways.[24]

To begin with, we admire technology. We are very adaptable in shaping daily routines to new machines and generally come to rely on this or that gadget—the microwave oven, jet air travel, voice mail, e-mail, cellular telephone, automatic coffeemaker, and the like. The admiration encompasses both the conveniences and opportunities machines add to daily life and the virtue of improvement itself. Technological improvement and personal improvement are widely seen as desirable and inevitable.[25]

Technology is complex, and technologically complex policy areas present special problems for democratic politics. Legislators and their committee staff have difficulty sorting out scientific, economic, and political ideas. The mass of citizens are unlikely, in present institutions, to understand the stakes in such policy areas.

Legislators and citizens do make sense of policy issues, however. When the details confound, deliberation and support are likely to be shaped by credible visions of the future. Ideology can be powerful here, even though the ideas are not clearly linked to policy.

For example, in the lead-up to the 1996 Telecommunications Act, most active participants—members of Congress, the Clinton administration, interest groups—spoke approvingly of broad citizen participation in the emerging telecommunications technologies. But what does it mean to participate? And why should people participate? Competing visions of participation were not carefully sorted out, and a compromise assortment of policies emerged.

One version of participation was presented by telephone and cable companies. Citizens are customers of regulated companies. They pay to use cellular telephones, to watch pay-per-view professional sports, to subscribe to basic cable plus premium channels, and to install a second telephone line in the home to handle the modem traffic. The world of information opens to citizens who purchase all the gadgets. Their stake in the legislative process was that of consumers.

The Clinton administration and several public interest groups believed that new telecommunications technologies would create a closer connection between citizens and government officials. They focused on the idea of public, educational, and governmental (PEG) access to the Internet. They accepted as an article of faith that on-line information about government was going to be useful to citizens. They believed that citizens would find it easier to contact their representatives through e-mail than through the regular mail or telephone calls. Congress instituted member e-mail, and within the first year of the service, members complained of being buried in e-mail messages. There was also talk of classrooms wired to each other, within schools and around the globe. Proponents argued that being linked to classrooms around the world would better prepare our children for tomorrow's challenges. This vision did not conflict with the consumer-oriented information highway of the telephone and cable companies. It added the idea that a few channels of cable systems and low-cost lines to schools and libraries, subsidized by other users, would allow PEG access to happen. Citizens who would rather do this than consume could do so.

A third vision of participation occasionally rose in the march to legislation. Some groups advocated a public model for the new technologies, essentially wanting to keep a regulated telephone system and wanting citizen use to be subsidized through higher prices on business customers. They were not influential in the politics of the 1996 Act.

These alternative understandings of participation were not seriously considered by the Congress, probably because of a prevailing sense of optimism for a technologically sophisticated future. There was widespread belief that the Internet and associated technologies were somehow the wave of the future. The commercial on-line services signed up millions of customers—and watched as millions simply disappeared, for reasons the services do not entirely understand. Companies rushed to establish web pages during 1995 and 1996, but there was no consensus that such electronic access made a difference in business. The belief was there, and businesses and citizens seemed eager to sign up. Why they wanted to be a part of the trend was not entirely clear; these ideas were not carefully examined. The possibilities of the new technologies were minor parts of the deliberations on legislation passed in the 104th Congress.

One key part of the consensus underlying the entire reform effort was the notion that our nation's *competitiveness* in the global economy was at stake. A word used by Democrat and Republican leaders, public interest figures, and industry leaders, competitiveness advocates claimed that the new electronic services are the key to the emerging information economy, where most value will be created in the next century. The stagnation in incomes over the last generation is due, goes the argument, to our declining competitiveness. Unleashing our companies to compete at home will make them stronger and better able to compete in the world economy.

But the claims about competitiveness were vague and poorly justified. The argument is a political concept generally rejected by economists.[26] When policy advocates say competitiveness, they usually mean productivity, economic growth, or reduction of the trade deficit. Loose use of the concept acts like a talisman that keeps economists and other uncomfortable critics at a distance. It is a word used to halt thinking about policy.

Sloppy concepts like competitiveness obscure assumptions about technology and politics. Participants in the policy process can be arrayed along a continuum of determinism. A pure determinist believes that technology develops according to its own internal logic and that we have little choice about the next things to build. We can see the beliefs most strongly in military technology, where the argument asserts that the enemy will take the next step and so must we. Research makes some new development possible, and survival depends on taking that next step. The pressure for building the MX missile, a large MIRVed ICBM, relied on this argument.

At the other end of the continuum is the notion of no determinism, or completely open choice of technical development. Here one believes that technology can be forced or invented if we have a desire and that extant machines are the product of deliberate choices. Again, using an example from military technology, the technical means for reliable ballistic missile defense did not exist in the 1980s, but President Reagan made the Strategic

Defense Initiative the center of his strategic policy. Fleet pollution standards for automobile makers is another example. Congress believed that by setting a performance standard, they required the automobile manufacturers to invent the technology to meet the standard.

One variant of the no-determinism position has been called the "technology-push" view.[27] This is the notion that if the corporations or the government of a nation can invest heavily in the right technologies, that nation can be an economic leader in those technologies. By pushing the technology itself, the other things that make up economic leadership (product development, jobs, trained and knowledgeable workers, growth) would follow.

Government officials generally endorse the technology-push view,[28] with important implications for industrial policy. First, governments endorse this view because it is easy to do so. Business interests generally support tax breaks and outright subsidies. Citizens in the United States generally accept elected officials' claims that they are encouraging businesses to create new jobs, although such quiescence may be in part a product of such claims. The levers available to elected officials to manage economic growth are few and clumsy. Systematic investment in the infrastructure necessary to diffuse technologies is expensive. Small investments in research and development turn out to be easier than other alternatives to pursue economic growth.

Second, the citizens who are party to the politics of technology-push investments are generally people associated with large businesses. Most citizens are only faintly connected to the details of capital investment. For the purposes of government policy, those citizens are seen principally as consumers of new products that might come from the investments. Particularly with respect to telecommunications technologies, opportunities for citizen participation may be lost if the policy problem is defined as providing the right incentives to large capital. What Ithiel de Sola Pool referred to as "technologies of freedom"[29] become principally things to buy for entertainment and business.

Technological change is subject to human choice, and the technology does make some outcomes more likely than others. This mix of views is referred to here as soft determinism.[30] Reasonable people may disagree. It is important to ask why one holds a certain view and to examine the consequences of holding one view as compared to another.

The three following guidelines for understanding the politics of technical change are a guide to asking questions about beliefs of policy actors concerning technology issues. There is an inherent bias in the principles, which is that claims of tehnological determinism, particularly with regard to public policy, require clear justifications. This bias is toward soft determinism and attempts to err on the side of democratic consideration of policy claims about technologically sophisticated issues.

All Technical Choices Carry Political Consequences

Some Americans have built communities with careful attention to this rule. Some Amish towns of southwest Pennsylvania are full of an unusual mix of machines and farm animals chosen to allow their citizens to live a particular way. Farming is expensive to enter these days, and farms have to be profitable to survive. Yet the Amish are able to buy new farms for their children and run profitable farms. Many use tractors, and they do employ machines in fields. It may seem odd to see a horse-drawn carriage in a field fitted with a motor that runs the sickle-bar mower or thresher. In farming communities of central Pennsylvania, the Amish have the reputation of putting up the best fences. Groups of Amish will come to a farm and fence a field. They arrive in pickups, unload their chain saws, and drive tractors with pile-driver attachments. They know that some machines will alter the way they live and make it difficult to remain distinctively Amish. But other machines allow them to keep Amish social and religious customs and run profitable farms.

The existing telephone system is another example of the political consequences of technical choices. Telephone technology is built to enable individual users, designated by separate numbers, to call and receive calls from other individual users. Telephone receivers are usually designed to fit one human ear at a time. Individuals have the choice of whom to call, when to call, and whether to answer a call. One telephone set can be used to call any other telephone set. Calls are private.

It did not have to be this way. Telephone technology could easily have been developed instead for broadcasting, with receivers built to address occupants in a room. The receiver could have looked and functioned more like a radio, and numbers could have been assigned by location or any other criteria. Service to each location could have been competitive, or by unregulated monopolies. The expense of current household basic service is not metered in the United States but easily could have been, with bills based on direct costs attributable to each minute of use. For decades, household basic service was subsidized by long-distance and business users, and it did not have to be.

Without subsidy of household service, many fewer households would have telephones. We might instead have more public telephones or more party lines (several households on the same line, much like several extensions in the same house), or local metered service. In high-traffic urban areas, specialized services, such as access to competing telephone companies or access to a limited set of destinations, might be available to compete with the higher-cost single, private lines.

A similar issue is found in computer networks, such as the Internet. Is a news story written for distribution on the Internet like a newspaper story or a television broadcast? The former is protected from regulation by a strong body of case law based on the First Amendment to the Constitution. The latter is heavily regulated, and illegal behavior can be punished by loss of licenses, fines, and even imprisonment. How do we use the technologies? How do we think of them? The technology requires political choices, one way or another.[31]

A technology we take for granted and use a great deal is the outcome of decisions made by government and businesses. Particular government officials decided that certain kinds of regulations made better political sense than others. The businesses, which were also influential in the making of government regulations, decided that certain kinds of technical options made more money than others. Opportunities for making money are affected by political rules. Each could be very different.

The current telephone system emphasizes individual use and choice. I can have close contact with people who do not live near me and avoid contact with my nearby neighbors if I so wish. Without such easy access to distant friends, my neighbors and I might have more of a shared life, which could be good or bad but certainly different. My private line makes me a telemarketing target for businesses, nonprofit organizations, political parties, and burglars. I may, of course, choose to keep my number secret from these people (and from my neighbors). Social relationships and commercial opportunities would be different under a different set of technical options. These are political consequences.

This suggests that a deliberately political evaluation of technologies is possible. We can ask, How do we want to live? How shall we make use of the technical possibilities of this invention? Those are political questions. That is the point: technical choices have political consequences.

All Rules About the Costs of Technologies Are Political Rules

The cost of telecommunications devices and services are never "true." For sixty years the field has been heavily regulated, both in who may enter the business and what prices may be charged for goods and services. No one can tell how the industry would have developed without these, or with different, regulations.

One example of this problem is in the notion of *separations,* used by regulators to apportion controlled prices of linked services. If a local telephone company customer makes a long-distance call, the message may travel over the local lines, through a regional telephone company, on to a long-distance telephone company, and then back through a regional company and a local company that serves the number called. If the call costs $1, how much of it should go to the first local telephone company? How much to the first regional company? Accountants attempt to separate the relative contributions of the different companies and apportion the $1 accordingly. Detailed methodologies are used for separations studies.

The problem is exacerbated if the various companies offer several services, some with regulated prices and some without, some by themselves and some as a conduit for other companies (such as long-distance operators). How much should a single service cost? How much should a long-distance company be charged, for example, for access to the local network of customers? How much should local customers be charged for access to the long-distance carriers? Should a customer of a new service, such as voice messaging, be charged the incremental cost of adding that one service?[32] Or should the customer be charged all direct costs of providing a service, which may include other costs of running the entire network? Should long-run marginal costs of a service determine price? Or should there be subsidies, in effect transfers of the costs of one service to another?

Some of these questions are about accounting conventions that represent attempts to draw neat lines where the real world combines and overlaps. Some of these questions are about policies—people making judgments about the rules others must follow, presumably to achieve some desired end. In both types of situations, the notions of cost are political—imposed by people trying to make the world turn out the way they want.

There is a more fundamental level of the issue of costs of technologies. The notion of "cost" is malleable and can be shaped to profoundly different notions of how the world should be ordered. Cost is a concept that we use to judge other ideas, like competitiveness (competition is good), fairness (also good), and adequate returns on investment (company bankruptcies are bad).

Consider the following dilemma faced by regulators of local telephone service. It is now technically possible to bypass the local telephone company network of lines and switches. Cable television companies can offer telephone service over fiber-optic lines and coaxial cables, and wireless carriers can offer cellular telephone service to local customers. In both cases, local customers can be offered access to long-distance carriers and other services not offered by the local telephone company. Should regulators allow these other carriers access to the customers of the local telephone company?

Until implementation of the 1996 Act, regulators have generally said yes to the cellular telephone companies, and no to the cable operators. One of the main reasons cellular operators could offer their services to anyone was because they did something the local telephone company could not (offer mobility), and because the high cost of cellular technology meant that it did not compete directly with local telephone company services. But prices for equipment change, access to the electromagnetic spectrum, and entry into markets were regulated. Local telephone companies could offer mobile service, they could charge what the market would bear for access to their lines, and companies could combine to offer services now offered by separate companies.

At the time of passage of the 1996 Act, courts have interpreted existing laws to mean that combinations that allow complete bypass of local telephone companies should be stopped. Such moves would impose heavy costs, of a sort, on local telephone companies.

Cable television operators have usually been told they may not offer local telephone services. There is a trade-off here. If cable operators can offer telephone services, should telephone companies be allowed to offer television services? The cable operators do not want the much better capitalized telephone companies to compete on their turf. They argue that the costs faced by the two types of companies are different—such competition is not fair.[33]

There is a still more fundamental notion of cost that is virtually always ignored by regulators. We can always ask if a policy change leads to a better world, one we would rather have. Often a technical change involves a shifting of costs, so that a new thing appears to be better but only because the costs are shouldered by someone else.

One example of this effect of technology lies in the construction of the interstate highway system. Its many benefits are enjoyed by lots of people—life is, in general, much better because of the wonderful ribbons of concrete. Yet some of those wonderful benefits come by letting people who cannot move to the suburbs or travel to work shoulder more of the burdens of older urban areas. The members of the middle classes can live better in part because they now avoid those costs of the cities. Many of the benefits of the cities are still available to them—they can drive in to see major league baseball, go to concerts and museums, shop, work, eat in diverse ethnic restaurants, and then drive back home.

Computerization of the workplace often is accompanied by such cost shifting. A secretarial job that used to involve meeting the public, knowing how to operate a variety of machines, knowing the filing system, and so on, may become more "productive" by having a lower-paid person stare into a cathode-ray tube typing pooled correspondence, while voice mail greets the public. Are worsened working conditions considered a cost? Are we better off if an organization pays less for its help and employs fewer people?

These are questions about what we value and how we want to live. That is the point: Rules about the cost of technologies are political.

One Technology Is Chosen over Another by Political Criteria

The choice of technical means to an end are seldom dictated by available technologies. Rather, the situation forces one to choose. By what criteria do we make choices?

We have many possible services available through the Internet. For a while during the early consideration of the legislation that became the 1996 Telecommunications Act, the Clinton administration referred to the Internet as a model for the National Information Infrastructure (NII). Competition made sense because it delivered more of everything to everyone—it was a costless goal. More services, and more sophisticated services, will be available if more money is available to pay for them. One obvious way to make more money available is to adjust charges for use of the Internet and make users pay for access to each type of service. The first feature of a competitive system is that the property is private.[34] The logic is simple and is endorsed by documents produced by the Clinton administration on the NII.[35] But the Internet does not have to be privatized. We can find value in the less commercial developments. One argument for a public Internet is that it allows less costly access to discussion groups that may seek to be politically influential. Do we want to endorse a technology that encourages more grassroots political activity? Another popular activity on the Internet has to do with sex. Do we want to regulate a technology that encourages more talk about sex and the trading of pictures and names?

The different visions of the Internet may be fed by competing notions of freedom. Advocates of a free or cheap unregulated meeting place may wish to encourage political participation, believing that the more participation the more empowerment of individual citizens and the stronger our democracy. Advocates of a privatized Internet may place a higher value on the private enjoyment of personal independence and so want the widest array of high-end services. Depending on our values, we can do many things with the Internet. There is no one best way.

These three principles were virtually absent from consideration of the 1996 Act. That makes the politics of technology something of a spectator sport, and that is unfortunate for the content of policy.

The Rest of the Book

Chapter 2, the first of two historical chapters on telecommunications policy, describes the period from the invention of the telephone to 1993. It covers the era of regulated monopoly, the first breakup of AT&T during the 1980s, and the attempts to make policy prior to the 103rd Congress. Chapter 3 continues the narrative through the 103rd and 104th Congresses, culminating in passage of the Telecommunications Act of 1996. Both chapters use concepts from the political model to describe developments. Chapter 4 is an attempt to answer the question, How did deregulation come to dominate policymaking in telecommunications? Other industries had significantly different experiences in the era of deregulation. Why did deregulation come when it did, in the form it did? Chapter 4 uses concepts from both models to describe the effects of ideas on policymakers. Chapter 5 is a description of the new regulatory regime created under the 1996 Act. The first two years under the law show it is more accurate to describe the new situation as the reregulation of the industry. The regulatory hand of government has a lighter touch, but it is still there. Chapter 6 discusses ways to evaluate telecommunications policies, particularly with respect to the distribution of resources and opportunities and the consequences for democracy. Continuous improvement in policy may require different designs in policymaking institutions.

Notes

1. The official title of Public Law 104-104 begins, "An Act to provide for a pro-competitive, deregulatory national policy framework." In this book it will be referred to as the Telecommunications Act of 1996 or, simply, the 1996 Act. A description of the content of the bill is found at the end of Chapter 3.

2. Perhaps the first to use this terminology were Cohen, March, and Olsen, "A Garbage Can Model of Organizational Choice."

3. See Solomon, *Passions.*

4. Kingdon, *Agendas.*

5. Ibid., pp. 12–13. The evidence for this assertion, a comparison over time of officials' reports that deregulation was important, is fairly dramatic.

6. Sharp, *Dilemma of Drug Policy,* p. 16.

7. S.173, the Telecommunications Equipment Manufacturing Competition Act, passed the Senate on June 5, 1991. See the following articles by Mike Mills: "Baby Bells' Fate Dangling Before Congress, Courts"; "Bells' Bid to Make Equipment Gains in Both Chambers"; "Senate Votes to Eliminate Ban"; "Two Powerful Chairmen Duel."

8. The section on courts and implementation in Chapter 5 of this book focuses on the CDA.

9. Weir adapted Kingdon's model to a historical approach in her *Politics and Jobs,* emphasizing interactions between the streams.

10. Examples of this dynamic are given in Derthick and Quirk, *Politics of Deregulation;* and Horwitz, *Irony.*

11. Accounts of the Reagan administration's regulatory policies are in Salamon and Lund, *Reagan Presidency;* and in Eads and Fix, *Relief or Reform?*

12. Approaches to policy and program analysis are described in Quade, *Analysis for Public Decisions;* Stokey and Zeckhauser, *Primer for Policy Analysis;* Drake et al., *Analysis of Public Systems;* and Williams et al., *Studying Implementation.*

13. The analogy is suggested in Meehan, *Reasoned Argument.* A similar approach is taken in MacRae and Wilde, *Policy Analysis.* Additional examples of applications are discussed in Hatry, Winnie, and Fisk, *Practical Program Evaluation.*

14. An original discussion of the topic is Lindblom and Cohen, *Usable Knowledge.*

15. Many people in social science hold the notion that empirical and normative questions (or, as the distinction is sometimes made, "fact and value") should be approached differently. Yet the intellectual apparatus for testing the two types of

claims is similar. The fact that people disagree about desirable ends does not in principle bar us from collecting knowledge about the outcomes of pursuing one or another course of action. A way to face the problem is to restrict normative claims to instances where policies change the lives of actual persons. Quality of life variables can be systematically investigated. See, for example, King, Keohane, and Verba, *Designing Social Inquiry.*

16. A case that illustrates this problem is Meehan, *Quality of Federal Policymaking.*

17. Meehan, *Reasoned Argument*, p. 158.

18. Meehan, *Ethics for Policymaking,* p. 11.

19. Ibid.

20. Standards for arguments are discussed in ibid., pp. 118–119.

21. Ibid., pp. 107–119.

22. The loose construction of values, so that they do not offer clear guides to choice in actual situations, is not impossible to overcome. Bardarch incorporated an approach to value analysis in his *Implementation Game,* especially in the appendix on writing implementation scenarios. An approach to coping with value ambiguity in the enforcement of regulations is offered in Bardarch and Kagan, *Going by the Book.* When a society lacks consensus on values, general guidelines are not likely to have much meaning. An example of learning limited lessons from cases and extending the lessons to classes of cases is Dworkin, *Life's Dominion.*

23. See the account of the origins of the idea of the National and Community Service Trust Act of 1993 in Waldman, *The Bill.*

24. This section is inspired by ideas from Spence, "Theory of the Politics of Technology." See also Winner, *Autonomous Technology.*

25. For social histories of technology in the United States, see Kaason, *Civilizing the Machine;* Haber, *Efficiency and Uplift;* and Noble, *America by Design.*

26. See Krugman, *Peddling Prosperity.* Krugman points out the following: About two-thirds of our economy consists of things that are not traded. Our slow productivity growth (real growth per worker has been slow since 1973) would be about the same if we ignored traded items. Low productivity is a problem, but international trade does not make it worse. We have seen some countries increasing productivity faster over the past two decades, but that should cause a dollar decline and lower prices for those goods, leaving us with about the same consumption we would have if those countries were not growing faster. Those international competitors, like Japan and Germany, have seen "deindustrialization"—the reduction of manufacturing jobs—on about the same scale as in the United States. The decrease in manufacturing due to trade with higher-productivity-growth countries is on the order of 2–3 percent. Higher productivity is desirable because it increases living standards, but government policies do not affect it much. The highest productivity comes in highly automated manufacturing, like cigarette making and oil refining. Electronics and software are by comparison not prone to high-productivity growth.

27. Hills with Papathanassopoulos, *Democracy Gap.* This book is particularly useful because of its comparative approach and its detailed discussion of how emerging technologies affect democracy.

28. Ibid., p. 3.

29. Pool, *Technologies of Freedom.*

30. Ibid., p. 5.

31. In subsequent chapters, the CDA, part of the 1996 Act, serves as an example of these First Amendment choices.

32. One example from 1997 was Caller Identification, where a regional Bell company charges $7 per month for a service that costs, incrementally, a mere $.07 to provide.

33. The 1996 Act, under Title III, describes the conditions for such competition.

34. The economics of the Internet are the subject of a section in Chapter 5 on the Internet and NII.

35. See, for example, the administration's account in White House, *National Information Infrastructure.*

2 The Evolution of Telecommunications Policy

From the beginnings of electronic communications, the U.S. government has been involved in making rules service carriers must live by. In important ways, the telecommunications companies helped to shape the evolution of these rules.

The industry began small and fell under existing laws. For the most part, these involved contracts, patents, and antitrust law. With both early telegraph (1836) and telephone (1876) services, companies competed for business and developed strategies that brought them into conflict with each other and with government.

The original filing of a patent for an early telephone by Alexander Graham Bell, on February 14, 1876, became the focus of hundreds of lawsuits.[1] That same day, but hours later, Elisha Gray filed a notice of intent to apply for a patent on a device that could convey speech (Bell's original invention could not). The timing was the focus of a protracted legal fight. It is possible that Gray's device could not have carried speech, and it is possible that Bell amended his application after reading Gray's. But it was Bell, along with a series of partners, who formed telephone companies from the mid-1870s to the end of the century. For this entire period, Bell's business rivals accused his companies of illegally obtaining their patents and exerting improper influence over government officials, and Bell companies sued rivals who allegedly infringed upon patents—perhaps 600 lawsuits in all. These early disputes were settled according to the adversarial procedures of courts. Bell himself was discouraged by the suits and after 1878 was not an active partner (except as a witness in trials) in the telephone businesses that bore his name.

Bell did understand the future of the telephone and should be considered as something of a visionary. In 1878, he wrote about cities in which homes and businesses would be linked through a single telephone network and linked to other cities through long-distance lines. The services, he assumed, would be priced so that virtually all households and businesses could afford to have a telephone. This would change the nature of cities, businesses, and social life.[2]

One key Bell victory came a year later, in 1879, in a dispute with rival Western Union, the telegraph company. The two companies fought over telephone patents well before Bell's vision of a telephone as more than a local, or even private, machine was widespread.[3] Local telephones and long-distance telegraph services seemed, at least to Western Union, to be the likely system of the future. And Western Union officials, believing Bell would win a trial, agreed to a contract that assigned the basic patents for telephone technology to Bell. Bell's vision paid off, and the monopoly on basic patents lasted until 1894.[4]

Patents are granted to inventors so that they may receive the economic benefit of their creativity. Users of the invention must meet the terms of the patent holder for the life of the patent—at the time of the early telephone, for seventeen years. Yet the technology does not in itself dictate the course of applications. The early Bell companies, in particular American Bell, chose to use its patents in courtrooms, suing companies that attempted to offer telephone service. For the most part, it did not attempt to beat the early competitors by offering cheaper and better services.[5] The public reputation of the company suffered where it had a monopoly. More independent companies cropped up after the expiration of the basic Bell patents, and the Bell companies argued against competition in front of state regulatory bodies. Competition did arise in many towns, mostly away from the East Coast.

Most of the Bell companies were local telephone companies, but one in particular, called the American Telephone and Telegraph Company (AT&T), focused on long-distance service. This was based in New York, and politics helped make it the center of the growing Bell system. American Bell, the chief company, was based in Boston. In that state the legislature had to approve corporate plans to raise capital; it also limited corporations in their ownership of subsidiaries. To find more lenient laws for raising capital in 1899, American Bell transferred its assets to the New York company, and the modern American Telephone and Telegraph Company was formed—a holding company that controlled businesses in each phase of the telephone industry.

The new company faced a great deal of competition—by one count, 500 telephone companies existed at the turn of the century,[6] and independent companies operated more than 40 percent of telephone sets.[7] Most of the competition was from local or regional telephone companies, and there were several manufacturers of telephone system equipment. The Bell system was the most successful for several reasons. The main issue was interconnection. The separate systems were not connected to each other because AT&T refused to comply. Part of the trouble was that rival telephone systems were constructed to different technical specifications because of AT&T's unwillingness to license its patents. If two systems existed in one town, the Bell customers could talk only to other Bell customers. A business that wanted a line to a wide range of customers needed to subscribe to both companies. In addition, Bell could interconnect its several systems and its long-distance service. Some state legislatures attempted to require interconnection, but AT&T fought in court and generally won.[8]

These were bitter battles. Merchants wanted as many potential customers as possible and felt pressure to subscribe to more than one telephone service. Household customers wanted to be able to call their friends, social circles, and the businesses they frequented. This led in some towns to a technical marking of class divisions. These disputes helped build an alliance of groups and a public mood that regarded the telephone company as an unscrupulous operator, as a natural monopoly that needed regulation.

Electoral politics sometimes figured in these contests between Bell and its competitors. Local government control of franchises was subject to the vote in some states. The rules about the cost of the technology could be explicitly political.

During this first phase of telephony, some important ideas were at stake. How should legislators and administrators see the new services? In what direction did the public interest lie?[9] Nationalization was one option, enforced competition another. Local and state government franchises for telephone service were still another. In a remarkably short time between 1880 and 1894, the number of telephones in use grew from close to zero to about 270,000. During the next thirteen years, when competitors to Bell companies could use the basic technology, the number of telephones increased to about 6 million. The telephone gained acceptance as a tool businesses and many households simply had to have.

What rules would guide the new technology? At the turn of the century, the country was in a period of consensus: competition seemed to be a good policy for enjoying the new possibilities of the telephone.[10] The idea of nationalization or national or state regulation had not captured the imagination of any significant portion of the public by the turn of the century. It was an era of laissez-faire capitalism, and except for the beginnings of antitrust activity, regulation of services like the telephone was simply not a national issue. One sign of the times was the growing willingness to regulate electric utilities, indicated in Supreme Court decisions. The concept of a public utility, invented only in 1877, took some years to develop.[11] The concept of a regulated utility, that a business with regulated prices has a right to a fair economic return determined by government experts, was not developed until 1898.[12]

Familiarity with telephones bred the movement to regulate. AT&T acquired a reputation as something of a bully, driving competitors out of business through its superior bargaining position of having the long-distance lines needed by local systems. There was another side to this story. During the period 1894–1907, the Bell proportion of all telephones in the nation declined from more than 80 percent to about 50 percent.[13] But AT&T held to its strategy of giving no quarter to competitors, and its unsavory reputation spread. State legislatures soon sought to control AT&T by requiring interconnection between systems.

At times in a corporation's history, leadership matters a great deal. The ascendancy to the presidency by Theodore Vail in 1907 led to important changes in the ideas by which AT&T operated. For the first few years of his leadership, the mission of AT&T was to become the monopoly telephone company. It did so by acquiring independent competitors and the nearest thing to a long-distance competitor—the Western Union Telegraph Company. The public displeasure at AT&T's monopolistic behavior grew, both in response to AT&T gobbling up telephone and telegraph services and from its steadfast refusal to interconnect.

The public mood was harsh with regard to AT&T. It was the Progressive Era, a mostly urban movement of the early twentieth century, when reformers sought to clean up the corruption of machine politics, restrain corporate power, and bring about reform in working conditions, moral issues, and urban poverty.[14] The city of Cleveland became famous for reforms in government that included taking over utilities like electricity. The state of Wisconsin became famous for passing rules to limit electoral fraud and for regulating corporations. The depression following the panic of 1907 convinced many politicians of the need for greater regulation of the economy. Eugene Debs, the socialist candidate for president, polled more than 900,000 votes in the 1912 election. Woodrow Wilson won that election on a campaign that focused on the need for using government power wisely to counter the threats to liberty and free enterprise posed by the giant corporations. Popular magazines and newspapers regularly ran series that detailed business abuses of power and the need for regulation.

In 1912, the Department of Justice (DOJ) began an investigation based on a complaint by a rival telegraph company and several independent telephone companies that AT&T was violating antitrust laws.[15] Vail understood where a reputation as a corporate bully would lead.[16] The prevailing public mood about corporations, Progressive elected officials, sympathetic bureaucrats, and offended businesspeople in many congressional districts presented AT&T with a powerful proregulation coalition. The grounds for the fight were not of AT&T's choosing.

Through negotiations with DOJ, Vail and AT&T decided to act in a way that was perceived inside the company, and by politicians such as the president of the United States, as statesmanlike. In a letter that became known as the Kingsbury commitment (after AT&T vice-president Nathan

Kingsbury), the company promised to relinquish control of the telegraph company under investigation, to allow independent companies to connect to the Bell network, and to acquire independents only with the approval of its regulators—at that time, the Interstate Commerce Commission (ICC).[17] This was a dramatic reversal of company policy and should be seen as the beginning of the political vision of the telephone as a natural regulated monopoly. Vail turned out to be a visionary leader on a par with Bell. He understood the economics and the technology of the telephone and the politics of making rules for both.

From then until 1921, the company's leaders worked to legitimize the idea of a natural monopoly. They would work closely with regulators. The company would receive antitrust exemption to manage a system consisting of its own components and noncompeting independent carriers and would receive a fair and reasonable return on its investments; in turn it would run a technically advanced, reliable system available to as many people as possible—what we still call "universal service."[18] AT&T leaders helped to shape a consensus among politicians and regulators who would clearly have been dissatisfied with continued company reluctance to cooperate in the creation of a smoothly functioning nationwide telephone system.[19] A new assumption had entered the regulatory arena: a regulated monopoly, working closely with government officials, could effectively deliver a national service.

Vail's pursuit of the vision of a regulated natural monopoly appears all the more politically wise when compared to the idea that was perhaps the greatest threat to AT&T: the idea of nationalization. In 1913, the new U.S. postmaster general, Albert S. Burleson, advocated that the Post Office Department take over the telephone system ("postalization"), similar to what had been done in most of western Europe.[20] Although there was no general political movement toward this, the European example and the advocacy of some national government officials suggest that the rules of telephony were by no means preordained by the technology. It is possible that the option of postalization pressured AT&T into the Kingsbury commitment.[21] At the time the AT&T leaders were influential in their DOJ negotiations, they were willing to concede considerable economic power to regulators, and the prevailing ideology in the nation still held a central role for private enterprise. The monopoly may have appeared to be natural, but it did not appear to be naturally nationalized.

Nationalization received a boost by way of the extraordinary powers assumed by the national government during World War I. In 1917, Congress set up the War Industries Board to organize the industrial might of the country to war needs. The railroads were put under the jurisdiction of the U.S. Railroad Administration. Government encouraged industrial combination and cooperation out of what had been just a few years earlier a climate of trust-busting. A strange dynamic occurred in which government sought more control over industry at the same time that industrial power became more concentrated in a few hands. Some of this had to do with the institutional changes during the war. Government was creating new institutions for industrial management, and this put government officials into regular contact with industry leaders. The corporate executives were the experts in industrial matters and generally shared the national goals of mobilization and victory. The proximity of the regulated served to tame the regulators.[22]

The dynamic is illustrated in AT&T's experience. The postalization idea found new institutional support during the war, including the secretaries of war and of the navy. AT&T was not even invited to the hearings on the matter before House and Senate committees. In mid-July 1918, Congress passed a resolution granting the president control of the telephone system, with the intent of having it run by the Post Office Department.

Yet on meeting, AT&T and postal officials got along very well.[23] Vail impressed Postmaster Burleson as an unselfish and patriotic man who was entirely reasonable about the wartime needs. The negotiations eventually produced a contract and relationship that gave AT&T benefits it had been unable to secure from federal and state regulators, including consultations on rate-making issues and a guaranteed return on investment,[24] and AT&T managers retained operating control of the company. Before the company was formally returned to the AT&T board of directors after the war, rate increases that state regulators refused to approve were instituted by the national government. It was a sign that the new consensus was formed at the national level, with state regulators following.

The national government did regulate the Bell system prior to World War I. In 1910, the ICC was given jurisdiction over the telephone industry in the Mann-Elkins Act. The law was introduced to strengthen the ICC's control over railroads, and the telephone and telegraph carriers were first added in a floor amendment in the House. Both AT&T and independent companies favored the legislation,[25] making it, as part of the wave of new regulation passed in the prewar Progressive years, rather uncontroversial.

The postwar view was evident in 1921, when Congress expanded the jurisdiction of the ICC to include policing AT&T's acquisition of other companies.[26] The trade-off was that AT&T could acquire other companies. The idea was supported by independent telephone companies, many of whom wanted to sell out to Bell. This considerably lightened the regulatory burden on AT&T, since more of its important battles would be fought in one venue. During this period, the strongest regulatory limit on AT&T was probably antitrust, such as when AT&T attempted to dominate radio and motion pictures but failed.[27] During this period, most regulation of AT&T occurred in the states, where state utility commissions had power over setting rates and granting franchises for local service. AT&T was generally successful in arguing its point of view before state commissions, and during this period it was perhaps the most profitable corporation in the nation.[28] State utility commissioners came to agree with the concept of natural monopoly and the practical outcome of a single system run by AT&T.

The Communications Act of 1934: New Institutions, Light Regulation

The Great Depression brought with it a new era of governmental regulation. The Roosevelt administration came to Washington with a supportive legislature and administrators who believed in an activist federal role in rebuilding the economy. And these administrators brought with them a new ethos for public administration—one that stressed efficiency, clear lines of authority and management control, and accomplishment of organizational goals.[29] Supporters of reorganization justified it as a way to make government more effective and efficient, but what was really at stake was control of policy. President Roosevelt and his advisers pursued reorganization of the executive branch, including the grouping of like activities under single agencies.[30] Reorganization made it more likely that national government activities would come more directly under the control of Roosevelt appointees. They would in turn direct the activities of civil service employees who were viewed as technically competent and politically neutral, able to serve political controllers of either party.

In the 1930s, telecommunications policy rode the tide of reorganization without major policy debates. For the most part, the Communications Act of 1934 was a consolidation of the Federal Radio Commission and the ICC jurisdiction over telecommunications under the umbrella of a new agency called the Federal Communications Commission (FCC).[31] The only controversies surrounding the bill, which were not major, involved antimonopolists who wanted a new framework for the regulation of broadcasting. Their ideas were not widely shared, and alternative approaches to broadcasting did not reach the institutional agendas of Congress and the president.[32]

The 1934 Act applied what was, for federal regulation, a recently developed standard of "necessary and desirable in the public interest" for approving new services and carriers, and a "just and reasonable" standard for carrier rates and practices.[33] These are vague standards and require details for application not found in the act. What is perhaps notable about the 1934 Act is the degree of delegation of quasi-legislative and quasi-judicial powers to an administrative agency. These issues were not raised at the creation of the FCC. Its creators assumed that the neutral competence of the experts employed in administrative agencies would forestall such difficulties. The administrative thinking of the time did not recognize these issues as serious problems.[34]

The 1934 Act provides an example of how emerging technologies challenge political thinking. Most of the media were new growth industries, and the telephone and broadcasting had become a part of everyday life. The long-term and wider consequences of the technologies—why they are designed a particular way, what the social consequences of the new gadgetry might be, who pays the costs—were difficult to understand. The people who most clearly understood the issues were those closest to the business. They understood the machinery, the economics of building and selling a system, and how rules were made at different levels of government.[35]

The government regulators in the new FCC did not generally come from business. They were a reconfiguration of existing agencies, consolidated into a new building with many of the same officials, enforcing existing law, and directed by law to produce new approaches to regulation. The early FCC is often considered a conservative organization.[36] It did set out to study the telephone industry[37] but was critical only toward some issues. Prevailing compromises with the industry generally accepted the notion of a horizontal monopoly, of an emerging nationwide network of Bell operating companies owned by AT&T and linked together by the AT&T long lines division. The high costs of entering the business and the earlier experience with rival unconnected systems made it seem like a natural monopoly. AT&T had the huge advantage of operating a recognized company and providing established services. The company held patents that were especially crucial in large systems. It linked local networks together through its own long-distance lines, and critics had long charged that the connection fees amounted to a huge transfer of revenue from the operating companies to the parent corporation. AT&T had already established rights of way for its wires. Potential competitors would have to cope with state and local rules barring competition and negotiate connection with the nearby AT&T facilities.[38]

The natural monopoly question became somewhat complex due to a competing idea: special regulatory problems might be presented by a vertical monopoly. A vertical monopoly occurs when a firm controls the complete range of manufacturing, sales, and service of a product. The regulatory problems are due to the firm being able to configure products or charge itself prices for goods and services in ways that avoid the reach of regulators. AT&T controlled the manufacture of equipment through its Western Electric subsidiary and claimed that it could not allow potential competitors to make equipment that might cause problems to the telephone system. Yet potential competitors could ask, as long as patents and technical requirements were licensed and respected, Why should AT&T forbid them to manufacture equipment? The results of the FCC study were generally ignored as political attention was riveted on gathering momentum toward war in Europe. The priorities enacted, though not deliberate, were that the FCC protected AT&T by shielding it from competition and by letting it take the initiative in the setting of rates. This pattern held until the 1970s.[39]

Part of the pattern was due to the approach to regulation adopted by the early FCC. We can think of the available options as lying on a continuum between negotiations among regulators and industry officials, and formal public hearings on questions about rules and rates, operations, and competition issues. The formal hearings lend themselves to the collection of evidence and points of view on specific questions and policy issues, and invite adversarial treatment of controversial questions. Negotiations—the style used by the FCC—lend themselves to rapid adjustment to changes in the industry but lack the structure of hearings that enable other interests to monitor and take part in the regulatory process.[40] They are not inherently adversarial. The FCC would find over the ensuing decades that policy is nearly impossible to make if the regulator does not have reliable knowledge about the industry.

Why couldn't the FCC generate reliable knowledge about policy? One obvious reason is that regulation of a national system, consisting of many separate businesses under the AT&T umbrella and independent carriers as well, is a complicated undertaking. AT&T possessed a very large staff to run the organization, and the FCC staff was always minuscule by comparison. The early FCC study that focused on vertical monopoly issues kept 300 researchers busy for years.[41] In practice, FCC officials often waited for AT&T to report earnings and then would consider rate adjustments. This occured in the context of a federal system, where state regulators controlled rates for local services. AT&T spoke with a unified and authoritative voice.

Some issues were simply unsolvable in principle. In the matter of rate regulation, for example, even if the FCC had a figure for a reasonable rate of return on investment, how could it know the real costs of service to a customer? AT&T's equipment was acquired from its own subsidiary, the local carrier was likely an AT&T subsidiary that connected to the AT&T long-distance network, and the local customer found many of the numbers it called in an AT&T telephone book. With so many different organizations in the network, and telephone calls flowing among them, what are fair rates and how is the revenue to be apportioned among the different companies? In the jargon of the FCC, the various businesses within AT&T had to be analytically "separated" so that the cost of each could be considered in rate making, and when independent carriers were involved, the calculations of separate business costs and revenues were called "settlements."

State utility commissions had jurisdiction over local rates, and the FCC controlled interstate rates. Further complications arise from the FCC's role as protector of the public interest, guarding the values of reliable and universal service—each with its own engineering and cost implications. The FCC was simply not capable of filling the role of knowledgeable expert, and so had to rely on negotiation with accounting counterparts from AT&T.

The separations issue requires a detailed explanation, since so many later issues depend on it.[42] A single call within the telephone system might pass through the equipment of several companies operating under many jurisdictions—yet the caller pays one bill. How should the money from the customer be separated into separate shares for the several companies? Here is an example from the time period we are discussing. The Yelm Telephone Company was an independent local operator. It was connected to the telephone network through Pacific Northwest Bell (PNB), a subsidiary of AT&T. General Telephone and Electronics (GTE) was an independent telephone company serving most of a neighboring county. It had direct long-distance connections to AT&T and was linked to PNB. When a GTE customer calls someone across the country, the call will be completed through AT&T long-distance services, linked to the ultimate receiver by a structure similar to the Yelm or GTE local companies. GTE links up with Yelm, and other companies within the state, through PNB. If a GTE customer makes that cross-country call, for a total charge of $1, how much of the revenue should go to AT&T? To PNB? If a Yelm customer calls the same place across the country, for a total charge of $1, how much should go to AT&T? To PNB? How should the revenue be allocated if a Yelm customer calls a GTE customer? Regulators need to know how to answer these questions in order to determine the fair rate of return for the different telephone companies involved.

The answers depend on several key assumptions. Perhaps the most important one is how we conceive of the switching involved in a telephone call. Yelm Telephone operates switches that connect its customers to each other; PNB operates switches that connect its customers to long-distance lines within the state and to the national lines run by AT&T. They in turn have a similar set of switches at the other end of the line to a cross-country customer. The switches connecting local exchanges to long-distance lines are called "boards" in separations jargon, a term left over from the old days when telephone switches were actually attached to boards. In the jargon, the telephone set in a customer's home or business is called a station. A simple diagram of the system is shown in Figure 2.1.

In Figure 2.1, if Y_1 calls Y_2, it is a local call, and a regulator has a fairly simple job of setting an appropriate rate. If Y_1 calls B_1, it is a long-distance call. If we think of Y_1 calling B_1 as a board-to-board call, the

Figure 2.1 Exchange Station and Board Connections

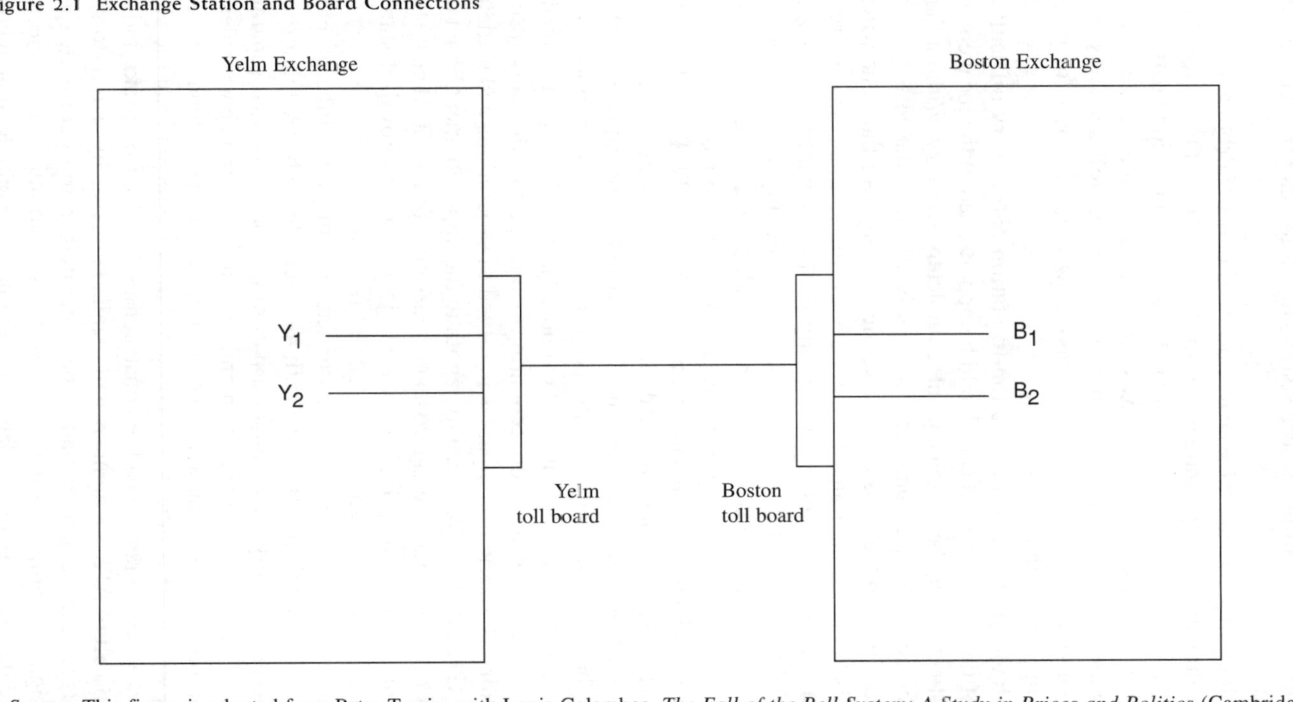

Source: This figure is adapted from Peter Temin, with Louis Galambos, *The Fall of the Bell System: A Study in Prices and Politics* (Cambridge: Cambridge University Press, 1987), p. 21.

portion of the call between Y_1 and the toll board is considered a local service, and the portion that goes between the boards is considered a toll call. If we think of Y_1 calling B_1 as a station-to-station call, the entire call is a toll call.

Calculating the cost of a board-to-board call is fairly easy to do. The local company already charges the customer for local service. We can choose a simple calculation, such as the board connection costs as a proportion of total local company costs, and arrive at an estimate of the cost per minute for long-distance service. Local versus toll accounts are kept easily enough. Or we could simply ask how much it costs for PNB and AT&T to provide that service.

Calculating the cost of a station-to-station call is very difficult. How much of the cost of the toll call should be apportioned to the local company? The distinction will be, at some point, completely arbitrary. Without the clarifying board-to-board assumption, admittedly arbitrary, the costs of each call are mixed in with the costs of other services going over the same wires.

This became important in the history of rate setting. First, there is the issue of whether the company in the long-distance business will charge too much for the toll call. Since local service is already virtually paid for—that is, the marginal local costs of the toll call are very small—with board-to-board logic it is the long-distance company that collects the lion's share of the fee. Telephone companies such as PNB and AT&T could use the argument to justify higher rates. Advocates of lower rates wanted to apply the station-to-station logic, because it justified a lower price for the services. The issue was fought in the courts, and the FCC decided to adopt station-to-station calculations, and eventually, in 1943, AT&T agreed.[43]

Setting the standards for accounting is only part of the work of implementation. The various companies involved in separations and settlements (Yelm, GTE, PNB, AT&T) had to negotiate the apportionment based on estimates of nationwide average costs per customer or on actual cost studies. The application of the principles was subject to the approval of state and, in the case of long-distance rates, federal regulators.

The movement to station-to-station accounting solved the problem of how to apportion the costs of one call, but it created other regulatory problems. AT&T was organized under a parent company and had separate divisions for long-distance operation and regional telephone companies. The corporation used board-to-board accounting, which corresponded to the divisions within the company that collected the revenue and ran the various services. Regulators then had to construct a second set of books and in effect undo all of AT&T's numbers and recalculate costs by station-to-station methods. Capital expenses had to be separated from operating expenses and assigned in proper proportions to interstate and intrastate services. The FCC did this on the basis of relative use so that, for example, if an increasing proportion of telephone calls from a local exchange were long-distance toll calls, a greater proportion of system expenses would be apportioned to the long-distance services. The process was enormously complex and required a thick manual to control the assumptions of regulators.

The negotiation process was also tied to subsidies within the telephone system. The tradition of charging less for home than for business users dates back to Alexander Graham Bell's first sale of private telephones and was carried on under FCC supervision. Rural users (who were often served by independent carriers) were subsidized by urban users. Justification of such subsidies relies on assumptions embedded in approaches to regulation and are connected to the practical details of regulation. For example, AT&T could show that the highest demand for services, and the vast majority of their traffic, was in the local exchange, but the rate structures supporting universal service require long-distance users to pay a disproportionately high share of system costs. Urban and business customers present higher demand for telephone service than do rural customers. The cases seemed contradictory: Should heavy demanders pay a higher price? Should the lower unit cost of serving urban and business customers result in lower prices? Such arguments are laden with assumptions that are subject to dispute. One important assumption underlying both examples is that the U.S. telephone system has a long tradition of unmetered local use based on monthly lease rates—and metered local usage would have made the subsidy questions much simpler. The idea of metered local usage is entirely sensible if we believe that price and usage are connected, but this was never acceptable before state regulatory commissions.[44] Alexander Graham Bell started the tradition of a fixed price for unlimited usage in order to encourage use of his invention, and both users and regulators resisted any movement to metered service.

The rules about the costs of the technologies emerged out of a complicated policy process, but sometimes the political power behind decisions was transparent.[45] In 1950, for example, the FCC bent to direct pressure from members of congressional oversight committees. In an exchange of letters, the message from Congress was that too many of the costs of the telephone system were being borne by household users and too few by big companies that use a lot of long-distance services. The FCC responded with a careful explanation of its separations process. But the Congress ordered the FCC to change, and it did. More of the costs of the system were shifted to long-distance services—this at a time when the costs of local services were going up (due to rising wages and a higher proportion of single-user lines) and the costs of long-distance services were dropping (due to improved switches and higher-capacity lines).

Perhaps the main effect of subsidies lies in the altered incentives offered to customers and potential competitors. Long-distance and most business services were becoming more and more overpriced. The impulse to subsidize universal service certainly helped to spread telephone usage, but it also created a powerful constituency of niche competitors that would attempt to make inroads into the AT&T monopoly.

The story of the early style of FCC regulation is subject to a variety of interpretations. From a certain point of view, AT&T appears as a powerful industrial giant, able to pursue its own ends and push aside duly constituted public authority.[46] One account calls AT&T leadership virtuous but describes an organization that, due mostly to the dynamics of a large organization, behaves as a determined and acquisitive organism largely out of effective public control.[47] Still another view suggests that these judgments miss a central point:[48] the system worked very well, and that had a powerful effect on the perceptions of regulators.[49] AT&T could count on many friends from a wide variety of national government agencies because of services provided to them, especially during wartime. State regulators were generally much less able than the FCC to cope with the complexities of the company and were for the most part service oriented.

The Postwar Era: The Development of Antitrust and Tighter Oversight

A major regulatory development in the postwar era was in antitrust policy. The 1939 FCC study of AT&T had identified the equipment manufacturing monopoly through Western Electric as an important regulatory problem. An attorney on the original study who went to work for DOJ's Antitrust Division heard from there complaints from state utility commission officials that emphasized the difficulties of regulating a company whose costs were unknown.[50] DOJ filed suit in January 1949, asking for divestiture of Western Electric and opening up of the market for telephone equipment—including reasonable leases on patents held by the company.

AT&T's approach to the case was to negotiate where it had political strength. It lobbied its biggest customer, the Department of Defense, to support its side of the case, and after the 1952 election it put its arguments to a more supportive Republican administration. The suit was settled in a 1956 consent decree that allowed AT&T to keep Western Electric, but with important provisos: AT&T and Western Electric would be limited to the telephone business, and Western Electric patents, including the transistor, would be licensed to other businesses for reasonable royalties. This meant that AT&T saw itself, and was accepted by the government, as a natural vertical monopoly. It was to rely on regulation, not the possession of patents, to protect it from competition.[51]

Here is one place to see the role of ideas in the policy process. Among the arguments AT&T advanced in its defense was that the company's vertical monopoly kept costs down and supported technical innovation. As we can see in hindsight, this is precisely the opposite of the general understandings that drove policy in the 1980s settlement and in the 1990s.[52] The early 1950s were still two decades before economists and policy specialists agreed that a regulated monopoly, compared to a competitive situation, causes higher costs and slower technical innovation. AT&T was regarded as a regulated monopoly, subject to control within the public realm. As the regulated telephone company, AT&T was not precisely private and not precisely public, but was in some sense semipublic. The definition of public interest and the cost and outcomes of company policies were now, in principle, the stuff of politics. Over time the company lost control of political forces that defined its role and appropriate public policy.

That these issues emerged at approximately the same time also points to the importance of ideas in the policy process. Holmes Baldridge was the FCC attorney who became head of the litigation section of DOJ's Antitrust Division. The notion that AT&T should divest itself of Western Electric, contained in the original FCC report of 1938, was championed by Baldridge. He convinced Attorney General Tom Clark to pursue the suit.[53]

Politics often responds to changes in technology and ideas. For example, one of the conditions of the 1956 decree was that AT&T maintained its telephone monopoly at the cost of its entry into other businesses, such as computing. Its work in advanced electronics (subsidiaries invented the transistor and the first computer based on them for the Department of Defense) would have made the company an important player in the new computer industry. The company may have merely wanted to maintain its focus on telephones and failed to predict the importance of computers in communications, but the line between computers and communications quickly blurred. Companies that could develop computer switches could enter AT&T businesses as manufacturers and equipment sellers and make equipment that businesses could use to augment services by AT&T. There were certainly economic incentives for companies to do so. This dynamic was played out in microwave technology as well. Technical developments exposed faults in the boundaries of AT&T, and the FCC had to decide how to settle the ensuing disputes.

This dynamic is illustrated in the cases of the Hush-a-Phone, the Above 890 microwave decision, the Carterphone, and Execunet.[54] The Hush-a-Phone was a small shield that snapped onto a telephone handpiece. It was supposed to direct the user's voice into the phone and shield it from other noises. The Hush-a-Phone company had sold the attachments for almost thirty years, but in 1948 AT&T notified stores that carried the device that it was illegal. AT&T had long concerned itself with interconnection, the linking of machines and networks to its equipment. FCC policies supported AT&T's role as the main protector of system quality and generally considered interconnection restrictions as reasonable. After hearings in which AT&T showed that the device interfered with the quality of transmissions, the FCC agreed the device should be illegal. The Hush-a-Phone company appealed the FCC ruling in federal appeals court. The court sided with Hush-a-Phone, ignoring the criteria used by the FCC. The appeals court was not bound by the methods and criteria used by the FCC[55] and was, from AT&T's perspective, a risky venue in which to pursue its goals. But that is one of the consequences of defending one's values in the political realm. The case was a sign that political forces beyond AT&T's control—the outcomes of public hearings, ideological shifts in Congress, the emergence of new potentially competing businesses—were successfully entering the regulatory regime.

The Above 890 decision[56] concerned the newly developed ability of companies to transmit long-distance messages by microwaves. Banks, credit companies, insurance companies, oil companies, national manufacturing companies, and others regularly sent data by what were called "private lines." These lines, which went from one company installation to another without going through AT&T's long-distance switches, were relatively expensive telephone lines, and businesses could save money by purchasing their own microwave equipment. When the FCC began hearings in the early 1950s on the use of the microwave portion of the electromagnetic spectrum, the business users of the new microwave equipment banded together to influence the FCC. For the most part, the case pitted big businesses who wanted the costs savings and security of their own systems against AT&T in its role as the provider of common carriage communications—in a system that relied on AT&T making money off of some customers to fund the public values of the network. In 1959, the FCC accepted the arguments of the private users. The decision applied only to a business's internal communications, not connection to AT&T's lines, but it opened the door to the building of new and eventually competitive long-distance networks.

The Above 890 decision signaled a turn in the procedures of the FCC.[57] The informal negotiations process had been used for over two decades in part because of the lack of a significant constituency with an interest in alternative FCC policies. Yet here was a major group of businesses, led by the Motorola Corporation, arguing that restrictions on manufacture of equipment and existing rate structures were in violation of law. To handle the contending sides, the FCC had to use its formal hearing process, which was a contentious and uncertain political venue.

And the case implied a dramatic turn in the content of FCC policies. Companies could acquire their private-line services elsewhere if AT&T did not offer just what they wanted. One way a potential competitor could differ was on price. This meant that if some source other than AT&T offered the same service but at a lower price, the company could buy it. Although the Above 890 decision prohibited companies from sharing these non-AT&T private lines—which would, in effect, be setting up an alternative telephone company—it undermined the systemwide assumption about the costs of providing universal service. It had long been national policy that AT&T would provide universal service and that they would pay for the system by subsidizing some users at the expense of others. The increasing levels of subsidy during the 1950s was not AT&T's doing—it was a result of congressional pressure on the FCC to limit rates charged to households. The Above 890 decision let the largest payers in the subsidy system leave. The FCC did not interpret this as a major shift in policy.[58]

AT&T did regard the decision as a major change. It responded with a proposed rate structure that would offer private lines to large customers based on what it would cost them to build their own lines. For many corporate customers the discounts ranged from 50 to 85 percent. They called the new rate structure TELPAK.[59]

This posed a huge problem for regulators, perhaps more so than the separations issue, and for many of the same reasons. The appropriate rate for a service was not simple to determine. It depended entirely on the assumptions used to define the cost of a service. The AT&T system had been built largely on the notion of return on investment. If AT&T received, say, 5.29 percent return on its capital investment each year, its rates were about right. With regard to particular services, such as private lines, the rates were aimed at average price. Regulators grouped similar users into a class, and all paid the average rate for a service. The notion of average price was adjusted to include system values, such as the need to subsidize some users, and so the resulting rate structure supported many values. For example, the separations process produced a price for a company calling between its offices in separate cities. The private-line business had been priced near those station-to-station rates because both types of services were included in the averaging calculations. The values that entered the separations debate[60] influenced private-line prices. Yet some of the users knew they could build their own private lines more cheaply. To compete for the business of these users, AT&T used a cost-based pricing scheme in TELPAK. For a given capacity line, AT&T would figure how much it would cost per mile to construct a private line and would charge each user based on the number of miles actually used.

This approach made sense to AT&T. It was indeed the only basis on which it could compete for the new private-line business. Yet to some regulators and to officials unfamiliar with past policies, the huge price cuts suggested that AT&T had been historically overcharging their customers. Since there was no agreement among various government institutions about the right way to price services, AT&T was open to charges that it had behaved wrongly.

Yet if the FCC were to allow AT&T to implement TELPAK, it would discourage entry into the business by new firms. AT&T would win most of the contracts. Motorola's complaint was based on the idea that AT&T's new rate was aimed specifically at killing competition by charging less than the actual cost of the service. By encouraging competition and making services available at the lowest possible costs, the FCC would end up with few alternative carriers. That bothered FCC officials who were becoming increasingly worried about the size and power of AT&T. The FCC apparently valued competition and judged the quality of competition by the number of competitors in a market. Although AT&T was proposing a shift toward marginal cost pricing, favored by most economists,[61] the problem remained that AT&T was seen as a big powerful company in the early 1960s.

Another important case from this era was the Carterphone case, decided by the FCC in 1968. The Carterphone looked like an early modem, with a cradle for a telephone receiver. It connected a telephone to a two-way radio and so raised the interconnection issue once more. Oil companies, with their far-flung, remote, and temporary sites, were important users of the Carterphone and argued their business required the devices. Technically, the Carterphone was a tough case to judge. It was an electronic device, but its output that interconnected with the AT&T network was a human voice. Why shouldn't someone be allowed to attach something to the network, as long as it did not harm it? The principle was important to AT&T's monopoly on equipment manufacture. It was a clear sign that at least some of AT&T's customers wanted equipment not offered by its Western Electric subsidiary, and that independent manufacturers were able to build more sophisticated devices that performed some of the work formerly handled by AT&T's switching machines. In 1968, the FCC ruled that companies could connect to the network and that AT&T had to provide standards for such equipment.

A New Regulatory Regime and the Capture Thesis

The Carterphone decision represents a turning point in the regulation of AT&T. After a relatively brief period during which the company held a special status as the monopoly common communications carrier for the nation, technical and political developments showed that the distinction could not last. Outsiders could build machines that performed valuable services, and AT&T could not respond to all such demands. The regulatory process was open to the arguments of interests who wanted the newer, and usually cheaper, services. And the notion that the public was served by the monopolistic AT&T was cracking.

Within two months of the June 1968 Carterphone decision, a new company, Microwave Communications, Inc., known as MCI, began to form a national network of affiliates to deliver long-distance microwave service.[62] MCI had petitioned the FCC for the right to be a specialized carrier as far back as 1963 and had proposed a microwave link between Chicago and St. Louis. AT&T had opposed the request. The FCC found for MCI, yet did so in a 4 to 3 decision that characterizes the shifting thinking about the telephone system. The three dissenters objected mainly for the effects the decision would have on long-term policy for the AT&T network. If the near-term policy was to allow construction of telephone projects that were technically feasible and did not harm the network, it would only be a matter of time before their interconnection policy became a casualty of such new businesses. The national network was supported by prices that subsidized some users, and the decision allowed an exit to those who did not want to subsidize others. In principle, the majority in the case did not see a hard and fast barrier against connection to the local telephone networks—a move that would undercut the entire logic of the AT&T-regulated monopoly. The case did turn on quality issues as well—companies complained that AT&T did not offer them the data transmission services they needed—but the vote was split along policy lines. It could be said that the majority did not fear the growing forces of competition and saw instead an opportunity to counteract AT&T's monopoly power.[63] Although the vote was close, two things seemed to guide commissioners' thinking. The inroads into AT&T's business seemed at the time a quite small percentage of company revenues. This notion that the big company could afford it was coupled with growing popularity of the idea that it is wrong to protect companies from competition. Popular ideas of the role of corporations in American life were changing.

Policy experts were poles apart on the appropriate approach to regulation. The capture thesis—the belief that regulated companies had effectively seized control of their regulators—was widespread, and the developing consensus on an antidote to capture turned out to be equally challenging: competition, aided by enforcement of antitrust law.[64] A 1970 panel discussion pointed to the widening gulf.[65] The MCI private-line services had been approved because they were different from AT&T services (mainly, lower quality) and so were not competing. Well, what if MCI did offer services similar in quality to AT&T and charged less for them? How should AT&T respond? One answer applied the existing framework of FCC policy and asked about the effects on both firms. AT&T should be allowed to lower its prices to compete with the new firm. Otherwise, the FCC would be in the business of allocating markets to companies, a power it did not have. Yet if AT&T lowered its prices to the point where it wins and drives MCI from the market, the FCC would have failed to protect a company from predatory pricing. The implications of the MCI decision were an increase in political pressure on the FCC to do something about the consequences of lowering barriers to new competitors entering AT&T businesses. Ironically, its regulatory authority would grow due to an attempt to allow limited competition.

A second answer was provided by William Baxter, an economist who would later be the Justice Department official to settle the antitrust suit that resulted in the dismantling of AT&T. He argued that markets should be allowed to operate: a new company may try to make inroads into markets, and it may fail. The process leads to lower prices for consumers, a few failed firms, and pressures for the development of new and improved services.

This dichotomy among views toward regulation put the FCC into a quandry. Its decisions could only reflect the confusion in the wider political stream. This was illustrated in the 1978 Execunet decision. MCI wanted to offer services to its private-line customers that included interconnection with AT&T's local telephone switches.[66] The FCC ruled that it could not do so without a compelling logic beyond precedents. MCI appealed the case, and an appellate court reversed the decision.[67] The court found that the FCC had no compelling argument behind its policies. Rather, the clear trend in their policies was to open the telecommunications business to precisely the type of service proposed by MCI. The FCC had tried to open only specialized markets to competition, but technical developments were to continually change the boundaries between services.

These pressures led the FCC and federal courts to move more toward competitive principles in making policy. The issues were complex, at one point leading the FCC to admit that, in a rate-setting case, it could not determine AT&T's cost of serving a consumer.[68] This conclusion was in a sense obvious, given the different assumptions possible for understanding the cost of particular services. Once competitive prices came into use in some services, the rates set under other criteria made less and less sense. AT&T was a wealthy and powerful organization, but it was in the business of subsidizing most of its customers. The politics of state rate setting precluded any possibility of resetting rates according to more competitive criteria like marginal costs. State commissions would not stand for the rate increases of 50 percent or more that would accompany more rational prices, and the economically rational method of metering local call usage was unacceptable to state regulatory commissions. AT&T officials felt they had to compete in developing markets—telecommunications was, after all, their business—but when they met and beat competitors' rates, they were accused of anticompetitive behavior.

There was really no way for AT&T to get out of this dilemma. They had been a willing partner to the construction of a regulated monopoly. The policies that had chipped away at that system were myopically applied, and both regulators and AT&T officials were surprised when others did not share their views of the industry. During the 1960s and early 1970s, public ideas about regulation turned increasingly against the interests of large corporations. The disparate forces were reflected in the ways AT&T was treated by different government agencies.[69] In conflicts with MCI following the Execunet case, for example, AT&T was accused by MCI of misusing its monopoly power to hurt a competitor. The FCC saw MCI as a customer of AT&T, since MCI's complaint was about the conditions under which it could interconnect with the Bell network. The FCC had to ask whether the conditions and prices applied by AT&T were appropriate compared to other customers. DOJ's Antitrust Division looked at the same events and saw MCI as a competitor to AT&T. Their different procedures and standards left AT&T in the position, in the eyes of the national government, of having no clear public purpose.

AT&T was really not prepared for the changes in its regulatory regime. The company chairs, H. I. Romnes and later John D. deButts, did not fully comprehend the political climate of the time.[70] They were perhaps more focused on service and organizational efficiency. During 1969, for example, AT&T's service to New York City proved to be seriously deficient; several local exchange failures became national news, and top officials knew the problem was not isolated. Those problems were effectively addressed by AT&T, but the FCC and DOJ were less interested in service standards and efficiency than in perceptions that AT&T was a powerful organization.[71]

The FCC's method for reaching decisions evolved during this period and complicated their regulatory task. Like many federal agencies, they moved away from negotiations toward more formal hearings that sought to broaden opportunities for participation in administrative decisions.[72] The changes actually raised barriers to widespread political participation. The agency's quasi-judicial proceedings did not meet judicial standards of evidence or protection of the rights of individuals or corporations. The FCC procedure of lumping all material about a case into a "docket," literally a list of everything received without reference to their relative importance or influence on decisions, is not a proper record of what the agency actually did in a case. The danger in the procedure lay in the possibility of insiders knowing who were the important players and which were the important documents, information hidden from the general public.[73] The danger may be hypothetical in the sense that the public seldom rises to take an interest in complicated technical issues that come before administrative agencies. When this occasionally happens, sifting through dockets without an insider's distinctions of significance is a daunting task.

DOJ suffered from poor leadership during the Nixon years. Nixon's first attorney general, John Mitchell, was regarded as exceptionally partisan while in office. Soon he resigned to head Nixon's 1972 reelection campaign, and he was indicted for obstruction of justice when he was attorney general. His successor, Richard Kleindienst, was forced to resign in April 1973 over charges he had lied to Congress in April 1973 as part of a Nixon administration effort to stall the growing momentum toward impeachment. The new attorney general, Elliot Richardson, lasted only until October 20, the so-called Saturday Night Massacre. Nixon had ordered Richardson to fire Watergate special prosecutor Archibald Cox. Richardson refused and resigned. Deputy Attorney General William Ruckelshaus also refused the order and resigned. Solicitor General Robert Bork, the third-ranking DOJ official, fired Cox and became acting attorney general. In December 1973, Nixon nominated Ohio senator William Saxbe for attorney general. His chief qualification was perhaps that he was a member of the Senate and could be confirmed. The crisis of leadership left DOJ without any clear policy direction. The institutional turmoil was to have profound consequences for AT&T.

In 1974, the Antitrust Division of the Justice Department filed suit in federal district court alleging that AT&T had used its monopoly power to exclude other manufacturers from making customer equipment and to exclude long-distance competitors from interconnections.[74] This suit would later, in 1982, lead to the breakup of AT&T. The announcement of the suit was something of a surprise to company officials. They had been talking with DOJ officials for some time and were assured that discussions would come before any suit was filed. That did not happen, and AT&T officials were stunned.[75] To underscore the point that the government's approach to regulation lacked any clear vision, other members of the Justice Department and of President Ford's cabinet reported that no policy discussion had taken place regarding the suit. Attorney General Saxbe may have made the decision by himself.

AT&T was a monopoly, but it was allowed to avoid antitrust rules because of its regulated environment. By limiting the businesses AT&T could enter, the FCC became the buffer between the company and antitrust regulations. Ironically, it was the FCC's earlier moves toward competition that put AT&T in antitrust jeopardy. Since the company was now engaged in some competition in providing long-distance services, manufacturing equipment, and pricing the access of outside services, there was a danger the company would use proceeds from its monopoly businesses to subsidize its competitive ones. That was essentially what DOJ alleged in its 1974 suit. The FCC's oversight turned out to be no protection from antitrust. Even though the FCC employed many more experts on AT&T than did DOJ's Antitrust Division, it was not effective in helping AT&T make its case.

Looking at AT&T, DOJ, and the FCC at the time of the filing of the antitrust suit, one realizes that it is no exaggeration to say that there was no consensus on policy. There was no agreement on what the preferred world of telecommunications should be and no shared sense of how to get there. The issues that reached the institutional agendas got there through the entire range of avenues depicted in the political model in Figure 1.1. Policies were made without apparent consideration of effects with regard to the rest of the system. Over a period of two decades, the FCC had made decisions that helped create competition in specialized services (like private lines) and equipment, while still claiming support for universal service and reasonable rates for the large mass of household consumers. Its relations with AT&T had grown increasingly adversarial.[76] AT&T had not altered its vision of itself as a regulated natural monopoly, and this put it directly in the path of the Department of Justice.

Congress Gets Involved

In 1976, Congress began considering the issues raised by the new competitive pressures, largely because AT&T presented convincing arguments that telecommunications policymaking had no center. The FCC, courts, and DOJ had pursued actions that, in the view of AT&T, had usurped the role of Congress in setting national policy.[77] From AT&T's point of view, the bill that was the focus of early hearings in the fall of 1976[78] was an opportunity to discuss the problem of institutional authority. The bill was commonly referred to as the Bell bill because it contained no compromise. Instead, it seemed to turn back the clock to an earlier time: no one would be allowed to compete with AT&T in interstate services, the existing rate structure was necessary for universal service, new carriers that wanted to offer service had to show that AT&T would be unable to provide the same services in the future, and the FCC would be deprived of jurisdiction over regulation of terminal equipment.

Congress had little policy expertise in telecommunications issues. The generation that had passed the 1934 Act had long departed. Perhaps half a dozen members were at all knowledgeable about the issues. Members of the House Commerce Committee's subcommittee on communications were part of a new core of officials who took seriously the new arguments about deregulation. Perhaps more important, they and their staff were not consulted in AT&T's drive to introduce and collect sponsors for the bill. The hearings did not go well for AT&T. In a sense, Congress was the wrong place to press their point, although they desperately needed legislative relief. Their main argument was that monopoly was good for universal service and for system reliability. Bell officials essentially argued that the telephone system worked well because AT&T was dedicated to providing the best service and the latest technology at affordable prices. In 1976, virtually no consumer groups testified at the hearings, so AT&T was in effect the only voice that claimed to represent the average residential consumer.

This argument did not sit well with committee members. Monopoly was difficult to defend in principle. Also at the hearing were independent company operators, such as the head of MCI, who argued that AT&T tried to use its tremendous monopoly power to crush his company. FCC officials also explained that the telecommunications business would work better with competition and that they were committed to competitive policies.

In retrospect, AT&T was right in substance, however clumsy in tactics. They responded to FCC charges by pointing out that the present turmoil in the industry and the antitrust action were the result of a series of steps that chipped away at the 1934 Act framework. The FCC had listened to the interests of businesses that sought to take advantage of the incentives inherent in the regulated rates. It amounted to an incremental but substantial change in the law.

Opponents' arguments did point to the weaknesses of regulated monopolies. Most companies, like MCI, arose to provide services that were not offered by AT&T. These nascent services had grown to where they were overlapping those offered by AT&T, and AT&T had expanded its services to counter their growth. Representatives of some of the new technologies (such as the beginning of the Internet) claimed that AT&T was seeking to compete with their services. Together, the AT&T opponents convinced members of Congress that the trend toward competition and deregulation, built on new technologies, could not be undone. The committee stopped the bill by the time of the 1976 elections, an election that highlighted arguments about excessive government regulation.

As the 95th Congress convened in 1977, Representative Lionel Van Deerlin (D-CA) and Senator Ernest Hollings (D-SC) began new hearings in their committees, but they were not limited to the Bell bill. Their committees expanded their inquiries into a wide range of issues, intending a complete reconsideration of the Communications Act of 1934. Each would come to support the trend to deregulation that spread through the Congress in 1978.

AT&T responded to the hearings as they did the year before. It was a sign that the company had not read the political winds. In 1977, Congress was not going to accept their claim to represent the interests of consumers. The Consumer Federation of America (CFA) gave testimony at the hearings, and they too claimed to speak for consumers, but in a way that was very different from AT&T.[79] The interests of consumers included competition by new companies in areas such as the manufacture and sale of equipment, and calls for special subsidies for low-income people and PEG organizations (including consumer groups like CFA). It was a voice that said consumer interests lay with the opponents of AT&T.

One of the important features of congressional policymaking is that, compared to institutions like courts and the FCC, a wide variety of actors can influence policy. Sometimes this creates new and surprising developments. For example, while the FCC worked against the Bell bill in the 94th and 95th Congresses, their testimony helped to convince Van Deerlin to embark on a complete rewrite of the 1934 Act. His idea of a new competitive era included abolition of the FCC.[80] Some in Congress wanted to control policy rather than leave it in the hands of the FCC and the courts. Yet one of the reasons cited by House Judiciary chair Peter Rodino Jr. for not moving on a similar bill in 1980 was that he did not want to undercut the pending DOJ suit against AT&T.

The regulatory politics clearly moved further toward competition. President Carter appointed Charles Ferris, who believed in the procompetitive policies, to head the FCC in 1977. Economists played a bigger role in FCC policymaking and brought with them a near-unanimous endorsement of increased competition.[81] Changes occurred quickly, as in a 1978 FCC decision to begin a program to certify competitors' equipment for use on the AT&T network and the 1979 FCC decision that enabled MCI to offer competitive long-distance service. AT&T was an important actor in the policy stream, but until it accepted the developing consensus, it could act only to block legislation.

In 1979, a new CEO took over at AT&T with the express charge of getting it ready to operate as a competitive company.[82] The company's leadership recognized, perhaps belatedly, that it had reached the end of an era. Its most profitable businesses were being picked off by new competitors; the regulatory processes needed to approve company responses were slow and the outcomes uncertain; the company was not allowed to enter the new information businesses that it knew would be the future of digital communications. And it was faced with an antitrust suit and repeated attempts to legislate a new future for AT&T. Perhaps a decisive factor in the change was the proposed Communications Act of 1978. Senator Hollings sponsored the bill, and although AT&T was able to block the legislation, it showed that congressional committee members, the specialists who in an earlier decade had shared AT&T's view of the world, had now come to see the virtues of the new procompetitive policies. AT&T's leaders could finally see the basic problem. In terms of the model in Figure 1.1, the problem, policy, and political streams were coalescing under similar ideas. Within six months, the plans were made to have Charles Brown replace deButts as chair. The new leader made it his mission to develop a new ethos at AT&T.

The Breakup of AT&T

The transition was not immediate. AT&T wanted to fight the antitrust suit that had been filed in 1974, but events caused them to reconsider. Despite turnover in key Antitrust Division personnel and the death of the first assigned trial judge, the case moved to trial relatively quickly. This was an exception to antitrust cases during the 1980s. DOJ completed its case, and AT&T asked to have the case dismissed. The judge, Harold Greene, refused, and his opinion was so strongly worded that it shocked AT&T. It was clear the judge believed that the Justice Department had a strong case, and AT&T attorneys concluded they would probably lose at the district court level. This was the situation in late 1981.

AT&T hoped for a negotiated settlement with the new conservative Republican administration, but the Antitrust Division head, William Baxter, was determined to support the suit. Baxter had taught at Stanford Law School where he was known as a supporter of the Chicago School economists. Whereas traditional Republicans had a reputation for being friendly to business concerns, this was a new brand of conservative. Baxter supported market forces per se rather than the interests of particular businesses. He had acquired a reputation for saying government antitrust law was poorly applied and that the only reason for antitrust was to promote competition. He did not see bigness as bad. Regulation was to blame for economic inefficiencies. Baxter may have been to the right of most telecommunications policy specialists, but he was in an important position.

Baxter's idea was to separate the regulated from the competitive parts of AT&T, and he declared at a news conference in April 1981 that he was prepared to litigate the case "to the eyeballs."

Politically, the suit was a complicated situation. AT&T did not want to break itself up, and it had several allies in the Reagan administration. But Baxter was the top DOJ official on the case (his superiors at Justice had excused themselves because of possible conflicts of interest—AT&T stock was held by more investors than any other in the world). AT&T supporters in the administration tried to urge the Defense Department to argue that the case should be dropped because a dismantled AT&T would imperil national security communications. A White House task force was ready to ask the president to order Baxter to drop the case. Senate Republicans cooperated and passed legislation that would allow AT&T to establish competitive subsidiaries for some businesses, thus sidestepping divestiture. But Baxter was an intelligent and forceful man. He was effective at explaining what he saw as defects in the Senate legislation, and he did not wilt under the pressure. He simply won the argument before the president and his top advisers. He tried to have the suit settled as part of a 1956 consent decree from an earlier antitrust case against AT&T, which opened the possibility that Judge Greene would not have jurisdiction over the case. Judge Greene was likely to impose harsher treatment on AT&T than would Baxter. Overall, the situation was complicated, and AT&T could end up considerably worse off than under Baxter's divestiture idea.

In January 1982, AT&T and the Justice Department agreed to the divestiture and settled the suit. Some details were left to be worked out, but the outlines were clear: AT&T would get rid of its local operating companies (which later were formed into the seven RBOCs,[83] such as U S West and Nynex) but would keep its long-distance services, Western Electric, Bell Labs, and its Yellow Pages. The long-distance services would still be regulated by the FCC. AT&T would be able to enter into new businesses such as computer applications in communications and wireless services. The settlement, officially an extension of the 1956 consent decree, became known as the Modified Final Judgment, or MFJ.

At the time, AT&T leadership understood that the divestiture agreement could not last. In congressional hearings on the proposed settlement, AT&T chair Brown predicted the outcome would be regulated companies providing universal service, competitive companies, and access fees charged for the competitive companies to gain access to regulated businesses. The proposed system would put in place incentives to develop the technology to bypass local telephone service, whether by cable lines, cellular radio, or microwave equipment.[84] Regulated companies may not survive in a competitive atmosphere. But competition spells the end of the public policy of universal access. Such changes in the vision of AT&T leadership was part of the ongoing shift in public ideas. One way to describe the change is as a redefinition of the public interest, "a shift away from a concern with stability and a kind of social equity to a concern with market controls and economic efficiency."[85]

After divestiture, much of the telecommunications business was still regulated. The RBOCs were heavily regulated and could not sell long-distance service outside of small designated areas. There was still much work for the FCC. The local telephone companies were subject to state regulation, which included regulated rates and entry. This was to become a crucial issue as technologies developed that erased the old boundaries between local and long-distance services, and between telephone and other information technologies such as cable and broadcast television. The settlement endorsed competitive markets in long-distance and equipment manufacture. The private-line business was growing, and companies were no longer dependent on AT&T for their telephone equipment. The cable television industry was growing and largely came under state and local regulations.

Why had deregulation in telecommunications come through administrative agencies and courts rather than through legislation? As with the airline and trucking industries, the accelerating movement of the regulatory agencies toward deregulation sent troubling signals to regulated companies. The pace of deregulation could not be controlled, and the timing and cost of decisions were unpredictable. The regulated companies generally believed they could achieve a better balancing of interests in their direction if they consented to legislated deregulation.[86] But not AT&T.

This is perhaps all the more surprising in that the 1982 consent decree established an ongoing supervisory relationship of Judge Greene's court over AT&T and the RBOCs. AT&T and regional Bell appeals to enter new businesses or change practices covered by the consent decree were to come before the court instead of the FCC. While Judge Greene did have the authority to end restrictions on the companies if he believed that competition would work properly, if allowed, he had a reputation for toughness. The only major restriction the RBOCs succeeded in lifting by 1984 was the bar against them offering information services. At about the same time, Congress passed the Cable Communications Policy Act, which forbade local telephone companies from delivering cable television services. This was a telephone issue because collectively the RBOCs had a strong political voice, and they knew about the possibilities of bypass. They needed to stay competitive in the developing businesses, and they had an interest in long-distance services and cable television. While legislation was introduced in 1985 (by Representative, now Senator, John Breaux [D-LA]) to take jurisdiction away from Judge Greene's court, it did not succeed. Most congressional leaders believed the problem of telecommunications was under control.

One factor that precluded legislation was AT&T's rather late resolve to become a competitive company. It takes time to change a company ethos. For example, one of the reasons AT&T was such an effective power in the Congress was that it had important economic interests, in the form of the local telephone company, in every legislative district. In a sense, the divestiture cast these local interests adrift to make their own way. The new company was looking at other businesses when it thought of the future. By this understanding, Baxter's offer was a better deal than AT&T could expect to emerge from the Congress. The policy window opened briefly, and AT&T jumped through.

The episode is a stark example of the consequences of a fragmented policymaking process. Multiple venues and avenues of influence have among their virtues an ability to encompass a wide range of interests, ideas, and arguments. The argument can be made that this is what democracy looks like in a modern and complicated state. The other side of that coin is a policy chaos that no sane individual would design. Ongoing FCC oversight of AT&T was heading in the direction of more competition. DOJ's Antitrust Division pressed the argument that during this same period, AT&T used its monopoly power in prohibited ways. DOJ presented this argument in a court that works by its own rules and acts quite independently of DOJ. The outcome of the case hinged on several assumptions about the behavior of affected parties, some of which turned out to be wrong. The RBOCs were still closely regulated by state utility boards and commissions, which in turn have enormous influence over the financial situation of the RBOCs. Under the divestiture agreement, the RBOC leadership turned out to be surprisingly able to adapt to a more competitive environment and petitioned the court for hundreds of waivers from line-of-business restrictions.

A simple way to make sense of the policy fragmentation is to focus on design and results. The 1982 consent decree was intended to settle the problems that gave rise to the dispute between AT&T and DOJ's Antitrust Division. Clearly, it did not. In less than a decade, nearly all telecommunications interests saw the need for comprehensive legislation. The ongoing relationship between AT&T, the RBOCs, and the court showed that the issue of monopoly power would never die so long as it was given a hearing. At the same time, the FCC's authority was continually challenged by competing claims over forces loosed by the MFJ. From this view, the divestiture policy was an abysmal failure.

A second feature of telecommunications politics is that so few people care about it. The issues are technical and complicated, and it is difficult to see how they are related to the reliable and generally low-cost instrument most citizens use to make calls. There was no driving force behind a consensus among the community of policy oriented professionals. The policy stream was highly fragmented. As Martha Derthick and Paul Quirk put it, new policies were made when AT&T, recognizing the futility of further challenge, stopped challenging them.[87] After divestiture it took a full decade for the regional Bells, with their local affiliates, and cable television companies to resolve a vision of a competitive world that might work to their advantage. By then a coalition could form around key interests, and legislative control of policy was once again possible. That is the subject of the next chapter.

Notes

1. Accounts of the story are found in Goulden, *Monopoly,* pp. 33–36; Brooks, *Telephone,* pp. 46–47; Stone, *Wrong Number,* p. 35; and Brock, *Telecommunications,* p. 90. Brock lists the date as February 17. Brooks perhaps provides the most reliable history in the sense that he had the greatest access to AT&T files; he is at times quite critical but overall conveys a positive view of the company. A balanced critical history is in Horwitz, *Irony*. Temin, with Galambos, *Fall of the Bell System,* made extensive use of interviews with AT&T officials and regulators and provides

detailed accounts of important regulatory issues; but the book focuses more on the recent history of AT&T.

2. Bell's vision of the future of telephony is recounted in Pool, *Forecasting the Telephone,* p. 21.

3. Early leases of telephones sold the customer the use of and service for a private instrument that was connected to one other phone. The concept of wiring phones into a switching center, so that a local caller could connect to any other on the exchange, took a few years to develop.

4. Brock, *Telecommunications*, p. 109, notes that Bell companies had by that time amassed around 900 additional patents on various parts of phone systems and could use those in patent infringement cases even after the basic patents had expired.

5. Brooks, *Telephone,* p. 103.

6. Stone, *Wrong Number*, p. 45. The story of the early development of AT&T and its handling of the competition is also told in Goulden, *Monopoly,* and Horwitz, *Irony*.

7. Brooks, *Telephone,* p. 108.

8. Ibid., p. 114.

9. Horwitz, *Irony*, makes the argument that later stages of regulatory conflict centered on a battle over which definition of the public interest became legitimate. The point is made for this early stage in Stone, *Wrong Number*, p. 45. Goulden, *Monopoly*, offers several examples of state politics over these issues, pp. 67–72.

10. The point is suggested in Brock, *Telecommunications*, p. 122; and Brooks, *Telephone*, pp. 111–112.

11. In *Munn v. Illinois,* the Supreme Court found that a state legislature could set standards for the use and price of a business's facilities—in this case, grain elevators. The regulation could reasonably protect citizens from harm done by the owner of private property if the public had an interest in such protection.

12. *Smyth v. Ames*.

13. Brock, *Telecommunications*, p. 124, notes that Bell service was primarily in the center of cities, whereas their competitors served mainly small towns and rural areas. Some farmers connected telephones via their barbed-wire fences. Brock (p. 111) cites the demand for such crude local systems as evidence that subsidies for isolated areas are not needed, whereas Goulden, *Monopoly*, p. 62, uses the example to illustrate Bell companies using their monopoly power to overcharge subscribers.

14. For a history of Progressivism, see Hofstadter, *Age of Reform;* and Weibe, *Business and Reform.*

15. In Chapter 5, we see that this form of political pressure on Justice Department policies has endured for more than seventy-five years.

16. For his change of direction, Vail achieved an unparalleled reputation within AT&T. See von Auw, *Heritage and Destiny,* pp. 308–309. Vail's willingness to assert a public role for AT&T is reminiscent of the business leaders described by Arnold, *Folklore of Capitalism,* who are steadfast in their public principles, believe they have a unique ability to understand the principles, and are often politically effective.

17. The letter is reprinted in U.S. Federal Communications Commission, *Telephone Investigation: Proposed Report* (Washington, D.C.: Government Printing Office, 1938), pp. 139–141, brought to my attention in Horwitz, *Irony*.

18. See Brooks, *Telephone*, pp. 143–144.

19. The ability of early-twentieth-century business leaders to mobilize political resources was described in Brady, *Business as a System of Power*.

20. Horwitz, *Irony*, pp. 100–110; Brooks, *Telephone*, pp. 148–149.

21. This is the argument of Horwitz, *Irony*. It is not suggested in Temin with Galambos, *Fall of the Bell System*, or in Brooks, *Telephone*. Since Postmaster General Burleson, who took office in March 1913, established a committee to look into the matter during that year, and the Kingsbury commitment was dated December 19, 1913, such a relationship is certainly plausible. We should remember that at the time, antitrust laws seemed to be very strong in the wake of the government's success in its 1911 antitrust suits against Standard Oil of New Jersey and American Tobacco.

22. Weinstein, in *Corporate Ideal*, argued that business leaders successfully worked for regulation that would restrain the worst of corporate behavior. Part of his argument is a claim that business leaders successfully molded a popular ideology that worked to restrain the most radical bits of the labor movement while recognizing the need for all classes to share in the benefits of a growing economy. Compare Wiebe, *Business and Reform*, and Hofstadter, *Age of Reform*. They do not disagree with Weinstein over the active role played by business leaders in spreading ideas and supporting regulation of the worst excesses of corporations and unions; their accounts do not rely on class divisions to explain this behavior. See also Thimm, *Business Ideologies*, who claimed that business leaders adopted the rationalism of their factories as a value to be applied in American public life. They ultimately failed, he said, because there were not enough imaginative leaders the likes of Marcus Alonzo Hanna. This explanation accepts, in the concepts of Chapter 1, the determinist argument about technological change.

23. The account is in Brooks, *Telephone*, p. 152. See also Horwitz, *Irony*, pp. 101–102.

24. However, the return on investment was based on fixed capital rather than the actual cost of providing various services.

25. See Brock, *Telecommunications*, pp. 158–159. He relies on company reports and a speech by Vail to make the case that AT&T saw itself as providing a public service, and as such it needed protection from irresponsible corporations that would raid the more profitable parts of its business. Haber, in *Efficiency and Uplift*, p. 74, raised the possibility that the 1910–1911 railroad rate-making controversy fueled a tendency among political leaders to see these regulatory problems in terms of efficiency and proper organization, a similar notion to Vail's ideal of a responsible, efficient, and public-oriented corporation. Parkes, in *Recent America*, pp. 236–237, said the railroad rate-making controversy was the decisive issue behind the Mann-Elkins Act.

26. Horwitz, *Irony*, p. 102; Brock, *Telecommunications*, p. 156. This was the Willis-Graham Act.

27. Brock, *Telecommunications*, tells this story at the end of his chapter 6. The early history of the DOJ's Antitrust Division is told in Thorelli, *Federal Antitrust Policy*, and in Weaver, *Decision to Prosecute*.

28. Goulden, *Monopoly*, Chapters 4 and 5. The most exhaustive account of such practices was contained in the FCC's investigation of AT&T, popularly called the Walker investigation (after Paul A. Walker, head of the FCC Telephone Division): Federal Communications Commission, *Investigation of the Telephone Industry*.

29. A presidential commission on the new focus in public administration summarized its work in Gulick and Urwick, *Science of Administration*.

30. Seidman and Gilmour, *Politics, Position, and Power*, describe ideas about reorganization as an orthodoxy that adherents uncritically use in attempts to change government more to their liking.

31. See Robinson, "Federal Communications Act," pp. 3–24. There seems to be no evidence that the creation of the FCC was part of a trend to use the public power of the state to counterbalance the growing private power of monopolistic corporations, as suggested in Galbraith, *American Capitalism,* or in a softer version of the argument, to balance conflicting groups, as suggested in Leuchtenburg, *Roosevelt and the New Deal.* Perhaps the rapid pace of the New Deal Congress shortened debate, but if these accounts are accurate, one would expect some mention of the dangers of corporate power in the debate records. Conkin, in *The New Deal,* argued that the New Deal agencies, including the FCC, were the product of an entrenched class system defending private economic power in the face of imminent class warfare. If that was going on, it escaped the stated concerns of large and small communications companies, legislators, and administrators involved in the creation of the FCC.

32. Robinson, "Federal Communications Act."

33. Ibid., pp. 14–15. The phrases from the act appear in S. 3285, Public Law No. 416, 73rd Congress, Title II, section 201 (a) and (b), and many other places in the act. See, for example, sections 214 and 215. The bill is reprinted in Paglin, *Legislative History,* and section 201 is found on page 927 of that work.

34. By the end of World War II, the delegation issues were widely recognized as important, and this recognition led to the passage of the Administrative Procedures Act (APA) in 1947. For a description of the APA and of the evolution of administrative thinking, see Schuman and Olufs, *Public Administration,* pp. 461–466, and chap. 4 and 5.

35. See Pool, *Forecasting the Telephone,* p. 156.

36. Horwitz, *Irony,* p. 127; Brock, *Telecommunications,* p. 179. Horwitz writes, on p. 128, "The regulation of telecommunications was essentially protective because, despite problems, the system *worked*."

37. Brooks, *Telephone,* pp. 196–199. The FCC proposed report was issued on April 1, 1938, and its implications were that government should more directly regulate rates and order competitive bidding by AT&T on equipment purchases. Brooks notes that AT&T stock value dropped as a result of the controversy. The company responded to the FCC charges and enlisted the support of other government departments. The FCC was persuaded to delete the strong policy recommendations from the final report issued in June 1939.

38. Brock, *Telecommunications,* p. 177.

39. Horwitz, *Irony,* p. 129; see Brock, *Telecommunications,* pp. 179–180; Goulden, *Monopoly,* pp. 84–86.

40. Horowitz, *Irony,* p. 134. A discussion of different styles of regulatory oversight and the consequences for policy and the quality of relations between regulators and industry is in Bardarch and Kagan, *Going by the Book.* Despite its strengths, a negotiation approach is difficult to justify in the U.S. political system because the prevailing notions of legitimate authority rely heavily on procedures and formal recognition of the rights and standing of interested parties. See Rohr, *To Run a Constitution.*

41. Federal Communications Commission, *Investigation of the Telephone Industry.*

42. This is based on Temin with Galambos, *Fall of the Bell System,* pp. 19–27. See also Horwitz, *Irony*, pp. 133–135.

43. The key court case involved the state of Illinois. The Illinois Bell company alleged that the state-required rates were confiscatory, that is, did not allow a reasonable return on investment. See *Smith v. Illinois Bell Tel. Co.* The FCC decision

was described in Temin with Galambos, *Fall of the Bell System,* pp. 22–23, and became codified in the FCC's *Separations Manual*, October 1947.

44. In metered local usage, a customer is billed by the load put on the telephone network. Calls are charged by the minute, and calls that use several switches in the network (such as long-distance calls) are charged at a higher rate. People who lived in England during the late 1970s and the 1980s may recall the telephones with odometer-like counters, which clicked off the units of network usage during each call. Regulators believed, and still believe, that U.S. citizens are attached to the idea of single-line fee for unlimited local use.

45. The example is from Temin with Galambos, *Fall of the Bell System,* p. 25.

46. Goulden's *Monopoly* takes this tone.

47. Danielian, *AT&T.*

48. Brooks, *Telephone*. The point is emphasized in Horwitz, *Irony*, p. 128.

49. A sense of the enormous range of inventions and organizational issues that helped form the Bell system is found in a multivolume set, *A History of Engineering and Science in the Bell System,* edited by S. Millman. Issues such as the physics of switches and procedures for quality assurance are explained in detail in the various volumes. See Fagen, *The Early Years;* Fagen, *National Service in War and Peace;* Schindler, *Switching Technology;* and Millman, *Communications Sciences.*

50. Brooks, *Telephone,* pp. 231–238; Goulden, *Monopoly,* pp. 86–103; Horwitz, *Irony,* pp. 141–143; Brock, *Telecommunications,* pp. 187–194.

51. An interesting question, raised by Horwitz, *Irony*, pp. 142–145, is why AT&T would agree to stay out of the computer business at a time when they knew it would be an important industry. He argues that a regulated company becomes risk-averse and that AT&T's assertion that it wanted to focus on communications does not tell the whole story. This is consistent with the relationship between regulatory policy and leadership transitions at AT&T and underscores the importance of ideas held by company leaders. For a detailed and introspective discussion of AT&T leadership ideals, see von Auw, *Heritage and Destiny,* pp. 373–396; von Auw was an AT&T vice-president and assistant to the chairman of the board from 1969 through 1981.

52. See Horwitz, *Irony,* pp. 142–143.

53. Brooks, *Telephone,* p. 234.

54. The cases are discussed in Brock, *Telecommunications;* Stone, *Wrong Number*; Goulden, *Monopoly;* and Horwitz, *Irony.*

55. Stone, *Wrong Number,* p. 124, argues that this is an early case of judicial activism and implies that the court went well beyond any principles contained in the 1934 Communications Act or other statutes. It does illustrate one of the difficulties in implementing policy under a separation of powers constitution.

56. The Above 890 decision, rendered by the FCC, *Allocation of Frequencies.* The "890" refers to megacycles, and 890 megahertz is the lower limit of the microwave portion of the electromagnetic spectrum.

57. Temin with Galambos, *Fall of the Bell System,* p. 29.

58. Ibid., p. 31.

59. Ibid., pp. 28–40; Brock, *Telecommunications*, pp. 207–210. The TELPAK rate structure went into effect in 1961.

60. See notes 42 and 59.

61. One of the more accessible descriptions is Wenders, *Economics of Telecommunications,* chap. 4. See also Viscusi, Vernon, and Harrington, *Regulation and Antitrust,* chap. 15.

62. The history of MCI is told in detail by Cantelon, *History of MCI.* This is an MCI publication marking the company's twenty-fifth anniversary. Critical treatments include Temin with Galambos, *Fall of the Bell System,* pp. 47–51; Brock, *Telecommunications*, pp. 211–232; Horwitz, *Irony,* pp. 226–235.

63. Brock, *Telecommunications*, pp. 211–212, emphasizes the policy dispute. Horwitz, *Irony,* p. 227, adds to it the notion that an important idea had changed: AT&T was now seen as a powerful company that had captured its ersatz regulator, and that more liberal FCC appointees wanted to establish a new direction.

64. The argument linking the capture thesis to ideas about competition is developed in Pertschuck, *Revolt Against Regulation.* For an influential assertion of the capture thesis, see McConnell, *Private Power.*

65. Panel discussion, "The Role of Competition in Transportation and Communications," *Antitrust Law Journal* 39 (1970): 487–489. This source was brought to my attention in Temin with Galambos, *Fall of the Bell System,* p. 2.

66. The FCC's *Execunet* decision *[MCI Telecommunications Corporation v. FCC].*

67. Ibid.

68. This happened in the case of a tariff AT&T submitted to the FCC to counter the prices offered by MCI. See AT&T 74 FCC 2d 1 (1979), recon., 85 FCC 2d 549 (1981). The example is cited in Crandall, *After the Breakup,* pp. 27–28.

69. The point was made by Temin with Galambos, *Fall of the Bell System,* p. 109.

70. Ibid., p. 111. Romnes became chair and CEO in February 1967, and deButts followed him in April 1972. For a discussion of their views of regulation and competition during this period, see von Auw, *Heritage and Destiny,* pp. 73–79.

71. von Auw, *Heritage and Destiny*.

72. See Schuman and Olufs, *Public Administration;* Bardarch and Kagan, *Going by the Book*.

73. This possibility was described in *Home Box Office, Inc. v. Federal Communications Commission,* discussed in Seidman and Gilmour, *Politics, Position, and Power,* pp. 151–152.

74. The case was settled as a modification of the 1956 antitrust action against AT&T, *U.S. v. American Telephone and Telegraph Co.*

75. Temin with Galambos, *Fall of the Bell System,* p. 110; von Auw, *Heritage and Destiny,* pp. 107–108. An extended account is in Coll, *Deal of the Century.*

76. Temin with Galambos, *Fall of the Bell System,* p. 114.

77. This account relies on the interpretations of Persons, *Energy and Telecommunications Policy,* and of Temin with Galambos, *Fall of the Bell System.* Persons uses an exhaustive reading of the hearings record to reconstruct the development of ideas in congressional policymaking. Temin interviewed many AT&T, DOJ, FCC, congressional, and other officials to construct a history of recent policymaking. They each support the notion that several factors drive the policymaking process: changing technology, changing public ideas, organization dynamics, and elections. Compare their systematic attention to the record with Tunstall, *Comunications Deregulation,* and that of Coll, *Deal of the Century.*

78. H.R. 12323, the Consumer Communications Reform Act of 1976.

79. Persons, *Energy and Telecommunications Policy,* pp. 105–106.

80. Temin with Galambos, *Fall of the Bell System,* observed "the contrast between Van Deerlin's bill and the Bell bill could not have been more complete," p. 130.

81. Horwitz, *Irony*, p. 238. Derthick and Quirk, *Politics of Deregulation,* cite a bibliography of more than 150 studies that point to the failure of regulation and the benefits of competition.

82. See the account of the policy discussions within the company and the resulting stance toward legislation in the 1970s in Temin with Galambos, *Fall of the Bell System,* pp. 142–159.

83. Pronounced "are-box."

84. Quoted in Persons, *Energy and Telecommunications Policy,* p. 139.

85. Horwitz, *Irony*, p. 16.

86. Derthick and Quirk, *Politics of Deregulation,* p. 203.

87. Ibid., p. 256.

3 Major Legislation Emerges

An Unstable Era

The breakup of AT&T did not establish a stable regulatory framework for telecommunications. From the start, powerful forces worked to destabilize policy.

One important force was the emergence of digital technologies. The AT&T divestiture settlement emerged at about the same time as the invention of the personal computer. Over the next ten years, the explosion of digital technology dissolved the barriers among regulated businesses. If electronic signals are put in digital form, the machinery for sending and receiving such signals can handle virtually anything. Voice telephone services, fax transmissions, the audio and video portions of cable television, on-line data services, signals from a business or home security system, papers delivered at a professional conference, etc., are all essentially the same thing from the standpoint of digital transmission. The signals can be sent through wires, through cables that convey light, or through various frequencies of the electromagnetic spectrum.

As more and more nonvoice data travel through a communications network, charging by the minute for use of the network makes less and less sense. The amount of data sent or received becomes the key issue between buyers and sellers.[1] Yet the existing regulatory framework had organizations and sets of rules responsible for cable television, long-distance telephones, local telephone service, and broadcasting based on the old technologies and separations between these businesses. The remade AT&T was prospering under the new arrangements, and the leadership of the RBOCs wanted to participate in the new possibilities. Altogether, in the decade after the breakup of AT&T telecommunications, sales of goods and services doubled to about $160 billion, as large as the markets for automobiles and trucks.[2] The field had become one of the biggest and most dynamic in the economy.

The regulatory regime of the divestiture era, summarized briefly at the end of Chapter 2, continued to generate strong political support for policy change. The divestiture agreement included large important roles for the federal court overseeing the divestiture agreement, under Judge Harold Greene, and for the FCC. In 1988, for example, Judge Greene decided that the RBOCs had an effective monopoly on local service; there was, in effect, a "bottleneck" between customers and a range of services offered by RBOC competitors, who were not allowed to compete in long-distance services. The RBOCs had argued that AT&T was, in effect, bypassing their facilities and making use of direct transmissions among major customers, such as banks and insurance companies. Since AT&T was providing what amounted to local telephone line service for these customers, should not the RBOCs be allowed to compete in long-distance service? Judge Greene received a study[3] that convinced him that the local telephone bottleneck was real and that fair competition could not yet take place. The competing interests were to argue for years on whether the local bottleneck existed, but as long as the divestiture agreement was in effect, the opinion that mattered belonged to Judge Harold Greene.

The FCC had plenty to do in the divestiture era, and the agency became the center of many political conflicts. Virtually every AT&T price change became a political issue. If the proposed price of a service seemed too high to the FCC or to competitors, the company could be accused of exercising its power as a member of an oligopoly (rather than as a monopoly, since it no longer had a monopoly in long-distance service).[4] If the proposed price seemed too low, AT&T could stand accused of predatory pricing—of lowering prices below economically efficient levels in order to drive rivals out of business or to discourage the entry of new competitors.[5] Although the evidence suggests that AT&T did neither of these, the decisionmaking process was subject to formal complaints and hearings. The FCC process was more quasi-legislative than quasi-judicial in nature, which opened the process to a wide variety of political interests.

One example of the difficult role for the FCC reached the courts. Common carriers like AT&T had to file rate change proposals with the FCC, but the agency had the discretion of dropping this requirement for "nondominant" carriers like MCI. AT&T objected to this exception for a competitor. Since they were the only "dominant" carrier, all of their competitors enjoyed this freedom. MCI and others could influence AT&T's rates in proceedings before the FCC but were free to set their own rates outside of such political scrutiny. AT&T filed suit, and the court of appeals and the U.S. Supreme Court agreed with the company on the grounds that the FCC was able to modify requirements for carriers but not simply drop them.[6] The extensive administrative procedures and litigation surrounding such decisions in the divestiture era provided the contending parties with powerful incentives to back policy reform.

The cable television industry also operated under FCC regulation.[7] In 1992, Congress passed a law that asked the FCC to set cable prices at levels that would have been produced by competition. Only 1 percent of cable customers had the choice of a second cable provider, and evidence from those cases suggested that most users paid about 30 percent more when served by only one carrier. The FCC issued rules that were to reduce cable rates, but cable companies pressed suit. The extended rule-making procedure, with court tests, caused the FCC to institute a price freeze on regulated cable rates. In the year after the price reductions, the FCC approved conditional price increases. As long as cable companies added a half dozen or so new channels to their service, they could raise prices back where they were before the price reductions. No one was happy with the situation—cable customers saw the companies raise prices back where they had been, cable companies endured two years of uncertainty about their revenues, developers of new networks (the content providers for cable) were put on hold while the conflicts played out, and the FCC was constantly accused of indecisiveness.[8] The FCC also became the focus of efforts by cable television companies to thwart telephone company entry into cable television services.[9]

The possibility of telephone company entry into cable television provides a case that illustrates the ways politics and technology interact. The issue before the FCC was whether telephone companies could act like cable companies and offer specific content, or whether they were common carriers and could not regulate what goes out over their wires. To compete for cable television business, of course, the telephone companies wanted to offer packages of channels for monthly fees. In the belief that such services would be allowed, telephone companies and cable companies completed a series of mergers in the early 1990s, but early experiments did not work out well. Telephone companies were able to try new technical innovations that cable companies simply could not afford, such as the idea of a video dial tone from which a customer could call up a variety of services, such as pay-per-view movies and Internet service. The regulatory questions raised by cable defenders were reminiscent of the separations issues from telephone regulation: Were the telephone companies going to subsidize these new services from their other businesses, some of them unregulated? If so, they were acting to thwart competition. Consumer groups got into the debate and wanted the FCC to make rules that would keep telephone companies from charging their customers for the capital investment for such networks.[10]

An important development that propelled telecommunications politics to national attention was the widespread acceptance of the ideas of competition and deregulation. These notions became popular in the 1970s and by the early 1990s were the cornerstone of the economic policies of both political parties. The decisive shift in public ideas came during the Reagan years, which marked a change in generally accepted views of public administration and civil service. Reagan declared "government is the problem" and took apart most of what was left of the 1930s theories of administration. During the debates over the 1996 Act, Republicans were joined by a majority of Democrats in discussing the FCC as if it had to be told exactly what to do. The political leanings of its commissioners and employees were suspect. Indeed, more conservative members of Congress envisioned an effective end to the FCC a few years after passage of the 1996 Act. Both the Republicans and the Democrats had come out for deregulation,[11] but apparently for different reasons. Ideas entered the political stream in a variety of ways. Several sources of ideas identified within the Clinton administration are described below.

1. The Clinton administration subsumed many policy initiatives under the rubric of technology policy and emphasized the need for such policies to support private sector investment and growth.[12] The administration wanted to focus on economic policies and believed that their largest effect on the economy would come through coordinating policies toward various industries, expanding access to foreign technical information and ensuring international protection of intellectual property, subsidizing high-risk research, and easing regulatory burdens on businesses. Several key concepts running through the policy initiatives were "competing in a global economy," "working closely with industry," and constructing a "National Information Infrastructure."[13] Administration policy papers claimed that technology was the engine of economic growth, the key to national productivity, and the path to maintaining U.S. leadership in many industries.

2. The Clinton administration took some steps beyond policy coordination to establish what some call an industrial policy—a code word for designating some industries and technologies as important enough to justify special subsidies and encouragement. High Definition Television (HDTV) and flat-panel displays are examples of such policy. Administration officials justified such bald intervention in markets as necessary to the nation's economic security.[14] A billion dollars was planned for the flat-panel displays alone. What was billed as deregulation was a complicated mix of policies, some of them embracing an active and interventionist role for government.

3. Part of the administration's technology policy was the NII initiative. Clinton's 1992 electoral strategy included an appeal to high-growth businesses in the south and west that worked in the new digital technologies. Democrats knew that to win in the 1990s they had to find a convincing progrowth plank in the party platform. The NII was not simply about telecommunications deregulation. The administration believed that the Internet would grow into a major commercial network and was in some ways

a new form of commerce. Its Information Infrastructure Task Force focused on mostly technical and economic issues, with little direct concern for the ultimate end-user or the possible social and behavioral challenges that might emerge out of major technical change.[15]

4. Clinton vice-president Al Gore was appointed the head of a task force, "Reinventing Government," an initiative to put more information about government into citizens' hands and to streamline agency operations. The broad goal was to make government more efficient and more responsive to citizens. Gore emphasized the role of technology in such plans and piggybacked on the administration's NII.[16]

In sum, the administration was primarily driven by a goal of economic development, and they believed that new information technologies were the key to such growth. Their support for deregulation has to be seen in this context to understand why the two parties came to have such uncritical support for a policy initiative sponsored largely by industries. As long as a policy was credibly linked to the new information technologies and the construction of an NII, Clinton administration officials in several departments could be counted on for support.

Many of the ideas in the administration's policy initiatives had been growing in the policy stream for years, under the rubric of an "information revolution." The term lacked a clear definition, but discussions of the subject focused on the role of new communications technologies in nearly every nook and cranny of society.[17]

A similar drive was working in the Congress, although without the broad scope of administration initiatives. The approach to deregulation legislation that had ended in 1981 produced some expertise and sympathy for new initiatives. One report from Congress's Office of Technology Assessment (OTA) in 1990[18] urged the leadership to support deregulation in stark terms:

> If Congress fails to act decisively and generate broad support, the opportunity to make deliberate choices about new communication technologies—and about the nature of American society itself—will be overtaken by rapid technological advances, the hardening of stakehold positions and alliances, and the force of international developments and events.[19]

The OTA report did not embrace deregulation and if anything emphasized that social choices will be made through markets, with unfortunate consequences, unless Congress acted soon. The report suggested that the quality of democracy and the distribution of political and economic power were at stake and within the legitimate reach of policymakers. It is not surprising that the Congress did not embrace the report. Indeed, in 1995 and 1996, the Republican majority moved to abolish the OTA, convinced that it did not produce analyses that were useful to its market-oriented goals. Yet the report was a sign that the debate was nationwide and had reached Congress. Elected officials were becoming aware of the issue and forming opinions.

The 1992 election of Bill Clinton and Al Gore helped bring this new wider approach to technology and telecommunications issues to the political stream. Al Gore had been a U.S. senator from Tennessee, and he had specialized in various aspects of technology policy. He introduced the Supercomputer Network Study Act of 1986[20] and in 1988 introduced a plan for the National Research and Education Network. It was endorsed by the Congress in the High Performance Computing Act in 1991[21] and was a major step in popularizing the notion of an "information superhighway." One of its provisions was to encourage upgrading of the lines connecting federally subsidized supercomputing sites in the Internet environment to 3 gigabits per second, about sixty times the then current capacity. This amounted to federal standards setting in an upgraded network and reflected Gore's developing notion of an NII. The following year, Gore introduced the Information Infrastructure and Technology Act of 1992, with the intention of making the network more available to K-12 education, libraries, health care, and industry.[22]

Al Gore had long championed the notion that communications technologies were the foundation of economic development and would become a major business environment. President Clinton assigned him the responsibility of coordinating federal policy in the area.

The developing technologies had consequences for the strategies of the major telecommunications companies. The RBOCs and cable companies had come to realize that, without competition and entry into new businesses, they could soon be out of business. The new wireless services (pagers, cellular telephones, satellite transmission) enabled companies like AT&T to begin to bypass the local carriers. The future clearly belonged to the companies that could offer services that encompassed a wide range of the technologies coming out of the marriage of computers and communications. For a time, the cable companies saw themselves as viable alternatives to the local telephone company to bring a wide array of services to homes and businesses. The RBOCs saw themselves in a strong position, since they would, if allowed, stand to gain in the near term from offering new services (like long distance) to their large customer base. In a sense, the different industries joined forces for deregulation, although they were to differ on particular provisions in legislation. Over the decade after divestiture, it seemed all the major interests came to want legislation, although for different reasons.

Were they influenced by ideas, beyond a narrow calculation of interests? The argument is developed in Chapter 4 that telecommunications company leaders helped build, and were themselves influenced by, the rhetoric of competition and a new picture of corporate dynamism and the emerging technological possibilities.

Still, any legislation would face formidable barriers. Democrats in Congress were still worried about the power of trusts, such as the RBOCs appeared to be, and Republicans generally favored removing restrictions as soon as possible. Judge Greene said publicly that he worried that the old AT&T monopoly would be reconstituted under competitive rules. Moreover, to say the Democrats controlled the 103rd Congress is more formal than actual truth. Individual members and different committees were responsive to different interests. The lineup of interests to be reconciled was formidable:

• Members of the Clinton administration and Congress wanted to pass telecommunications policies that promised to foster economic growth, while at the same time preserving some remnant of the universal-access policy. Important voices in the administration differed on how to balance these goals and the interests of constituents.[23] The administration favored managed competition, by which they meant the FCC needed increased flexibility to decide when increased competition would be feasible.

• Cable television companies wanted to be able to offer local telephone service. They feared the RBOCs would have a distinct advantage in immediate head-to-head competition. They wanted rules about the degree of competition needed before telephone companies could compete with them. Some also wanted to have simpler rules on buyouts of cable companies. Most of the cable industry installed their lines on poles belonging to telephone companies, and they wanted to continue to do so at low cost. They also wanted an end to regulation of their rates. Perhaps the biggest concern of the cable companies was about which set of rules would apply to them. Telephone companies were called "common carriers" and the regulations governing their industry required equal access to all suppliers of programs. Cable companies did not want to be required to give such access to competitors.

• The RBOCs wanted to be free of the restrictions of the 1982 consent decree and to provide long-distance service, offer cable television, and manufacture equipment. They emphasized that AT&T and other long-distance carriers were developing the means by which to bypass the regional and local telephone networks. Democrats tended to fear large companies more than did Republicans and so would differ on conditions under which the Bells would be able to acquire cable companies. They would still be regulated, and the Bells pushed for price caps rather than profit controls imposed by most states. Senator John Breaux (D-LA) and Senator Packwood were helpful to the RBOCs. The Bells thought legislation introduced by John Dingell (House Energy and Commerce chair [D-MI]) and Jack Brooks (House Judiciary chair [D-TX]) waited too long for them to get into the video business. Since the Bell companies ran the regional networks most long-distance and other companies would need access to, competing groups lobbied for many requirements on the RBOCs. They were concerned about universal-service rules if free to compete in all lines of the telephone business. Who should pay for bringing the services to the low-profit customers in rural areas and to the poor? Moreover, the seven RBOCs[24] did not always agree on every issue. Their differences emerged as a key reason legislation did not pass in the 103rd Congress.

• Long-distance companies, such as AT&T, MCI, and Sprint feared RBOC competition in long-distance services before they were able to offer competitive local service. At one level, AT&T already offered that service through its cellular phone services and through data services to large businesses, but debates about the local bottleneck were unsettled. Long-distance companies wanted to keep the RBOCs out of their market as long as possible. The RBOC and local telephone company networks, which owned the lines running to most telephone customers, reasoned that once AT&T had its own access to those homes, fair competition with the RBOCs would exist.[25] The access fees paid by long-distance companies to local companies were at the time far above the cost of interconnection. But there was considerable disagreement over what constituted fair competition. Their allies were to include Senate Commerce Committee chair Ernest Hollings (D-SC), ranking Republican John Danforth of Missouri, and Communications Subcommittee chair Daniel Inouye (D-HI).

• Consumer groups wanted the RBOCs and companies that lease their networks to share the costs of building new digital networks. The idea was to have industry pay the capital costs, rather than passing them along to local rate payers. Consumer groups generally opposed price caps, as they commonly kept up rates that would have otherwise dropped. Some also wanted an option for customers who wanted only basic telephone service and did not want to pay for some upgraded multimedia service. Still another consumer group demand was subsidized telecommunications services for public and educational institutions (the so-called PEG access). The issues here were bandwidth and access and were essentially the universal-access policy aimed at the PEG institutions. That means that public-oriented uses, such as politics or community groups, should have access to high-capacity lines so that town meetings could happen electronically, politically active citizens could share information, and interactive video could come to schools.[26] Representatives Markey (D-MA), Wyden (D-OR), and Synar (D-OK) were helpful to the consumer groups.

• Broadcasters wanted to be able to use their "extra" broadcast spectrum (spaces between channels, originally in place because of interference problems that have since been eliminated by new technology) to offer additional wireless services. They also wanted fewer restrictions on the number of stations they could own. They were joined on this point by newspaper owners.[27] Representative Billy Tauzin of Louisiana (D in the 103rd Congress, R in the 104th) assisted the broadcasters.

• Media companies wanted to ensure open markets for their programming. If a national communications network made 500 channels available to consumers willing to purchase the services, program quality becomes an important issue. Media companies that own production studies and archives of movies and television programs wanted to have access to customers. This would enable them to collect more of the revenue that might otherwise go to cable companies.[28]

• Computer and software companies, like Microsoft and IBM (and also AT&T), favored an open-architecture information infrastructure. Open architecture means that just about any equipment could be attached to the lines and operate according to what customers want to do. If cable companies help to construct a large part of the carriage system, it is possible that special cable equipment would be necessary to make use of the signal. They wanted open-architecture rules put into the new law, which guarantees that any company could offer services over the lines going to customers' homes and businesses.[29]

• Equipment manufacturers were concerned about rules that favored one kind of technology over another. One bill required local telephone companies to use existing facilities (wires and switches) as much as possible when building their new networks. Corning, a manufacturer of fiber-optic cable, prevailed upon Representative Alex McMillan (R-NC) to change the provision. Corning employed a thousand workers in McMillan's district. Computer and electronics firms wanted a requirement that would make television set-top boxes (which might be served by a cable or telephone company) to accept programming from anyone, not just the local company.

• Unions were influential in communications firms, particularly the RBOCs. They favored a quick RBOC entry into cable television, a largely nonunion industry. They were also in favor of domestic content language in a Senate bill. The unions understood that the telecommunications revolution was bound to hurt them.[30] Unions are strongest in the public sector and in the older basic industries, such as automobile manufacturing and railroad operations. Newly developing industries are often slow to unionize for a number of reasons. As the old regulated monopoly gave way to competition among new firms, unions saw the proportion of organized jobs in the industry drop.

• State and local governments argued that they should continue to have a role in protecting consumers of telephone and cable television services. The rights-of-way used by communications companies were traditionally a state concern, as were cable television and telephone rates and the siting of communications equipment such as radio towers.[31]

• Civil libertarians and software companies objected to a provision, added late in the legislative debate, that would have required companies to monitor their networks for "obscene, lewd, lascivious, filthy, or indecent" material. They would become active in telecommunications policy debates that included the ability of government agencies to decrypt digital communications, the sale of encryption technology beyond the nation's borders, and a Senate bill rider that appeared to limit discussion of abortion on digital networks. The issues that brought these groups into the political stream are examples of how the legislative process often opens up a conflict beyond the boundaries envisioned by proponents of legislation.[32]

• Rural companies came under special attention. A group of senators that called itself the Farm Team feared that deregulation would end up costing rural constituents more. In principle, they were right. Outright competition in all telecommunications industries would mean that few competitors would trouble with high-cost customers in rural areas. These groups benefited from the cross-subsidies of the universal access policies of the previous generations. The Farm Team backed subsidies and limits on takeovers of rural cable and telephone systems.

The Clinton administration and both the Democratic-led 103rd and Republican-led 104th Congresses shared a rough consensus on general principles for legislation, but general principles are not policy. The agreed-upon principles were:

1. Public policy should endorse an information superhighway, although there was no consensus on what it would look like. The widespread interconnectivity of the Internet was the starting place for most visions of the superhighway, somehow involving a variety of means of access, two-way or multiway communication among users, and high capacity for services like video.
2. The network should be built and operated by private industry, with minimal government participation.
3. Existing regulations on communications companies, especially telephone companies, should be dramatically reduced.
4. Universal access was still important to ensure that rural areas and poor people were not left out of the alleged benefits of the new technologies.

The various interests found much to disagree about within the confines of these principles. For example, telephone companies and media companies regarded cable companies as too proprietary. The cable companies had built their own networks and had begrudgingly carried educational and public-access stations. There was a history of fairly acrimonious negotiations among content providers who wanted to put their programming on cable systems and the cable providers who wanted fees for carrying the services. Another example comes from universal access. The telephone companies believed that too much "cream skimming" had gone on over the previous thirty years, as they subsidized prices to some customers while new companies skimmed off the customers whose higher prices paid for universal access. Since the new companies had no experience and little inclination to begin their own support of subsidies, the telephone companies were wary of being left holding the bag. They were receptive to a Clinton administration proposal that all service providers pay a portion of their revenues into an account administered by the FCC, to be paid out to providers who subsidize whatever categories of universal-access users that could be agreed upon.

Still another important issue not settled by the principles was, for a privately financed system, perhaps the biggest of all. Who will pay for the capital costs of the new system? As the 103rd Congress got under way, the estimated costs of providing homes with a digital connection to a network amounted to about $1,500 per household. To amortize those costs over a reasonable period of time (reasonable for the private company that must report to shareholders) required something like $60 per household per month. That level of expenditure might be reasonable for customers if it included highly desirable services.[33]

The 103rd Congress Attempts to Pass Legislation

Congressional attention was focused on three bills. Representatives Brooks and Dingell introduced H.R. 3626,[34] which allowed the Bell companies to manufacture equipment, enabled them to enter long-distance services if approved by the FCC and the Justice Department's Antitrust Division, and established time periods for progressive increases in the long-distance services they could provide—increase services within their own territories immediately, sell services provided by outside carriers (such as other Bell regional companies) after eighteen months, and construct their own national networks after five years. This question of the timing and circumstances under which RBOCs could enter long distance and manufacturing, along with the companion notion of when they would be able to offer video services, formed the heart of the deregulation debate.[35]

Representatives Markey (D-MA), Fields (R-TX), and Bloucher (D-VA) introduced H.R. 3636,[36] which enabled telephone companies to enter cable television services in exchange for allowing competing telephone and video services over their lines and would have established a federal-state regulatory board to make universal access policy.

The bills brought policy differences among the various interests out into the open.[37] The RBOCs felt they were put at a disadvantage if they were not allowed to immediately compete in long-distance services. Long-distance companies insisted that such competition should wait until the local telephone company was already facing effective competition. The RBOCs replied that this would cause them to lose a great deal of their business before being able to compete at all in long distance.[38] They endorsed the principle of "incidental" long distance, which meant that if one of their customers wanted to call outside the company area, they should be able to carry the call rather than purchase the services of a company like AT&T or MCI.[39] They also endorsed clear standards for universal access—and they meant access, not actual provision of service—specifically for "advanced services" and not merely basic telephone and cable television, to be paid for by all providers, not just by them and the local telephone companies. As originally written, H.R. 3636 was vague about the definition of universal service and included a requirement only for subsidy by the local carrier.[40] Regional telephone companies wanted to be able to offer cellular service without regard to their current operating areas, since AT&T's recent purchase of the McCaw Cellular phone company enabled them to do the same. The long-distance limits would effectively keep them out of the video business as well, because the large computers they expected to use to sell video-on-demand services would need to reach a large area to make economic sense.[41]

The demands of other important interests presented a bewildering array to Congress. Large cable companies referred to the most desirable information highway as a toll road, with the highway manager collecting fees for the transmission of others' material. They also wanted an open-architecture standard so that they would not be at a disadvantage compared to regional telephone companies that own a wide variety of enterprises that enable them to offer a larger bundle of services than those available to cable companies.[42] Small cable companies were concerned that restrictions on mergers in H.R. 3636, put there to keep telephone companies from simply buying an existing network instead of constructing a new information highway, be relaxed for small carriers. The merger restrictions would severely limit the market value of their companies.[43]

Cable companies were also very concerned about their limited capital compared to the telephone giants. Ideally, they would have preferred to be able to raise their rates in order to generate the needed funds and enter telephone services, while the telephone companies were not allowed into their business.[44] Broadcasters made their case that the airwaves should be considered part of the information superhighway and that they were ready to provide a number of services if a few rules were relaxed, mainly on the types of service they could offer through the electromagnetic spectrum segments they currently occupied and limits on the number of media outlets they could own.[45] In response to large software companies like Microsoft, whose operating systems (like Windows) had come to dominate the personal computer business and who thought something like that might be acceptable on an information superhighway, smaller software companies wanted interoperability standards in place to discourage the dominance of proprietary systems.[46] A manufacturer of television set-top operating systems (the so-called addressable boxes used for pay-per-view cable television, which might be expanded into a general telecommunications server) argued that interoperability standards set to 1994 technology would do great damage and retard the development of innovative technologies.[47] And media production companies that produce programs emphasized the need to endorse particular standards for open architecture so that cable and telephone companies could not control (and charge for) the transmission of independent programming.[48]

This overview of the hearings showed that general agreement to principles did not, at this point in the policymaking process, matter very much. The hearings showed significant conflict over priorities. The process for making specific rules was going to involve compromises and would likely be clumsy. The most powerful interests endorsed processes in which, based on their experience, they believed they would be influential later. When such disagreements over priorities exist, policymaking is messy and not likely to produce clear and consistent consequences.

While these differences over H.R. 3626 and 3636 were being aired, Senators Hollings, Inouye, and Danforth introduced their own bill, S. 1822,[49] to complement and move beyond the house bills. S. 1822 allowed the RBOCs to compete in long distance as soon as they convinced the FCC that they faced "actual and demonstrable competition" and let them compete with video companies if they faced competition in the local telephone business. The universal-service concerns of the local telephone companies were addressed with an account similar to that advocated by the Clinton administration. The broadcasters were assured that the FCC would review the rules they were concerned about. Senate hearings mirrored the arguments heard in the House. The big difference seemed to be Senator Hollings's long-standing interest in telecommunications policy (dating back to the legislative efforts of the late 1970s) and his ability to encourage the RBOCs and AT&T to agree on the simultaneous competition supervised by the FCC.

S. 1822 was prepared in cooperation with Vice-President Gore's office, and Gore made several public speeches seeking to gain popular support for legislators willing to follow the administration's lead. The Clinton administration was placing more emphasis than industry on the value of universal service and challenged industry to agree to the central-fund idea.[50] In Gore's leadoff speech unveiling the administration's plan, he got the comedian Lilly Tomlin to reprise her role as Ernestine, the telephone company operator. In its earlier incarnation the comedy routine contained the joke "We don't have to care. We're the phone company." At the policy unveiling she asked whether the new information highway was for everyone or just for the elite. Gore's speech dangled an implied threat to the RBOCs and industry giants like AT&T: if industry does not effectively connect the nation to the new information technologies, strict regulation will follow.[51]

However, the administration did not always help its case. Because it saw technology policy with such a broad sweep, it supported initiatives that clashed and reduced the support of key interests.[52] For example, in February 1994, the FCC announced its intentions to have the cable television industry cut prices by a total of about $2 billion under authority granted in the 1992 law, sponsored by then Senator Gore, that increased oversight of cable companies. Within weeks, several planned mergers involving cable companies were called off because of the doubts about future cash flows. Telephone companies were entering into joint ventures with cable companies to build the capacity for new video services, but these came to an abrupt halt after the FCC announcement.[53] Another mixed signal came in antitrust policy. Deregulation and competition were understood by cable and telephone companies to mean that government would be less involved in economic choices and more tolerant of the structures that emerge from private choices. But the Clinton administration, particularly the head of DOJ's Antitrust Division, Anne Bingaman, believed in a more vigorous policing of the conditions of competition. Whereas the Bush and Reagan administrations had earned the reputation of being very lenient with antitrust laws, Bingaman opened many new investigations.[54] The administration spoke of competition but approached it through new, vaguely defined regulation.

These competing interests saw the bills before the 103rd Congress as their opportunity to influence policy in the strict sense—the rules by which government officials will act to force an outcome. For example,[55] computer and electronic industries won a provision to have the FCC investigate and make public ways to make television set-top addressable boxes open to any provider of services, not just those of the local cable company. Consumer groups won a rule that enables telephone customers to not receive "enhanced services"—and the higher costs that go with them—that may develop in the future. The enhancement route had been used by cable companies to increase rates, and regulators allowed them to charge more. A manufacturer of optical fiber cable was able to get language changed that would have required phone companies to upgrade "existing facilities" in building a new network. The company believed that without the rule they would be able to sell more fiber cable. Literally hundreds of such changes made it into the bills.

It seemed as if the deals would hold together and that a deregulation bill would pass in late 1994. However, on September 23, 1994, Senate Commerce Committee chair Hollings announced that this Congress would not pass such legislation. The move caught many by surprise.

The key dispute involved dissension among the RBOCs. Some of them had been successful in easing FCC restrictions and state government oversight and had come to believe that they would be worse off if legislation passed.[56] The economics of the industry put the RBOCs in a dangerous position. Since they collected about $36 billion in annual revenue, compared to $12 billion for long-distance companies and $10 billion for cable companies, a redistribution under deregulation was likely to affect them the most.[57] The upshot was that some of the companies, in particular Bell South, Ameritech, and U S West, were much less willing to agree to the limits imposed on them by the proposed legislation.

The final straw that broke the deals seems to have been a last-minute intervention by Senate minority leader Robert Dole (R-KS).[58] The story indicates the importance of communication, leadership, and dumb luck in the policy process. Dole had been sympathetic to the RBOCs and on their behalf was generating support for their position in relation to the long-distance companies. They wanted less regulation of local telephone companies and fewer restrictions on Bell entry into long-distance services. Dole met with Hollings on Thursday evening, September 22, and presented him with a list of requirements from his side of the chamber. Afterwards, Hollings and a Dole aide publicly disagreed on how flexible Dole was over the suggested amendments. The recalcitrant Bells suggested they were not bound by an earlier deal, which they claim was made not by them but by an association of local telephone companies. Hollings did not agree. The dispute between Dole and Hollings may also have been affected by the upcoming election, which was looking increasingly favorable for the Republicans. Dole may have been trying to deny a large legislative victory to the Democrats. Hollings may have wanted to blame Republicans for inaction. Neither man would say. Seeing no way to redo all the bargains before the end of the congressional session, Senator Hollings announced he would let the bill die. The ironic thing about the dispute is that, according to a lobbyist for the Bell companies, they had planned to ask Dole to back off on Friday. But they were a day late, and Hollings made his announcement. The RBOCs expressed shock at the outcome and tried to get the bill revived. They ardently wished to avoid blame for its failure.

There were other signs of trouble for the Senate bill during the 103rd Congress. Senators John McCain (R-AZ) and Packwood threatened to filibuster on the grounds the bill was too regulatory. Senator Howard

Metzenbaum (D-OH) threatened a filibuster because the bill was not regulatory enough.

The 103rd Congress failed to pass telecommunications deregulation, but it did demonstrate that a policy window had opened. The last important barriers to the Congress's decision agenda had been removed. The language of the debate was almost entirely procompetitive.[59] The alternatives considered were for the most part intended to encourage forces of competition. The interest groups showed a recognition that the agenda had opened and included deregulation. The many deals were a sign of their vitality. The ideological disputes had long been settled, with some exceptions (like the requirement to monitor networks for "obscene, lewd, lascivious, filthy, or indecent" material).

The failure to pass a bill during the 103rd Congress did not stop the economic and technological pressures that undermined the existing regulatory regime. An unprecedented expansion of wireless telephone services was erasing the very distinctions over which the long-distance and regional telephone companies battled. Within a month after Senator Hollings pronounced the legislation dead, Sprint, the third-largest long-distance company, announced an alliance with TCI, Comcast, and Cox enterprises, three major cable television companies. They were to expand their networks and offer wireless and wire telephone services. If the traditional industry giants remained at an impasse, they could easily lose huge portions of their market share as other companies developed the new technologies.

During all of 1994, as the Congress considered telecommunication legislation, the FCC had been engaged in what was described as the largest auction ever held. The bidding was on newly available portions of the electromagnetic spectrum,[60] previously used by the military but transferred to civilian use by the Clinton administration. Since 1986, Congress has authorized the FCC to auction rights to available wavelengths, and the newly available frequencies were seen as a way to encourage the development of new communications businesses. The RBOCs in particular understood that expanded wireless services made it possible for more people to bypass their local networks. The thinking at the time was that new sales would involve paging, cellular telephones, localized cellular phones that act like a cordless telephone with a range of just a few miles, data links to computers, and video services. The bundle of services would eventually be offered to customers over one network, and the RBOCs wanted to preserve their head start at constructing the new networks. They needed a new regulatory framework in place before such alternatives developed without them. In a real sense, the Senate let them down insofar as poor negotiating skills, quick tempers, and political cynicism contributed to the dispute.

THE 1994 ELECTIONS CHANGE THE CONGRESS

In 1994, the Republicans gained control of both houses of Congress for the first time since the Eisenhower administration. The election outcome stunned the Democrats, who had been leading most of the deals in the telecommunications legislation. The immediate effect of the shift was to make all the Democratic heads of congressional committees lame ducks. Interests that thought they would fare better under the Republicans had only to wait two months and new deals could be struck.

The Republicans in the 104th Congress were entitled to select new committee chairs and determine the size of committees and the proportion of Republicans to Democrats. This meant that generally more conservative members of Congress led the legislative debates, and more Republicans were influential in the committee processes.

One indication of likely changes came December 5, 1994, when incoming Senate Commerce Committee chair Larry Pressler (R-SD), replacing Hollings, announced that the entire legislative package—all the deals, not just the disagreements that stopped legislation—was up for grabs. He said it would be "a mistake to accept [previous industry deals] without asking if we can achieve the same goals in a less complicated way."[61] He went on to explain that too much regulation, especially focused on the FCC, was contained in the earlier bills. He made it clear that he favored a minor and steadily diminishing role for federal control of telecommunications.

A month later, Pressler circulated a discussion draft of a bill that included shorter time limits on competition than in 103rd Congress bills and allowed almost immediate competition for RBOCs if they opened their own markets to competition. This was close to the administration's position and was widely interpreted as sympathetic to arguments pressed by AT&T.[62] He also wanted a complete deregulation of cable television rates, citing the need to enable that industry to raise the capital necessary to compete in new services.[63]

The majority Republicans were widely seen as more sympathetic to the case of the RBOCs. In part this was because the argument of immediately freeing up markets, consistent with RBOC positions, sounded consistent with free market principles. The Heritage Foundation was influential with Republican lawmakers, so much so that AT&T flew in economists with rival views to explain to lawmakers the need for a gradual transition to competition.[64] House Speaker Newt Gingrich (R-GA) and Senator Pressler headed a private telecommunications conference on January 19 and 20, 1995, with Republicans and industry leaders only invited. Republicans also floated the idea of abolishing the FCC. Some months later, a conservative group that had worked closely with Speaker Gingrich, the

Progress and Freedom Foundation, published a report from a prominent telecommunications specialist who argued that the FCC should be abolished and replaced by an agency that merely collected data that might help federal courts and state regulators make decisions about antitrust and rates.[65]

The Clinton administration believed these conservative rumblings enough to declare their openness to arguments for greater deregulation.[66] The administration reissued an announcement of the formation of its Information Infrastructure Task Force, chaired by secretary of commerce Ronald H. Brown, and that it was currently involved in a reexamination of issues surrounding the NII,[67] but it was clear that the Republicans in Congress had seized the policy initiative.

The 104th Congress

It was clear that, whoever deserved blame for stopping legislation in the 103rd Congress, the new session would produce legislation less favorable to the RBOCs.[68] The legislation was reintroduced as S. 652 and H.R. 1555[69] and started out predictably more conservative. Yet majority control did not mean that Republicans would have smooth sailing. The administration had a clear agenda on the bill and would take credit for legislation similar to that undertaken in the previous Congress. The Republicans were not used to leading, and the business groups closely allied with them did not agree on all issues.[70]

The major interests involved with the previous year's efforts were anxious to pass legislation, but serious differences remained. The RBOCs and AT&T were at odds over the conditions of increased competition. AT&T insisted that RBOCs still enjoyed a monopoly, and the Bells adamantly denied it.[71] The RBOCs tied their legislative preferences to an assurance that they would invest $100 billion over and above the amount they would spend in the existing regulatory framework.[72] The FCC was vigorously pursuing its existing authority over rate regulation, ordering the RBOCs to reduce their access charges to long-distance companies.[73] The Bells found that the managed competition concepts guiding the FCC were usually not to their liking. The delay in legislation also altered investment decisions by major companies. AT&T and Bell Atlantic, for example, dissolved their deal to build a video network, in part because of the lawsuits over the regulated telephone competition issues.[74] It was clearly serious economic policy before the Congress.

The nation's largest broadcasters were lobbying heavily for reform. Anticipating legislation, two of the four national broadcasters merged with media companies to form multimedia conglomerates.[75] Broadcasters hoped to offer a wide range of services in the additional spectrum they anticipated would be theirs after a bill passed. Among the possibilities were cellular telephone and other communication services, video-on-demand, computer on-line services, and higher-quality digital television signals. No one really knew what role broadcasters could play in the future, but the companies were betting that, with the right legislation, broadcast multimedia companies could compete with telephone and cable companies for a wide range of services.

The addition of the broadcasters to the chorus of interests in favor of a bill certainly added to its chances of success. The mergers in broadcasting were part of a larger pattern of business moves that suggested the industry was living by rules the legislators had yet to make. Put differently, the Telecommunications Act of 1996 codified much of what people were already doing. A list of major business moves suggests a pattern:

- AT&T had two years earlier purchased McCaw Cellular, the largest cellular or wireless telephone company, in a big step toward building a national wireless network. Digital services of any kind could be transmitted over the airwaves.
- GTE Sprint made deals with three major cable television companies (TCI, Comcast, and Cox) in a move toward building a wired digital network. Together they submitted bids in a 1994 wireless spectrum auction overseen by the FCC.
- Several of the RBOCs (Bell Atlantic, Nynex, U S West) and the Air Touch cellular telephone company linked up to submit bids in the 1994 spectrum auction, in a move to build a national network that could offer a wide range of digital services. Air Touch had earlier been "spun off" as an independent company from its former owner, Pacific Telesis. The companies did not actually merge.
- U S West had earlier acquired partial ownership of Time Warner cable television.
- As the bill passed, Bell Atlantic was talking with Nynex about a merger that would encompass most of the East Coast's major cities.

The driving force behind the mergers was the perception by companies that they needed to get themselves into a position to offer four key money-making services as a package to consumers: local telephone service, cable television, long-distance service, and wireless telephone and other wireless services. The future one-stop-shopping telecommunications market will be very large.[76]

The stakes were huge, and the interested parties spent a great deal on making contributions[77] and hiring some of the best-connected lobbyists in the nation's capitol.[78]

• Howard Baker, former Senate Republican leader and adviser to President Ronald Reagan, lobbied for long-distance carriers. Clients included AT&T, MCI, and Sprint. He sought to increase the amount of time before the RBOCs could offer long-distance services.

• Marlin Fitzwater, former White House press officer for President Bush, also lobbied for the long-distance companies.

• Roy Neel, former deputy chief of staff for President Clinton, and before that an aide to Vice-President Al Gore for seventeen years, lobbied for an association of local telephone companies.

• William Diefenderfer, former deputy budget director under President Bush and a former top aide to Senator Bob Packwood, lobbied for the Bell companies.

• The WEFA Group produced a major study for the Bell companies.[79] Their forecast of the consequences of deregulation (which means letting the RBOCs go into any business they want) included 3.4 million additional jobs over ten years, a fall in the unemployment rate, an increase in real GDP growth by 0.5 percent annually over the next ten years, and over half a trillion dollars in consumer savings over the same period.

• Ray Marshall, former secretary of labor under President Carter, lobbied for AT&T.

• Richard E. Wiley, former chair of the FCC, lobbied for CBS and the Newspaper Association of America.

• Thomas H. Boggs, one of the best-known lobbyists in Washington, also lobbied for the Newspaper Association of America.

• Donald Jones, a telecommunications entrepreneur who owned radio stations and cable systems, worked as a "volunteer" in House Speaker Newt Gingrich's office (not as a staff member, and not as a lobbyist) to help the Speaker interpret technical issues of the telecommunications bill. He was listed in the "Smithsonian Campus on the Mall" brochure as the Speaker's telecommunications director. Ralph Nader and Gary Ruskin of the Congressional Accountability Project filed an ethics complaint with the House Committee on Standards of Official Conduct over Mr. Jones's role.

• A conglomeration of many groups of computer professionals, Internet companies, artists' associations, and public interest groups was headed up by the American Civil Liberties Union (ACLU) and lobbied against the Communications Decency Act portion of the bill.

The rhetoric of deregulation is important because it enables members of Congress to work with powerful interest groups and at the same time speak of their work for the public interest. As lobbyist Roy Neel put it, "Members of Congress don't think there are any good guys or bad guys in this. This is not about right or wrong. It's ultimately about money."[80] A controversy arose over the intense and sometimes secretive lobbying efforts that did not stop when legislation died during the 103rd Congress. And, to hear the participants tell it, the discussions of the emerging legislation was entirely bipartisan. On February 7, 1995, a letter was sent to Representative Thomas J. Bliley Jr. (R-VA), the floor manager of H.R. 1555, and Representative Fields, protesting the "closed-door sessions" between Republicans and industry lobbyists. The letter, signed by about forty public interest groups with a variety of opinions about the bill, implied that industry interests were excluding the public and shaping legislation by themselves.[81] Yet Senator Hollings had said that charges of partisanship were misleading. He, Senator Pressler, and Vice-President Gore said they were regularly conferring across the partisan aisles as the legislation developed, even though Pressler and Bliley were clearly leading the process.[82]

In one example of the contending sides' position taking, long-distance carrier lobbyists attempted to change the Senate bill's limits on RBOC entry into their long-distance markets.[83] S. 652 contained a fourteen-point "competition checklist" that would have the FCC certify that RBOC entry into a market would not decrease competition. Senator Strom Thurmond (R-SC) proposed an amendment that would have transferred such oversight to the Department of Justice, a forum that had been historically more concerned with the RBOCs' strength in local telephony. AT&T wanted to solidify its position and knew it had to do it through the Senate.

The competition checklist presents an example of the congressional role in policymaking. During the 103rd Congress, key members and long-distance industry officials wanted a "date certain" approach to market entry for the RBOCs and long-distance companies. The main function of a deadline is that decisions about market entry are made by Congress, not by the FCC, some other administrative agency, or a court. During the 104th Congress, the RBOCs were more influential, and the leadership's thinking on the institutional framework for deregulation was muddled. Is it better to compromise among industry rivals than to make a rule that guarantees the competition ostensibly sought in the legislation? The leadership in the 104th Congress agreed it is.

This was particularly true after last-minute changes in H.R. 1555 made it easier for the RBOCs to enter long-distance markets. The changes were drastic enough to convince AT&T and other long-distance carriers to defeat the bill entirely if they could not get their way. The strategy at the time was to remind everyone of the threatened presidential veto and to provide lawmakers with a justification for supporting the president in that eventuality.[84]

Cable television companies wanted to be free of regulation if a competitor was merely possible, not necessarily already selling services to clients. Existing rules said a company faced competition if half the households in its market could be served by a rival and if at least 15 percent of the households were customers of the rival. Consumer advocates argued that prices in the era of cable deregulation (1984–1992) nearly doubled and that close regulation was needed until real competition existed. Competition from the largest potential rivals, the regional telephone companies, was likely half a decade away.[85]

Some of the issues raised by public interest groups were deceptively important. For example, several groups wanted some standards inserted about the pricing of Integrated Services Digital Network (ISDN) service.[86] Proponents of the measure claimed that the special service should be regulated until the local carrier, in most cases a regional telephone company, faced real competition. The House was not sympathetic to the claims.[87]

Perhaps also significant was the type of issue that was not at all considered in the House and Senate bills. For years telecommunications policy had contained elements of affirmative action. The FCC auctions of available electromagnetic spectrum wavelengths included set-asides that in effect lowered the price of licenses to minority firms and may have been, in terms of economic value, the largest affirmative action program ever undertaken by the national government.[88] Another affirmative action provision took the form of a tax provision that allowed a company to avoid capital gains taxes when it sells major assets to a minority-controlled company.[89] House Ways and Means Republican members wanted to delete such affirmative action policies, and the Democrats in the 104th Congress did not even attempt to address the issue in the telecommunications bills.

The language of competitiveness helped hold together the consensus that made legislation possible. Part of the rhetoric of competitiveness is a claim that competition lowers prices, and even proregulation interests accepted this idea in legislative hearings. It also means deregulation, an idea endorsed by both Republicans and Democrats. By sharing common terms, the two sides could pass legislation that embodied principles but omitted complicated details of implementation.

The language of competitiveness may be a convincing new way to look at policy and organizational issues at the national level. The orthodoxy of reorganization brought in with the Roosevelt administration has, despite volumes of criticism, remained the basic approach for two generations.[90] Its resiliency is due to the clarity and simplicity of the ideas. The language of competitiveness has the same qualities, and historians of the future may describe the 1990s as the decade in which the traditional approach to organization and policy was fundamentally changed.

The language used in Congress to describe the deals shows the direct connection between the industry compromises and claims of serving the public interest. The economics claims reported above from the WEFA Group report were generally accepted in the Congress. In effect, to many members of Congress, accepting the legislative requests of the many big telecommunications companies amounted to a wise and public-interested fiscal policy. Few things done by the 104th Congress would have the promised economic impact of the Telecommunications Act. With the widespread agreement on the virtues of competition, businesses could appear to sound public-spirited. Chief executive officers from the seven RBOCs, the big long-distance companies, and the big telecommunications manufacturing companies issued a statement of support for the Clinton administration's NII technology initiatives. The policy would, said the executives, provide huge benefits to schools, health care, national competitiveness, and consumers. They announced their willingness to enter into a partnership with government to develop, with government grants, some of the key technologies for the future.[91]

Vice-President Gore, chairing a telecommunications summit, said, "We seek open and free competition in which any company is free to offer any information good or service to any customer. Why is that important? Very simply. Because competition lowers prices, increases choices, improves quality and creates jobs. Competition is the key . . . [that] will lead to new, higher-paying jobs and an economy better prepared for the challenges of the 21st century."[92]

Larry Irving, assistant secretary for communications and information of the Commerce Department, claimed the legislation would "unleash the promise of the Information Superhighway for all Americans." He reiterated "the objectives to which we are all committed—competition, investment, consumer welfare, and reduced government regulation."[93]

Members of Congress repeated the claims that new jobs would be created. Some said thousands of jobs, some said tens of thousands of jobs, and Representative Tauzin said it would create millions of new jobs.[94]

Representative Rick White (R-WA) said that "it's people, not the government, who are going to make the best decisions about technology. . . . No matter how many Rhodes scholars you have in the White House, they're never going to be smart enough to tell Bill Gates to drop out of Harvard and invent the software industry. . . . The market, not the government, is going to tell us what the next wave of technology is."[95] Representative Dingell referred to the then extant regulatory system as telephone companies "held captive by a federal judge . . . a good judge, mind you . . . [and] a group of Department of Justice attorneys. . . . It has been hard times for communications companies the last ten years."

The bill did have detractors, particularly aimed at the House leadership. Representative Marcy Kaptur (D-OH) said she was "ashamed" at the behind-the-scenes markup of the bill (several important provisions were added in a "manager's amendment," from the floor manager, which gets around open-committee session requirements) and the brief late-night debate. Senator Bob Kerrey (D-NE) called it a "contract with one hundred American corporations."

The bill's language was about technical issues and guidelines for the reregulation of telecommunications. Industry officials took great care in the precise language of amendments, but for the most part the controversies were lost on the general public. One exception was the so-called spectrum giveaway.

The rhetoric of competition does suggest position taking, but not always in a clear fashion. The complicated set of events that constitutes an open policy window was illustrated by Senate majority leader Dole's last-minute concern about the "spectrum giveaway." Dole was in the early stages of seeking the Republican nomination for president. Groups like the Council of 100 and the Consumer Federation of America received media attention at their announcements that the telecommunications bill contained this bit of "corporate welfare," which will enable broadcasters discretion in how to use spectrum freed up under new technology and fewer restrictions. Senator Dole took up the issue without sufficiently consulting the interested parties. The ideas themselves were powerful. His office issued press releases, and he made a televised speech on the need to end such special-interest concessions. His public stance lasted a little over ten days, by which time he understood the issue as worked out by several members of his party. He dropped his objections once he had elicited a promise from FCC chair Reed Hundt and from fellow congressional Republicans that the issue would not be decided before separate congressional hearings and legislation.[96] It could be said that interests corrected the ideas of Senator Dole, but the emerging consensus on the bill was based on a great deal of willingness among different interests to build policies they believed would actually work. The idea of deregulation was important on both sides of the aisle in Congress.

Competition is such a broad idea that it can encompass irreconcilable points of view. While agreeing on broad principles, the details of the legislation threatened to divide Republicans and Democrats. The White House released a threat of a veto, explaining that the Republican version of H.R. 1555 was "abhorrent to the public interest and our national well-being."[97] The administration's complaint noted that "one person owning the majority of the media outlets in a community is a threat to [our] very system of democracy," and that Republicans were replacing competition with consolidation. The specific differences were:

• The bill relaxed media ownership limits to the extent that a majority of local media outlets and 50 percent of television stations in the nation could be owned by a single company and allow "cross-ownership"—ownership of newspapers, radio stations, and television stations in the same market.[98]

• The bill virtually eliminated regulation of the cable television industry. Telephone companies would be able to purchase cable companies, which the administration interpreted as hurting competition. Cable rates could rise to what markets would bear.

• The House bill took the position of the RBOCs on the timing of opening up long-distance service to competition. The administration wanted the power to certify that specific RBOCs actually faced local competition before they were able to compete in long-distance markets.

• The House bill, unlike the Senate bill, did not include the administration's V-Chip proposal.

Claims to represent a general public interest take many forms. The language of competition was not used to support the CDA, an amendment that required on-line service providers to scan their networks for "obscene, lewd, lascivious, filthy, or indecent" content.[99] It was accompanied by sensational arguments. Senator Exon had an aide assemble a file (blue in color) of the most obscene and indecent pictures to be found on the Internet. It was on his desk for anyone to view—and he announced that a vote against the CDA was an endorsement of the pornographers. Public statements about the dangers of child access to pornography did get the attention of the major media outlets, but the issue was hardly central to the overall telecommunications bill. Conservative groups without much understanding of the Internet or the First Amendment were able to win passage of the amendment. The CDA adds little in the way of enforcement power against child pornography already contained in law. Within days of the presidential signature, the American Civil Liberties Union (ACLU) won a stay of enforcement of the CDA against the Justice Department. The U.S. Supreme Court agreed to hear the case and in June 1997 ruled that the CDA went beyond permissible limits on speech protected by the First Amendment.[100] The authors of the CDA attempted to impose a new and broad standard for obscenity, but federal courts did not let them.

The Senate passed their bill in June 1995, and the House followed in August. In the House, the complexity of the deals already embodied in the bill compelled the floor leaders to adopt a modified closed rule that limited debate to a few minutes.[101] The differences between the two versions were large enough to threaten an outcome like that of the previous Congress. Enough was at stake that major interests prodded members of Congress to make additional changes in the bills. By late December, the majority Republicans were in disarray over the concessions made to the administration. Part of the problem was a carryover from other issues. The Republicans and the administration were having trouble agreeing on a budget for the fiscal year that began the previous October, and that dispute led to temporary shutdowns of some government offices. Republicans differed over whether to use the shutdown tactic in their battle with the administration. On top of that, Vice-President Gore had said in interviews that the Republicans made changes in the bill that met all of the administration's objectives—in effect, claiming a complete victory for what had actually been long and laborious bipartisan negotiations.[102]

The disputes were over concessions made in conference committee and focused on issues as much as partisanship. House Republicans objected to several specific provisions endorsed by the conferees, including more stringent standards for ownership of media outlets and tighter standards and oversight for RBOC entrance into long-distance markets. Yet Senate rules provided more opportunities for opposition forces to influence legislation. The smaller (than in the House) Republican majority, along with Senate filibuster rules, made Senate concessions to Democrats necessary in order to find a bill agreeable to the disparate industrial interests.[103]

A large number of groups in the Internet community took particular exception to the CDA. Its regulation of on-line content was a dramatic increase of federal power over speech and expression. On February 7 and 8, 1996, many concerned groups switched their web page backgrounds to black as a sign of protest against the measure. While the move elicited some attention in the media, for the most part it passed unnoticed by members of Congress.[104] As Vice-President Gore noted, the issue would be decided in the courts. It is likely that many members of Congress understood its fate when they voted for the measure. Only twenty-one voted against the Telecommunications Act, and not all because of the CDA.

In general, the media did not pay close attention to the struggle over telecommunications legislation.[105] Citizens are unaware of many of the issues at stake. One crude indicator is an estimate that about one-third of telephone customers in the country still thought, in 1996, that AT&T was their local telephone company.[106]

The Telecommunications Act of 1996

The 1996 Act had several major parts:

- Title I dealt with telecommunications services. The RBOCs were allowed to offer long-distance service outside their areas immediately. Once an RBOC is in compliance with a "competitive checklist," a series of standards, competitors would have fair access to local customers within their areas as well. Competitors could put no unreasonable conditions on the reciprocal use of each other's parts of the telephone network. PEG organizations and low-income households were to receive subsidized access to services. The FCC was ordered to convene a joint federal and state board that would administer a fund aimed at subsidizing the universal service. State and local governments were prohibited from acting in a way that limits the ability of a company to enter any telecommunications market. The RBOCs could manufacture equipment, engage in electronic publishing, and after five years enter the alarm-monitoring business (except for the one company that already offers the service). The FCC had to produce a very long list of rules within a short time for carrying out these changes, described in Chapter 5. In short, the 1982 consent decree was overturned, and government agencies, chiefly the FCC, were ordered to make policies that would manage a transition to a more competitive industry.

• Title II set rules for broadcast services. Media companies were to have less stringent limits on the number of stations that can be owned by a single company, and broadcast companies were permitted to own cable companies. The FCC was required to make exceptions to rules that appear reasonable within single markets. The FCC was to license direct broadcast services. Broadcast companies were permitted to use some of their allocated spectrum for other services but were to allow the FCC to control and possibly auction the spectrum wavelengths not in use.

• Title III dealt with cable television services. State and local governments could not act in a way that limits the ability of a company to enter any market. Rate regulations were to disappear in three years, except for the basic services, which means airwave broadcasts and educational and public-access channels. Telephone companies were allowed to enter cable television businesses, but their video transmissions were subject to telecommunications regulation, and their video programming was to be subject to the same regulation as cable companies. Companies could offer "open" video programming (the notion of a video dial tone, where customers can dial what they want and not just flip through the package offered by one company). Small cable companies were freed from many regulations, as were companies that face real competition.

• Title IV focused on regulatory reform. The FCC was ordered to "forbear" from enforcing any part of the act if doing so did not protect consumers, and in those cases states were not to act in the place of the FCC. Title IV also stated that FCC regulations would be reviewed every two years. This would require the regular collection of data to enable the agency to effectively evaluate outcomes of its actions.

• Title V was alternatively entitled the Communications Decency Act of 1996. It outlawed the creation and transmission of "obscene, lewd, lascivious, filthy, or indecent" material "with intent to annoy, abuse, threaten, or harass another person" and prohibited sending such material to anyone under eighteen years of age. Title V declared it unlawful if one "uses any interactive computer service to display in a manner available to a person under 18 years of age, any comment, request, suggestion, proposal, image, or other communication that, in context, depicts or describes, in terms patently offensive as measured by contemporary community standards, sexual or excretory activities or organs, regardless of whether the user of such service placed the call or initiated the communication; or . . . knowingly permits any telecommunications facility under such person's control to be used for an activity prohibited." This part of the act also asked the FCC to implement a rating system for television programs, similar to the one used for motion pictures, so that interested parents could more effectively control their children's viewing.

• Title VI spelled out the fact that the 1982 consent decree, the terms under which the telephone industry had been regulated the previous fourteen years, were superseded by the act. The act similarly superseded other consent decrees in the industry.

• Title VII was full of miscellaneous provisions. The FCC is to implement a Telecommunications Development Fund, intended "to promote access to capital for small businesses in order to enhance competition," to promote technology development, employment training, and universal service in "underserved" areas. The fund would be financed through interest on proceeds from spectrum auctions. It also established the National Education Technology Funding Corporation, whose purpose is to "stimulate private investment in education technology infrastructure." It also contained some consumer protections against some types of fraud made possible by the overlapping network of telephone companies.[107]

• The act contained many implementation deadlines for the FCC. These are discussed in more detail in Chapter 5.

A few of the provisions in the act are, strictly speaking, policies. These take the form of rules expected to bring about a desired outcome when applied to a specified situation. For example, if a competing telephone company wishes to use the poles of an existing company, the new competitor must be allowed access on the same terms and conditions offered to other users of the poles, such as cable companies. Another example is in the rule requiring video services to scramble the signals of "adult" channels so that nonsubscribers would find them unintelligible. Yet there are just a few such rules in the act. Most of the provisions require the FCC or some other agency to make new rules.

The main effect of the act is to establish a new regulatory regime and require the FCC to make rules over a four-year period to establish the new system. By definition, no one knows what the policies will be. Policymakers had a general expectation that the new regulatory regime would be more competitive and that state utility commissions and federal courts would have less to do with telecommunications policies. Were those reasonable expectations?

Several things were clear at the signing of the act in February 1996. First, the FCC would be a busy organization. Interest groups, telecommunications officials, and attorneys would be working to influence the FCC's rule-making procedures. In a real sense, the politics of telecommunications begins anew but shifts to a different arena.

Second, the rules under which financial decisions were made in telecommunications industries would become clearer as specific rules were made by the FCC. As the bill came before the president, several major deals were already being negotiated between RBOCs, between telephone companies and cable television companies, and between broadcasters and companies they are now able to acquire.[108] The financial effects of opening more telecommunications industry decisions to market forces are, by definition, uncertain. Estimates of the act's effect varied widely. One estimate was that by the year 2005, the RBOCs would have about 37 percent of a $235 billion long-distance market, compared to AT&T's 31 percent, MCI's 13 percent, and Sprint's 11 percent.[109] At least one prediction was that large companies like AT&T could lose more than half their value unless they linked with firms that have huge customer bases.[110]

Third, the effects on ordinary people were far from clear. Whether considered citizens, consumers, or workers, markets affect people in surprising ways. For example, supporters of the act said that cable television bills would fall, but in the near term, citizens in most regions of the country would find their cable television and telephone bills going up. Some of the central questions about priorities and values are the subject of Chapter 6.

Deregulation policies had come to Washington in the late 1970s, but telecommunications had to wait nearly twenty years for a consensus among lawmakers. Why had the idea of deregulation come to dominate telecommunications policymaking? Why had it not come before? An attempt to answer those questions is found in Chapter 4.

Notes

1. Cairncross, "A Connected World," p. 33.
2. Gilpin, "Market Place."
3. Huber, *Geodesic Network.*
4. Part of AT&T's problem was that it was big, and the antitrust field is sensitive to the charge that bigness conveys inappropriate power. Current antitrust law requires a "smoking gun," such as a memo among competitors stating the agreed-upon price. Yet theories of oligopoly show that firms can easily collude without overt communication, and this notion is readily accepted in popular culture. See the discussion in Viscusi, Vernon, and Harrington, *Regulation and Antitrust,* chap. 5.
5. Ibid., pp. 462–465.

6. The word *modify* is found in Title 47 U.S.C. 203(b)(2). The case before the Supreme Court was *MCI Telecommunications Corporation v. American Telephone & Telegraph;* it was a 5-3 majority on the court.

7. The FCC had actually refused jurisdiction over cable television in 1959, asserting it was neither a wire service nor a broadcast service. By 1966, broadcasters had convinced the FCC that cable was engaged in direct competition with them and should thus be regulated. Cable television systems require physical hookups to each house, and state and local regulations for franchised monopolies became the default regulatory option.

8. See Andrews, "Cable Price Freeze"; and Andrews, "F.C.C. Approves New Rate Rises."

9. Andrews, "In Twist."

10. The Benton Foundation produced several studies of this issue, available at www.Benton.org.

11. The growing influence of the ideas of deregulation and competition is the subject of Chapter 4.

12. White House, "Technology for Economic Growth: Progress Report," December 1993, available from the White House Archives on the Internet. See also White House, "'95 Technology Administration Budget Highlights"; White House, Executive Order 12864; and U.S. Department of Commerce, *NII Advisory Council Report*, pp. 1–3.

13. U.S. Department of Commerce, *NII Advisory Council Report.* Several cabinet departments contributed to technology policy. See, for example, Commerce Department press release, October 12, 1994, "Public Institutions Receive Millions to Deploy Information Highway."

14. Bradsher, "US to Aid Industry"; U.S. Congress, *Electronic Enterprises;* White House, *Information Infrastructure;* and *CQ Almanac 1993,* "House Passes Competitiveness Bill," p. 241.

15. See White House, *The National Information Infrastructure.* The point was suggested in Howell, "Point of View."

16. White House, Office of the Vice President, "Telecom Summit."

17. See, for example, Ronfeldt, "Cyberocracy." An earlier version of this was a Rand Corporation study, P-7745, 1991.

18. U.S. Congress, *Critical Connections.*

19. Ibid., p. 4.

20. This was brought to my attention by Kulikowski, "File 3."

21. Public Law 12-94, December 9, 1991.

22. These are described in Ronfeldt, "Cyberocracy."

23. See White House, Office of the Vice President, "Telecommunications Policy Reform Initiative"; and White House, "Communications Act Reforms." The latter makes reference to S. 1086, sponsored by Senators Inouye and Danforth, which was superceded by S. 1822 when they were joined by Senator Hollings in February. The bills, described later in the chapter, supported a shift to fewer barriers to competition in telecommunications industries.

24. Ameritech, Bell Atlantic, Bell South, NYNEX, Pacific Telesis, Southwestern Bell, and U S West.

25. The major RBOC group was called the Alliance for Competitive Communications. It published position papers and issued progress reports on legislation through its Internet site at bell.com. For example, see Testimony Before the House Telecommunications Subcommittee, May 10, 1995, by Edward E. Whitacre Jr., chairman and CEO of SBC Communications, Inc., on behalf of the Alliance for Competitive Communications.

26. See Alliance for Community Media, Washington, D.C., "Public Interest Wins and Loses in House Vote on Telecommunications Conference Report; Public Access Preserves Earlier Gains," press release dated February 1, 1996; and Taxpayer Assets Project, Washington, D.C., Information Policy Note, May 23, 1995.

27. Sohn and Schwartzman, "Pretty Pictures." See also Carney, "Spate of Squabbles," pp. 3881–3883.

28. The Clinton administration's view of this controversy can be read in "Administration Comments on H.R. 1555: The Communications Act of 1995, and Related Legislation Before the House Commerce Committee," White House, May 15, 1995.

29. See Taxpayer Assets Project, Washington D.C., Information Policy Note, May 22, 1995.

30. See Goldman, "Telecommunications from Labor's Perspective."

31. James Bradford Ramsay, Deputy Assistant General Counsel, National Association of Regulatory Utility Commissioners, presentation to National Conference of State Legislatures Assembly on Federal Issues, May 9, 1996, Washington D.C.; National Conference of State Legislatures, Committee on Commerce and Communications, "Policy Statements on Telecommunications," distributed May 9, 1996, at NCSL Telecommunications Reform Summit, Washington, D.C.

32. American Civil Liberties Union, letter from Laura W. Murphy, director of Washington National Office, and Donald Haines, Legislative Council, delivered to the House Conferees with regard to S. 652 and H.R. 1555, December 5, 1995.

33. Businesses could readily calculate a median household communications budget. About two-thirds of nearly 100 million U.S. households subscribe to cable television, paying about $25 per month. Those same households have telephones, paying about $20 per month or so for basic services, and many are getting connected to the Internet at a cost of about $20–$30 per month. There are other services as well that drive the communications budget of some households to twice this amount, and equipment amortization pushes the figure much higher. It is possible that televisions, computers, and telephones of the future will somehow combine, and so it may be possible to tap into the amortization costs of family acquisition of these as well. Some cost shifting may occur, as people find they would rather spend money on the new interactive services instead of on video games, movies, sporting events, and so on. Altogether it seemed possible to achieve a median household commitment to telecommunications somewhere over $150. For the consumer market alone, the annual dollars spent would be anywhere from $60 billion to $120 billion. That was enough to begin thinking about having customers pay for the system, if the providers had desirable services.

34. H.R. 3626, the Antitrust Reform Act of 1993, 103rd Congress, 1st session, November 22, 1993.

35. See the testimony of Philip L. Verveer (January 26, 1994, House Committee on the Judiciary, Subcommittee on Economic and Commercial Law).

36. H.R. 3636, the National Communications Competition and Information Infrastructure Act of 1993, 103rd Congress, 1st session, November 22, 1993.

37. This account relies on the the following sources: (a) hearings records before the Congress, including the Senate Committee on Commerce, Science, and Transportation, March 1995; House Subcommittee on Telecommunications and Finance (of the Committee on Energy and Commerce), February 1994; House Subcommittee on Economic and Commercial Law (Judiciary Committee), January and February 1994; and House Commerce Committee, May 1995; (b) White House archives, especially the telecommunications documents housed under the Office of the Vice President; (c) media stories such as Andrews, "A Free-for-All in Communications," and pieces

appearing in the *Wall Street Journal* and *The Economist;* academic studies of current policy issues, such as the excellent collection in Drake, *New Information Infrastructure;* (d) analyses of the telecommunications industry published by private research groups such as National Economic Research Associates, Cambridge, Mass., and the WEFA Group, Burlington, Mass.; (e) news releases, speeches, and newsletters published by interest groups, officials, and trade associations, such as Washington Telecom Newswire, Alliance for Competitive Communications, Federal Information News Service, Electronic Freedom Foundation, Taxpayers Assets Project, the Telecom Post, the Center for Information, Technology, and Society, and officials in the Department of Commerce and the Department of Justice Antitrust Division.

38. See the testimony of James G. Cullen, president of Bell Atlantic Corporation (February 8, 1994, Committee on Energy and Commerce, Subcommittee on Telecommunications and Finance).

39. Testimony of James Cullen, president of Bell Atlantic Corporation (February 2, 1994, House Committee on the Judiciary, Subcommittee on Economic and Commercial Law).

40. Testimony of Gary McBee, chairman of the United States Telephone Association, representing the RBOCs, GTE, and many local telephone companies (February 3, 1994, Committee on Energy and Commerce, Subcommittee on Telecommunications and Finance).

41. Testimony of Richard W. Odgers, executive vice-president and general counsel for Pacific Telesis Group (February 2, 1994, House Committee on the Judiciary, Subcommittee on Economic and Commercial Law).

42. See the testimony of Edward D. Horowitz, CEO of Viacom Broadcasting (February 1, 1994, Committee on Energy and Commerce, Subcommittee on Telecommunications and Finance).

43. Testimony of David Kinley, president of Sun Country Cable and chairman of the Small Cable Business Association (February 2, 1994, Committee on Energy and Commerce, Subcommittee on Telecommunications and Finance).

44. See the testimony of Decker Anstrom, CEO of the National Cable Television Association (February 2, 1994, Committee on Energy and Commerce, Subcommittee on Telecommunications and Finance).

45. See the testimony of Edward T. Reilly, National Association of Broadcasters; and Al Devaney, chair of the Association of Independent Television Stations, Inc. (both on February 2, 1994, Committee on Energy and Commerce, Subcommittee on Telecommunications and Finance).

46. See testimony of Wayne Rosing, CEO of Sun Microsystems, Inc. (February 1, 1994, Committee on Energy and Commerce, Subcommittee on Telecommunications and Finance).

47. Testimony of Hal M. Krisbergh, president of the communication division of General Instrument Corporation (February 1, 1994, Committee on Energy and Commerce, Subcommittee on Telecommunications and Finance).

48. Testimony of John Hendricks, chair and CEO of Discovery Communications, Inc. (February 1, 1994, Committee on Energy and Commerce, Subcommittee on Telecommunications and Finance).

49. S. 1822, Communications Act of 1994, 103rd Congress, 2nd session, February 3, 1994.

50. As legislation neared passage, the Commerce Department issued a study showing, not surprisingly, that poor people have less access to telecommunications services, particularly high-end features available through modems. U.S. Department

of Commerce, "Falling Through the Net: A Survey of the 'Have Nots' in Rural and Urban America," July 1985.

51. This reading of his speech is suggested in "Gore's Law," *The Economist,* January 15, 1994, p. 72.

52. Andrews, "Clinton and Technology."

53. See Andrews, "Clinton and Technology"; and Gilpin, "Market Place."

54. Andrews, "Clinton and Technology," observes that in the last year of the Bush administration, four cases were opened; in the first fifteen months of the Clinton administration, fifty cases were opened. Antitrust Division head Anne K. Bingaman's views on DOJ policy prior to the passage of legislation were outlined in a speech she delivered at the National Press Club, Washington, D.C., on February 28, 1995. She argued that the division endorses careful management of the transition to competition, close monitoring of the outcomes of market choices, and evaluation of the acceptability of those outcomes. Although she argued that markets should decide what services are offered, and at what price, she referred to meaningful competition—where "every company will be permitted to compete in every market for every customer." From the standpoint of large telephone and cable companies, it was not good news.

55. These examples are from *CQ Almanac 1993,* "Stumped."

56. Some RBOCs were preparing to sue the FCC to be able to offer video services. See Cauley, "Baby Bells." Ameritech was in negotiations with the Justice Department to enable it, with the approval of a federal judge, to enter the long-distance market in metropolitan Chicago. See Andrews, "U.S. May Let a Baby Bell Widen Reach." Perhaps most important, several states were reviewing their approaches to regulation in ways that would prove favorable to the RBOCs. For example, see the Washington Utilities and Transportation Commission, "Alternative Regulation of U S West: Toward A New Paradigm," Olympia, December 1, 1993.

57. The figures represent cash flow, profits before taxes, and depreciation. Reported in Andrews, "Phone-Law Static."

58. Ibid.; *CQ Almanac 1993,* "Stumped"; analyses produced by the Benton Foundation, at www.benton.com.

59. This judgment is based on the hearings record. The hearings record for the 104th Congress, which did pass a bill, is reviewed later in this chapter.

60. Federal Communications Commission, "Auctions Fact Sheet"; Federal Communications Commission, "Modifications to PCS Band Plan"; Federal Communications Commission, "Competitive Bidding Procedures for Broadband PCS"; Federal Communications Commission, "Answers to Questions"; Andrews, "U.S. Seeks Military Airwaves"; Andrews, "Wireless Bidders"; Safire, "Greatest Auction Ever"; Andrews, "Sweeping Revision."

61. "Pressler Says All Deals Are Off, Everything's on the Table," *Washington Telecom Newswire*, December 5, 1994.

62. The point was made in the speech by the assistant attorney general of the Antitrust Division, Anne K. Bingaman, "Promoting Competition in Telecommunications," the National Press Club, Washington D.C., February 28, 1995.

63. Although the proposed legislation was aimed at superceding the 1982 consent decree, it did not propose to end all antitrust issues for the industry. For example, telephone company attorneys regularly meet to discuss their programs for monitoring their own compliance with law and regulations. This is an opportunity for prohibited collusion even under deregulated markets, and both regulators and company officials understand that scrutiny of such contacts will continue. See France, "Are Telecoms Discussing Compliance?"

64. Pearl, "Baby Bells."

65. Associated Press Wire, "Conservative Group Urges Replacing FCC with Less Powerful Agency," June 1, 1995, released on the listserve of the Center for Information, Technology and Society.

66. Pearl, "Clinton Weighs Backing Changes."

67. White House, "Fact Sheet."

68. See the statement of AT&T executive vice-president Alex Mandl, September 28, 1994, "AT&T Exec Says Legislation May Be Tougher on Bells Next Year," *Washington Telecom Newswire*.

69. S. 652, Telecommunications Competition and Deregulation Act of 1995, 104th Congress, 1st session, March 20, 1995 (introduced by Senator Pressler, the new chair of the Commerce Committee); H.R. 1555, Communications Act of 1995, 104th Congress, 1st session, May 3, 1995 (introduced by Representative Jack Fields, the new chair of the Energy and Commerce Committee).

70. Edmund L. Andrews interviewed several lobbyists who indicated the new role for business would require new behavior. They thought that business interests had experience at making changes in mostly Democrat policy initiatives but were relatively unskilled at shaping congressional debates and legislation. See Andrews, "Why G.O.P. Falters."

71. In addition to the lobbying efforts under way, these views were publicly aired in a televised exchange between Ron Stowe, vice-president of Pacific Telesis, and Mike Brown, vice-president of AT&T, on PBS stations, February 24, 1995, as part of a program entitled "Technopolitics."

72. The point was made in a discussion paper circulated by the Alliance for Competitive Communications, a group representing the RBOCs, entitled "Reinventing National Communications Policy: What's Needed and What's at Stake," and available from their Internet web site, www.bell.com.

73. *FCC Digest,* March 29, 1995. Later, RBOCs and cable companies were to ask the FCC to delay action on their video dialtone (VDT) regulations until the outcome of the 104th Congress's telecommunications reforms were known. See "An Information Age Plea to Washington: Let Congress Decide the Future of Video Dialtone," news release of July 19, 1995, news conference, Washington, D.C., distributed also over the *Telecommunications Policy Roundtable Forum* via their Internet listserve.

74. Andrews, "Bell Atlantic."

75. CBS was acquired by the Westinghouse Corporation, and by the time the bill passed, Capital Cities/ABC was about to close on a purchase by the Walt Disney Company.

76. See note 33. The telecommunications market for nationwide telecommunications networks is worth, as of 1998, somewhere between $60 billion and $120 billion annually. That estimate may be low. With capital and business expenses, the total amount spent on the industries was nearly three times that spent in 1996. Companies expect to create new services, such as video-on-demand, that will entice consumers to spend considerably more than currently. We should expect to see many more mergers as companies learn how to tap these markets.

77. Telecommunications interests spent $13 million in Political Action Committee (PAC) money leading up to the 1994 election, and about $20 million in the 104th Congress by the time the Telecommunications Act passed. Andrews, "Phone-Bill Lobbyists"; *Telecom Post*, August 6, 1995.

78. The list is gleaned from Andrews, "Phone-Bill Lobbyists"; Gary Ruskin, Congressional Accountability Project, Washington D.C., news release, November

15, 1995; and news release, Washington National Office, American Civil Liberties Union, Laura W. Murphy, director, December 5, 1995.

79. WEFA was formed in 1987 in a merger of Wharton Econometric Forecasting Associates and Chase Econometrics. See WEFA Group, *Economic Impact.*

80. Andrews, "Phone-Law Static."

81. The letter was dated February 7, 1995, and released to the press and on Internet listserves from several of the signing groups on the same day.

82. Assurances of bipartisan work on the bill are contained in, among other sources, the news release "Pressler Calls for Staged Opening of Telecom Markets," *Washington Telecom Newswire*, January 12, 1995.

83. "U.S. Senate Rejects DOJ Decision Making Role in Telecom," *Federal Information News Service*, June 13, 1995.

84. See *Telecom Post*, no. 17, October 26, 1995; Andrews, "Clinton Enters Battle."

85. The estimate is reported in Robichaux, "Cable Industry."

86. ISDN is a direct digital transmission over some medium, like telephone lines. Most computers that connect to other computers and the Internet over telephone lines do so through a modem that transforms the digital signal of the computer into the telephone system's analog format. The modem at the other end of the call handles the transformation in the opposite direction. ISDN permits vastly quicker transmission. The actual costs of ISDN transmission are a matter of dispute. Public interest groups claim that marginal costs to telephone companies are less than $10 per month per household for the service. Telephone companies claim that the cost runs from $32 to $184. The different estimates are reminiscent of the debates over separations policy, described in Chapter 2.

87. See "Ad Hoc Coalition to Press for Low Cost ISDN Service," *Taxpayer Assets Project-Information Policy Note*, May 9, 1995; "Consumer Project on Technology (CPT) Files Comments in FCC Inquiry on ISDN Prices," *Taxpayer Assets Project-Information Policy Note*, July 15, 1995. The FCC docket for its investigation into ISDN pricing was no. 95-72.

88. FCC, Report no. DC-2621, Action in Docket Case, June 29, 1994, "Commission Adopts Competitive Bidding Procedures for Broadband PCS" (PP Docket no. 93-253). The qualifications for minority ownership status are described in FCC, "Answers to Questions."

89. Andrews and Fabrikant, "The Black Entrepreneur"; Andrews, "Viacom's Cable Sale Threatened."

90. Seidman and Gilmour, *Politics, Position, and Power.*

91. From a press release issued by the companies and their trade associations, March 23, 1993.

92. Remarks released by the White House, Office of the Vice-President, January 9, 1995.

93. Testimony before the Committee on Commerce, Science, and Transportation, United States Senate, March 2, 1995. Released by Mr. Irving's office.

94. The brief House debate was televised on C-Span, August 2, 1995. The comments in this and the following paragraph were taken from that broadcast. Tauzin's claim of millions of jobs is supported by the ten-year estimate of the WEFA analysis *Economic Impact.*

95. Yet government officials err in such judgments. Congressman White later said his support for the Communications Decency Act was a mistake, based on a misleading characterization of the dangers of Internet pornography on the part of Senator Exon.

96. The Dole position on the "spectrum giveaway" is found in Dole, "Giving Away the Airwaves." The congressional controversy and his role in it are described in Andrews, "Digital TV, Dollars, and Dissent."

97. "Statement by the President on H.R. 1555," White House, Office of the Press Secretary, press release of July 31, 1995; "Statement by Vice President Gore on H.R. 1555," White House, Office of the Vice-President, press release of August 3, 1995.

98. Although the administration aimed this charge at the House bill, similar arguments were made against the Senate version as well. See, for example, Mills, "Great Radio Debate."

99. It was introduced by Senator Exon and Senator Slade Gorton (R-WA) as S. 314, Communications Decency Act of 1995, 104th Congress, 1st session, February 2, 1995.

100. Supreme Court of the United States, No. 96-511, Janet Reno, Attorney General of the United States et al., *Appellants v. American Civil Liberties Union et al.,* June 26, 1997.

101. The rule was adopted as H.R. 207, August 2, 1995. It was adopted, officially, at midnight on August 2, 1995, by a vote of 255 to 156. "Modified Closed Rule on Telecom Debate Agreed To," *Federal Information News Service,* August 2, 1995.

102. See Andrews, "Conference Accord." Compare to the previous day's coverage in Andrews, "Accord Is Reached." The subhead of this article read, "Retreat by Republicans."

103. The point was made in Andrews, "Accord Is Reached."

104. See Lewis, "'Darkness' to Meet Communications Bill."

105. This can be said about most policy issues that come before the Congress. The notable exception to this is the coverage in the *New York Times*, especially by Edmund L. Andrews, referred to extensively in this chapter.

106. "Washington's Wake-up Call," *The Economist*, January 20, 1996, p. 61.

107. For example, if a customer dials a toll-free number, the call cannot be routed to a pay-per-call circuit; in another example, a telephone company cannot charge calling card customers for services unless there is an agreement between the issuer of the card and the charging company.

108. The effects on business decision are treated in the last section of Chapter 5.

109. Forrester Research, quoted in "Washington's Wake-up Call," *The Economist*, January 20, 1996, p. 62.

110. Cairncross, "A Connected World."

4 How Did Deregulation Come to Dominate Policymaking?

The idea of deregulation in telecommunications has taken many forms since it first appeared in the nation's capital during the 1970s. By the mid-1990s, it was the guiding principle for policymakers. Why were the 103rd and 104th Congresses different from earlier legislative configurations that did not embrace deregulation? If, by 1992 or so, deregulation in telecommunications was an idea whose time had come, why had it come at that particular time? Why did it take until 1996 to pass legislation?

In this chapter I present an answer to these questions. The story focuses on the critical years leading up to the divestiture agreement and the 1996 Act—roughly, the twenty years from 1976 to 1996—and follows the approach described in Chapter 1, summarized in Figures 1.1 and 1.2. First, the chapter is organized by the concepts in Figure 1.1 (the political model)—those elements in the problem stream, the policy stream, and the political stream that mark activity of political actors who influence policy. Next, the chapter employs the analytical model depicted in Figure 1.2; I use this section as a device to see whether analysis was a significant feature in telecommunications policymaking. Third, the chapter considers the technological context, using the concepts introduced in the final section of Chapter 1 to present telecommunications as a case study that illuminates the politics of technical change.

A Political Description

The Problem Stream

The problem stream consists of government officials who routinely deal with indicators of problems and the events that bring problems to their attention.[1] Problems come to their attention in a variety of ways. In the case of telecommunications policy, the single most important development turned out to be the emergence of digital technologies and the way they changed business views of public policies.

Digital technologies challenged officials in government and in industry by skaking the foundations of current practices. For example, digital transmission opened up the possibility of bypassing the local telephone company loop. A regulatory framework built on the premise of separate telephone, cable television, broadcasting, and wireless communications left telecommunications interests in an uncertain position. It was not that large telephone companies were in imminent danger of extinction—in the early 1990s, the possibility of making local telephone companies obsolete was a mere guess—but to telephone company executives it was a possibility within the space of a decade if they did not adapt.

Digital technologies made possible the bundling of services, such as regular and cellular telephones, paging, cable television, and Internet connection. Business leaders believed that the first firm to market a "killer application," a bundle of services large numbers of consumers want to have, would make a lot of money. In an earlier era AT&T's linking of local companies via long-distance lines served as an example of this phenomenon. In the early 1990s, popular examples included Microsoft's good fortune at being selected to write the operating system for the IBM personal computer, McCaw Cellular's stringing together of local cellular radio licenses into a network, and Netscape's early success as the industry standard for an Internet web browser.

At the time, the fastest growing part of this digital possibility was in wireless telephones, such as cellular telephones.[2] The cost of single-line service was, as legislation was passing in 1995, as low as twice that of a telephone connected to copper wires. Ten years before, the service was simply not available, and crude early wireless telephones cost many hundreds of times that of regular telephones.[3] It seemed likely that as the costs of single calls continued to drop, cellular service would rival regular telephone service prices. Cellular telephones could become regular telephones.[4]

Pager technology was also changing rapidly at the time. Pagers could receive and display a wide range of information, from simple paging services to financial market price quotes. Data could be sent between computers, and businesses with far-flung and mobile installations could operate company message networks. These were expensive specialty services a decade before, and in the 1990s they were available to a mass market.

Once a transmission is digitized, there is in principle no difference, aside from volume of information, between a telephone call and a televised baseball game. If the conduit for the information is big enough, and the machines at both ends are capable of sending and receiving the information, the distinctions between cable, broadcast, and telephone companies disappear. This is dangerous news to telephone companies used to protection from competitors in a telephone business with annual revenues, during the time legislation was passing, of about $100 billion.

Did the Internet spur any of this? Certainly the three years leading up to passage of the 1996 Act saw an explosion of Internet activity; 1995 was a year when just about every imaginable type of business saw some urgency in establishing a home page on the World Wide Web. Why? It was not at all clear that companies knew what they were doing, only that it did not cost much and it could convey materials already produced to an audience not otherwise easily reached. Subscribers to Internet services buy things, starting with personal computers and on-line services. But by the mid-1990s, it was unclear whether these consumers would be a powerful independent market or would force businesses to adopt new strategies. Some companies, such as the Internet infrastructure providers and information-intensive businesses, believed the Internet would be a huge commercial opportunity,[5] but most businesses were unsure. The image of the Internet was a frequent feature in speeches on deregulation delivered by the president, the vice-president, and congressional leaders.[6] The rush to be on the web by businesses and government officials was a sign of an enthusiastic and positive view of technology in the United States.

Why should technical changes seize the attention of government officials in the problem stream? The changes challenge industry's and regulators' thinking by stretching the boundaries of policies. New technologies arise in a complicated web of choices that may be influenced by several factors, singly or in combination:

- An innovation may make a popular or emerging technology cost less and compete more effectively. In a classic example, the Ford Motor Company's application of assembly line technology changed the nature of manufacturing work in the United States and helped bring the automobile within the means of many citizens. In the telecommunications field, the development of computerized switching and microwave transmission in the telephone network dramatically altered the relative costs of local versus long-distance telephone calls. Businesses with a need to communicate over large areas encountered a dramatic drop in the costs of transmitting information. Companies founded on this new technology, such as MCI, were able to effectively compete with AT&T during the 1980s and 1990s. In a similar example, cellular telephones were made possible by several inventions, one of which was the digital switching that provided a more efficient way to use the available electromagnetic spectrum. These inventions made it possible to conceive of commercially viable cellular telephone networks. The building of McCaw Cellular, later purchased by AT&T, illustrates a new business made possible by such inventions. Digital switches also made possible the building of hybrid cable and fiber-optic systems. New ways to cram more bits of information into copper wires and coaxial cable were one of the promises that spurred mergers between telephone and cable television companies in the mid-1990s. Eventually, the 1996 Act removed many of the limitations on these companies, and they found themselves facing challenges by competitors who were better able to make use of the new technologies.[7]

• Sometimes commercial goals lead a company to choose technology *A* over technology *B*. Several examples support this model of technology change: (1) MCI grew largely because company leaders saw commercial opportunities in the regulated fee structure of long-distance telephone service. The cheapest way to build such a network, without having to purchase rights-of-way, etc., was to build a microwave network among large commercial customers. (2) AT&T saw itself at a growing disadvantage vis-à-vis the regional Bell companies, because the latter might enter long-distance service cheaply, while AT&T would find it expensive to offer local service. By acquiring McCaw Cellular, AT&T was able to tap into the fastest-growing local telephone markets otherwise barred to them by regulation. (3) The growth of the Internet during the early 1990s led carriers like AT&T and MCI to question their support of the technology. The most common way for each Internet node to operate was to set up a bank of modems on a line leased from a telephone company, which was connected to a "backbone" line that carried messages across the country and around the world. Many Internet users wanted use to remain "free" in the sense that once their part of the network was up and running, no further charges are levied for increased volume. They saw the backbone as a public resource. To the backbone provider this looked like a subsidy at their expense to the advocates of a free Internet. Since the backbone lines are provided by only a few companies, pricing schemes are regulated by the FCC and by state commissions. Attempts to increase prices for high-speed data lines are a move toward a private model of backbone services.[8]

• Sometimes commercial needs present problems that companies seek to solve, and in so doing find new technologies. For example: (1) Many companies sought to be part of Internet advertising during 1994 and 1995, but the commercial outcomes of this surge of advertising were unclear. World Wide Web pages, for example, could not become catalogs and markets until someone developed secure means for transmitting credit card numbers over the Internet. The commercial needs drove the quest for such software. (2) In the mid-1990s, digital technology offered real advantages over analog cellular telephones. Business customers could more easily fax, send, and receive computer files, as well as speak over digital networks. Cell phone companies could sell more services through digital networks. Yet nonbusiness users were reluctant to purchase the more expensive new equipment, and so the move from one technology to the other appeared to need five years' time. The cost of cell phones was, in a sense, too high because the quality of the service was too high. Lower-quality services at cheaper prices later proved to be popular.[9]

• A corporation with some degree of monopoly power may influence technical choice toward its interests. The regulated AT&T monopoly for years resisted the attachment of outside equipment to its system. Supporters of new innovations faced substantial and costly barriers. Not only did they have to shoulder the research, development, manufacturing, and marketing costs of an innovation, they also had to prepare to battle AT&T in courts and before the FCC.[10]

• Government policy may encourage or otherwise subsidize a technology. The French government decided it wanted its citizens to have ready access to government, business, and each other through "minitel" computer terminals. The United States government, wanting U.S. industry to lead the way in setting standards for and manufacturing HDTV, for years worked to encourage research and development in this field. These are a form of industrial policy and are examples of practices found in all our major trading partners.[11] In the late 1990s, the U.S. approach was to encourage private sector investment in communications networks and in particular encourage the use of the relatively cheaper (in the near term) digital wireless technology. During the 104th Congress, members used estimates from a study produced by a prestigious think tank that predicted vigorous job and gross domestic product (GDP) growth following deregulation.[12] Support for deregulation sounded to many like good public policy.

• Government policy may actively discourage a technology. In the decade prior to its breakup, the government of the Soviet Union drastically limited the availability of personal computers to its citizens. Information technologies enabled individual users to pursue many interests government wished to discourage. The government was less vigilant toward limiting video recorders, and an underground supply of videotapes enabled antigovernment groups to organize and keep track of news and art in the West. During the same period, the U.S. government was subsidizing the Internet.

• Technologies may be more or less consistent with popular values, and that may influence their adoption. Pornography in the United States is widely available, but also widely condemned. Many of its consumers must find it in anonymous or semiprivate situations. In the early 1990s perhaps more than half the bits of information traveling around the Internet were pictures with sexual content.[13] Pornography on the Internet became the subject of one of the most contentious debates leading to passage of the 1996 Act. The new technology was apparently suited to our culture's mix of high demand for and vigorous public disapproval of pornography.

• The degree of fit between popular values and a technology has another side. Many youngsters understand computers much better than do their parents. Conversations at social gatherings often turn to computers—it has been a common thread of male conversation in the 1990s. A generation earlier, the automobile enjoyed a similar popularity. Knowledge of cars, and the ability to work on them, was in an important way a badge of maleness. But the automobile changed, and fewer and fewer men understand how to work on them or possess the necessary and expensive diagnostic computers. Women now make most new car purchase decisions. America's love affair with the automobile is different now that one is more often merely a consumer and less often a mechanic. The popularity of home computers is difficult to explain by way of a narrow account of value focusing on productivity or the cost of an hour of computer entertainment. Computer literacy is part of a larger social movement toward the use of active information technologies.[14]

In addition, policymakers were faced with a widespread recognition of an ongoing policy problem. The breakup of AT&T left a lot of confused and disagreeable customers of telephone companies, due to the continued widespread popularity of low-cost monthly rates.[15] Public opinion was not highly informed on telecommunications issues but was sensitive to the claim that a better deal was needed. Telecommunications policy reform was directed in part at this public sentiment.

The Policy Stream

The policy stream consists of communities of policy specialists. As noted in Chapter 1, there is considerable crossover between the problem and policy streams. The special feature here is when developments turned into policy-oriented ideas. Perhaps technologies become important policy issues when important economic, military, or ideological elites see them as problematic. This seems to be the case in telecommunications technologies. This section focuses on elite academic professions and policy-oriented organizations in business and in the media.

The turning of academic opinion in the direction of deregulation happened over a period of twenty-five years. It began in academic departments of economics. One such department was at the University of Chicago, where such figures as Friedrich von Hayek, Milton Friedman, and George Stigler steered a generation of economists. Many economists beyond the "Chicago School" worked in regulatory issues. The field of economics moved from the belief that regulation is often needed to counter monopoly power and other market failures, to the conclusion that price and entry regulation is inefficient and can be replaced by better, procompetitive policies.

Analyses of market failure had to be balanced with analyses of government failure. This became the consensus in the field of economics.[16]

Strong beliefs in markets changed the way economists and other policy specialists conceived of relations between government and business.[17] Since the Progressive Era, the most common approach to economic and environmental regulation was to assume adversarial roles for government and industry. The new economic consensus mixed with political action by business groups to convince government officials to move to a less adversarial approach to regulation.[18] In telecommunications policy, the FCC applied some of these ideas but, as noted in Chapter 3, failed to see how its small inroads into AT&T's monopoly from the early 1950s to the late 1960s helped create new companies and powerful forces for telecommunications deregulation.

During this same period, many economists came to be employed in government service. This was partly due to the confidence most policymakers shared during the mid-1960s in our ability to manage the economy.[19] Part of it was also due to the efforts of organizations devoted to bringing some of the more procompetitive ideas out of academic departments and into the streams where policy is made.[20] These included the Ford Foundation, the Brookings Institution, the Olin Foundation, and the American Enterprise Institute.[21] One example of this carriage of ideas through institutions, certainly archtypical rather than average, is seen in the career of Stephen G. Breyer. He worked on a Brookings study of energy regulation and later took a job on the Senate Judiciary Committee's Subcommittee on Administrative Practice and Procedure, chaired by Edward Kennedy. It was Breyer who convinced Kennedy to emphasize airline deregulation. Kennedy, still supportive of the consumer movement, adopted the argument that airline regulation cost the consumer too much. The merging of conservative and liberal agendas in airline deregulation set a pattern followed in other industries. (Breyer became associate justice on the U.S. Supreme Court.)

The model followed by the American Enterprise Institute[22] suggests the possibilities for getting ideas into the policy process. First, a resident scholar would write a paper. The paper would then be sent to influential people who might mention the idea. For example, a Jack Kemp could be convinced to use the notion of enterprise zones in a speech. Next, an institute member would encourage newspaper columnists to write about the idea contained in the speech. The author of the original paper (in the case of enterprise zones, Stuart Butler) would write a book on the subject, which would be sent to senior White House aides. Finally, the idea would get into a presidential speech. At that point, the idea is at the door of policymaking institutions.

In this model, media outlets became part of the challenge to the old regulatory orthodoxy. The economists' and policy studies organizations' insights helped produce more vigorous reporting and editorializing by conservative and business-oriented media outlets. The preeminent source has been the *Wall Street Journal*.[23] Robert Bartley, who became editorial page editor in 1971, was responsible for some of the spread of ideas. He wanted to make conservatism more politically and economically respectable and hired reporters who shared his views. The supply-side economics concept, to give one example, was named and popularized by a reporter he hired: Jude Wanniski.

Wall Street Journal editorials from 1965 to the present illustrate the new emphasis during this period.[24] In the six years prior to 1971, the *Journal* published an average of 20.7 editorials each year criticizing the size or role of government. In the next six years, 1971–1976, the average jumped to 43.8 such editorials per year. This doubling is a matter of editorial focus and not an effect of the *Journal*'s increase in size. The number of stories in the paper about government actually declined by a little over 2 percent during the same time. These patterns continue to the present.

Still another part of the increasing influence of conservative ideas was the development of a coherent neoconservatism on the part of intellectuals like Daniel Moynihan, Irving Kristol, Nathan Glazer, Daniel Bell, and James Q. Wilson.[25] Neoconservatism was not one coherent ideology but a collection of ideas offered in opposition to prevailing notions in the academy and in policy circles. The 1960s found Democrats in control of the White House and holding large majorities in the two houses of Congress. The leadership of Lyndon Johnson and key members of Congress brought about an extension of government programs to offer benefits to groups that had traditionally been left out. Along with this went an increase in economic planning and an expansion of the role of government into concerns that had before been regarded as largely private affairs. School busing and affirmative action are two examples of policies that set off neoconservatives from the mainstream.[26] They were programs where freedom and planning necessarily collided.

Deregulation was a part of this neoconservative spirit. At times, the analysis was a relatively simple dichotomy between regulation and deregulation.[27] At other times, the analysis went well beyond that. For Eugene Bardarch and Robert Kagan the problem was a wider and more complicated phenomenon they called regulatory unreasonableness.[28] Regulators become unreasonable when they are tightly controlled by a central organization, out of fear the regulated industry would otherwise "capture" the regulating agency; when regulations are not case sensitive and must be applied even if not appropriate; and when norms discourage negotiations and cooperation to address problems because it might appear that regulators are backing down or being soft on industry. Bardarch and Kagan argued for a new consensus on seeking policy cooperation instead of an adversarial relationship between businesses and regulators. Their model for diagnosing and providing remedies for regulatory unreasonableness is a powerful model for making policy but does not lend itself to the simple rhetoric needed for brief political arguments. The literature on deregulation is an example of intellectual and political elites not exactly seeing eye to eye. In the case of the 1996 Act, the straightforward argument that competition is better than regulation was adopted by policymakers.

It is possible that in 2010, students of the policy process will look back and say the mid-1990s were a time when a pendulum was swinging back to a balanced or refined view of regulation and competition.[29]

Business views of the connection between economic forces and technological change can be illuminated by asking the question, When did major companies[30] begin to believe that the digital revolution in communications was the key to their future growth? AT&T certainly went through a major shift in leaders' and employees' self-concept in the time leading up to and after the 1982–1984 breakup period.[31] A broad company ethic of serving the average customer was strong until at least 1980, but then the situation grew complicated. It became clear to AT&T, and to regulators, that its remaining days as The Phone Company were few. The speed with which AT&T announced its second breakup, less than six months after President Clinton signed the 1996 Act, and the contents of company annual reports suggested that broad corporate strategy was scrutinized and redefined during the 103rd and 104th Congresses. The emerging convergence of computers, telephones, wireless transmissions, broadcasting, and cable meant that the company needed to redefine itself once again. AT&T's chair, Robert Allen, has made it the theme of his tenure to remake AT&T in an era of more competitive long-distance competition and possibly compete once again in local markets. Yet there are few signs the company leaders thought seriously about this prior to the 103rd Congress.[32]

Other companies had thought through the issues. MCI was the main company pressing AT&T in long-distance markets and so had long been preparing to compete on new territory.[33] Its financial incentives were directly created by the regulatory regime governing AT&T from 1968 until the 1996 Act. While microwave transmission technology was invented before the company was formed, the construction of the commercial network spurred technical development.[34] Another example comes from the RBOCs, which had been asking Congress to lift the restrictions on long-distance markets for five years prior to the 1996 Act. Their position presented an entirely different picture to AT&T and to regulators. For most people, the regional Bells were their telephone company, and AT&T strongly resisted their entry while retaining control of the local loop. Rather than spurring AT&T to competition, the reforms the RBOCs wanted encouraged AT&T to seek protection under the wing of the FCC and to attempt to block legislation in Congress. AT&T simply did not change its strategy to endorse competition until the technology and the congressional movement to legislation forced it to act.

The companies may have simply been following the then current bets on the financial future of telecommunications. Household technology budgets were changing, and companies were making estimates of how much money could be made. Millions of households are willing to spend as much for computer on-line services and cellular telephones as they do for cable television. Telecommunications companies understand that regular telephone service and cable television markets are almost saturated; they reach nearly as many households as possible. Growth will come in wireless and computer services and in new applications that offer enhanced or combined services. These might take the form of second and third telephone lines into a house to support computer services, or interactive cable services. The technologies most likely slated for commercial development are those that tap into the growing markets.

Cable television technology has been around for nearly fifty years, but business development of the possibilities has only recently made it the most popular way to receive television signals. It is a wealthy nation where most people prefer to pay $25 or more per month for many channels than to receive just a few over the "free" airwaves. The development of the cable business made it possible to conceive of the effective end of free broadcast television for most citizens. And as long as cable television's so-called second wire was in the houses of a majority of the population, the enhanced and combined services made possible by new switching and transmission technologies appeared to be a practical business venture. During the first half of the 1990s, it looked as if cable companies would compete with telephone companies.

The speed with which the current wires, switches, and computers that make up the information infrastructure will be replaced by newer technology is severely constrained by cost. Carriers are not sure what application will be popular with the majority of the nation's households, and so the technology needed to deliver it is uncertain. This means the movement to new technologies is going to be fairly slow and incremental, moving forward as carriers believe they are in a position to make money from particular applications.

There were consensus guesses about the most likely technologies in the near term.[35] Digital transmission would be needed to some point within carrier networks, which suggests the need for optical fiber, and the last bit of line into a customer's home or business might be coaxial cable, and in some cases copper wire. These so-called fiber-coax hybrid systems were expected to be popular because they involve less expense and risk than an all-fiber system. They were less expensive because they were, for the most part, already in place. During 1996, the year legislation passed, estimates of the cost of putting in new cable or fiber ran to about $1,000 per home passed on a newly installed line. This amount was based mainly on the actual conduit and the labor and machines needed to install it. Improvement in computer switching would not lower this amount by much. To amortize such an amount over its useful life requires a fee of about $30 per month. To that one can add the costs of whatever service a carrier can sell to each home.

These examples of the pressures on AT&T recall the key finding of Horwitz's study of telecommunications policy.[36] In the late 1970s, as the deregulatory trend was moving through Washington, the affected industries did not want deregulation. Trucking, airlines, and natural gas industries were deregulated as an outcome of a new and diverse coalition of interests using new ideas that resonated well in the Congress and with the public. Telecommunications was the exception during that period, because AT&T was strong enough to stop any legislation it did not like.[37]

Yet by the 103rd and 104th Congresses, AT&T and other major telecommunications companies did embrace more competitive policies. As suggested above, the key lies in the company perceptions of trends in technology, markets, and politics. The ambiguity of these calculations highlights the important role played by ideas in the policy process.

With each of these technical possibilities, politics loom large. Consider the technology assembled for cell phone networks. Regulations about radio licenses and the placement of transmission towers meant that a host of local licenses had to be acquired to form a network. The value was created in the network. One of the ways the 1996 Act lowered the cost of the technologies was to make local government treat all telecommunications companies equally. This was done in the knowledge that local governments were not yet ready to deal with the issues and to shoulder the costs of regulation over the siting of radio towers and rights-of-way.[38]

The pattern is repeated in every industry involved in telecommunications. Calculations of corporate interest take place under conditions of uncertainty that can be affected by public policy. The companies that supported the 1996 Act did not wish to add to their troubles, but they may have done so by embracing procompetitive ideas.

Ideas about deregulation came to Washington, D.C., in the mid-1970s but did not become part of telecommunications legislation until 1996. When the legislative machine started moving, it was not as a result of big scandals, and it was not because large segments of the public were protecting or seeking benefits. Instead, the changes occurred in steady public services that most citizens found satisfactory. Did interest groups drive the process? How influential were ideas? This analysis suggests that both were involved.

The Political Stream

One important political change prior to passage of the 1996 Act came from the electorate. Republicans held a nineteen-seat House majority following the election in November 1994, controlling the House for the first time since 1948. They had a working majority in the Senate. Democrats lost in droves, and for the first time, not a single incumbent Republican lost in either house. Republicans picked up fifty-three House and eight Senate seats. Yet in the face of this apparent sea change in political tides, the legislation that passed the 104th Congress was very similar to the legislation that almost passed the 103rd. Why?

Georgia Persons's analysis of earlier telecommunications legislation suggests an answer to that question.[39] Elections matter, but one must look at the dynamics of the committees in Congress. Although a new majority controlled the legislature, key committee people of both parties had been there a while and imparted stability to the political stream in Congress.

Lance LeLoup described this mixed effect of elections in his comparison of the roles of Congress and the president in national policymaking.[40] Particularly in an era of divided government, the degree of cooperation between the institutions will vary depending on the policy. In some areas (such as Medicare and social security policy), even legislators of the opposite party expect presidential leadership. In other areas, such as congressional committees investigating presidential ethics, members of Congress directly attack presidential leadership. Telecommunications belongs in a third category, in which bipartisan policy expertise or ideological agreement dominates policy direction. Welfare reform of the mid-1990s is another example of this type.

Why were the two parties so close to each other on telecommunications legislation? One possibility is that the parties are far apart on "cultural" issues that involve morality or values (such as abortion, the use of English versus bilingual instruction in public education, a flag-burning amendment to the Constitution) but are virtually identical on political economy issues (such as rules on the role of government in the economy and trade agreements). The institutional incentives within the Congress are important here. The leadership of each party has, over the past two decades, come to see budget resolutions as the center of policy directions, and this has led to stronger divisions among the parties.[41] Telecommunications policy did not involve congressional promises to spend more money. On the contrary, many legislators thought the bill would ultimately lead to the abolition of the FCC and budget reductions.

Republicans tend to favor deregulation, but Democrats have been key players in previous deregulation legislation. President Clinton and Vice-President Gore remained committed to telecommunications reform and included it in their broad approach to economic and technology policy. It was not party so much as experienced people that mattered. The 1994 election let the momentum for legislation continue because the key people did not change. The point emerges from a comparison of the 1992, 1994, and 1996 national elections.

The 1992 election was, among the three, most important to telecommunications deregulation. When he was a member of the Senate, Vice-President Gore worked for more than ten years on various aspects of technology and communications issues. He had come to see them as intertwined with economic policy and argued that economic development comes through technological development. The Democratic Leadership Council (DLC), of which Bill Clinton was a founding member, had embraced the idea in the 1980s as a way to garner popular support for Democratic party policies and win elections.[42] According to DLC members, the Democrats had become captives of a wide variety of interest groups, and the mass of voters simply did not have confidence in what the party stood for. A concept of economic development that relied chiefly on markets and technological innovation was at the center of many DLC conferences.

Democrats that controlled both the Congress and the presidency after the 1992 elections were set to consider at least one issue that traditionally had been advocated by the Republicans. Vice-President Gore and secretary of commerce Ron Brown publicly aired ideas about economic development through technology and markets in speeches and at conferences attended by industry representatives. They worked to make popular, in particular, the phrase "information superhighway" and tried to convince people that great economic benefits would flow from it.[43] The first major legislative effort of the Clinton administration, national health care, failed. One of Clinton's favorite projects, his Americorps national service program, passed only after significant compromise and outright subterfuge.[44] He considered it all the more significant that telecommunications legislation succeeded during the second year of his administration.

The 1994 election was vital to some policy areas—for example, both houses of Congress cut all appropriations for Americorps—but much less important to telecommunications legislation. The 103rd Congress narrowly missed passing legislation.[45] The 104th Congress did change the content of the bill, but its major points were virtually identical.[46] The committee chairs were in every case the ranking members on the committees that had reported legislation the previous year. These elected officials were up to speed on most issues, accustomed to the terminology of the debate, and had working relationships with the major interest groups. Floor managers of the bills did change, and this was probably important in rebalancing the effects of the bill more toward the preferences of the RBOCs. But this is difficult to judge.

The 1996 Act was not a high-conflict issue. It was not of a type likely to generate a great deal of public attention. In general terms,[47] the potential benefits were concentrated (the main benefits went to interest groups that could conduct business in new ways), and the potential payers were highly dispersed (consumers who would be paying the new rates). The incentives to organize were strong for the industry beneficiaries. The direct conflicts were generally between interest groups, such as the issues that separated regional Bell companies from the long-distance carriers. At the same time, the premises of elected officials led them to believe that important general benefits, such as the creation of new jobs, would accrue from passage of the act.

Elections are seldom straightforward referenda on policy issues. If elections in the United States are retrospective assessments of the incumbent's performance, with particular emphasis on the condition of the economy, the connection to deregulation policy is loose at best. For example, if growth of personal income is above 3.8 percent, incumbents nearly always win; if it is below 2 percent, incumbents nearly always lose. A variety of events can influence outcomes of elections in the middle ranges of these numbers. In 1994, the idea was widespread that citizens could not trust elected officials. Republicans were swept in on promises of meaningful change, although most voters had no idea what it was the Republicans proposed to do. If elections are prospective, then voters respond to forecasts of these outcomes. Either way, the evidence suggests policy is at best indirectly considered in the voting booth.

This pattern of behavior on the part of the electorate, of responding both to their material conditions and to public ideas, is not new. Views of imagined harms, of potential threats in the rest of the world, of the role of industry in public life, of the competence of government are not produced solely by material conditions. Leadership and the dynamics of generational change play a role in the evolution of public ideas. This was true in the Progressive Era, when national regulation of communications started, and it is true in the late twentieth century.[48]

The 1996 election figured somewhat in the timing of passage of the 1996 Act. Congress had failed to pass the legislation before the November 1994 election, and both parties were building a record for the following contest. Whereas the health care issue dominated the first year of the 103rd Congress, the issues that would compete for the attention of congressional leaders in the 104th Congress were fewer. Major issues at election time were taxes and the health of the economy—and several observers of Congress claimed that the policy debates had never been so polarized, encouraging both sides on an issue to exaggerate and mislead.[49] Regulatory issues were not contested in the campaigns, as both parties endorsed the phrases about making government smaller and more efficient, with a lighter hand on regulation of business.

No significant change in the balance of power in the national government came out of the 1996 election. Most incumbents won, including Democratic President Bill Clinton, Republican Speaker Newt Gingrich, and Senate majority leader Trent Lott; the Democratic party leaders in Congress also returned, and the distribution of seats among party members remained roughly the same. In sizing up the political effects of the election, leaders of both parties made reassuring sounds that the voters endorsed representatives who would work to find a bipartisan consensus on important issues.

Investors were happy with the results. The stock market surged ahead on election day as polls confirmed continuation of the status quo in Washington.[50] In retrospect, this was the middle of the longest post–World War II bull market, and it would get stronger in the eighteen months following the election.[51]

To compare the views of leaders across branches of the national government, President Clinton and House Speaker Gingrich each accepted the idea that technology somehow drives social change. They believed that the thing called the Information Age would provide a new basis for the economy.[52] Yet these views were not carefully thought out. They operated on the level of principles and were vague about policy details.

In the case of telecommunications policy, specialists widely understood that the transition to competition would cost customers money. For example, the expansion of cable television companies into telephone service required capital, and with rate deregulation, expansion would be mainly funded through increased rates. Yet both Republicans and Democrats persistently used the language of consumer savings. The principle of cost savings through competition deflected what experience and reason should have amply demonstrated. The same could be said in relation to residential telephone rates. Decontrol of prices and a weak definition of universal service in the 1996 Act meant that household phone service would no longer be subsidized through higher rates on business phones. Policy experts knew that local residential rates would rise, by most estimates in the neighborhood of 50 to 100 percent.[53] But elected leaders adhered to the principle that competition saves consumers money. In another example, policy specialists expected that the transition would cost many jobs and that a minority of the laid-off workers would find jobs at comparable pay levels.[54] But again, Republicans and Democrats shied away from the details of policies.

A strong consensus on public ideas sometimes leads to Orwellian results. The CFA and other consumer groups kept track of proposed local rate increases in the first months after passage of the 1996 Act.[55] They found that across the nation, telephone companies wanted to raise rates by an average of about $10 per month per customer. Some, such as U S West, had proposed to roughly double the charges per line for regular residential service. The CFA reported their findings to the press, and news media played the story prominently.[56] Roy Neal, of the United States Telephone Association (USTA), stated publicly that allegations of rate increases were "doomsday predictions" and that competition would lower rates. He claimed that the 1996 Act mandated affordable local rates and suggested that media calculations that the industry he represents was planning to raise local rates by $10 per month were untrue. His statement may have been precisely true, but it did not amount to a direct response to the CFA's claim. He did not mention his association's recommendation that price caps on local rates be applied at the level of 1 percent of a state's median income, a standard that meant some areas would increase just a few dollars while others would more than double. The language of competition was used by the USTA and other industry groups to deny what was plainly happening.

The period leading up to the 1996 Act was, by comparison with earlier decades, a conservative one. Republican resurgence and a Democratic move to the right served to bring more conservative politicians into positions of authority in the legislative process and into influential positions in the policy stream. We can compare the 1990s to the Progressive Era in its treatment of industry and social power. Progressivism was in large part a high moral crusade.[57] Its backers were conservatives who were influenced by rural Protestant values: antitrust and antiprostitution, antiliquor and anti–political bosses. They were against concentrated power and vice because each assaulted autonomous individuals who should be responsible for their own situations. In a later era, when government was plausibly more powerful, when citizens had grown used to and had seen positive sides to industrial giants, and when those large economic organizations were plausibly checked by competitive forces among other similar organizations, the same conservative impulses could endorse the idea of deregulation. The language of competition touched the same chord visited by the language of countervailing powers two generations before. This is testimony to the enduring importance of the core values of individualism in the United States.

Agreement on basic principles does not by itself produce policies. Interests found plenty to disagree over. One way to conceive of the march toward legislation is as a developing deal between the government and telecommunications companies. The terms of the deal were that government would regulate less, and in return the companies would respond to market challenges by investing in new technologies. Businesses would be stronger, have fewer political ambiguities injected into their decisions, and lower the costs of compliance with regulations. Government would get an investment-oriented economic policy. But the devil was in the details, and the incentives to companies could be somewhat perverse. They were wise to quickly settle into market niches where they could make money sooner than later and gain market share without taking big risks.

During the buildup to legislation during the 103rd Congress, Vice-President Gore and other government officials emphasized how competition would help put a fiber-optic connection within the reach of nearly every home in America. That turned out to be wishful thinking for the near term, and telecommunications companies backed off of their predictions for the extension of fiber to homes. Perhaps the grand example of the retreat was a proposed merger between Bell Atlantic and TCI that fell apart in 1994. The two companies found their strategies would for some time be based on the existing, competing technologies. Most estimates of technical possibilities changed substantially during emergence of legislation.

It was possible that the new technologies were not at all encouraged by procompetitive policies. Although few officials in Congress considered it at the time, it may have been that the high cost of fiber optic was a reason to recognize a new natural monopoly that would extend the cable, with the services it offered, to every home through something like the RBOCs or even local utility companies.[58] As was pointed out in Chapter 1, sometimes the first technology installed becomes the standard even if others are by many measures superior. But the old policy framework that had regarded AT&T as a natural monopoly had vanished, and the idea was not taken seriously for a moment by congressional and administration leaders in the case of the 1996 Act.

Government antitrust policy also affects the way businesses make economic calculations. In 1996, U.S. corporations spent more money purchasing each other than in any previous year. The leading merger sector of the economy was in telecommunications, continuing a trend that started in 1993. The Federal Trade Commission (FTC) and the Antitrust Division of DOJ were each convinced that the mergers in telecommunications were examples of businesses joining forces in ways that enabled them to compete more effectively. For example, if two RBOCs merged, they would probably realize some economies of scale and then offer customers better deals—customers that might be lured away by cable companies or long-distance companies entering the local phone markets. Regulators expressed some reluctance at big mergers, since it meant that in the future the merged companies might have otherwise competed with each other, but now would not. Such "might have beens" are harder to prove in antitrust law and have been largely ignored in mid-1990s antitrust policy. The Antitrust Division of DOJ spent more time investigating Microsoft, which purchased some businesses but generally grew by expanding its own product lines.[59]

In the emergence of legislation during the 103rd and 104th Congresses, telecommunications company leaders joined politicians in assumptions about rapid technical progress and dramatic economic benefits from deregulation. Agreement on these ideas contributes to substantial agreement among the forces at work in the converging streams in the policy process. Details of legislative compromises and business plans produced after the 1996 Act show us in retrospect that the ideas shaped the legislation but were much too optimistic about the future.

An Analytical Description

The analytical model presents a standard for evaluating policy.[60] According to the model, policy is defined as a rule to be enacted in a specific situation with the intention of achieving a priority, a more desirable outcome in terms of human well-being. The seven titles within the 1996 Act changed existing law in many ways—but were the changes clear enough guides to behavior to qualify as policies under this model? How clearly were various actors thinking through policy issues?

The Clinton administration and congressional leaders were trying to create a fair set of policies that delivered better and cheaper services to consumers, more opportunities for U.S. businesses, and more economic growth. They believed that markets would achieve these goals better than would regulation. But to go beyond these general formulas requires specific knowledge about policies, which implies reliable knowledge about the behavior of telecommunications firms under competition. The interests presenting their cases to the Congress generally did not understand policy this clearly.[61]

Telecommunications firms were, with some exceptions, unsure of what they should want. Markets were volatile, and the euphoria of the early consideration of the 1996 Act was driven in part by the fear of not being in on the next "killer application"—the next mix of technologies, sold as a package, that few consumers would do without.[62] The next killer application is inherently impossible to predict. Telephone companies learned this lesson from several attempts to recreate the video telephone. Consumers may not want something that is more efficient or saves time but may choose things for reasons that have more to do with their prejudices and traditions. No one knows the degree to which people react to price signals or tradition; firms are unsure of why consumers do the things they do. The technologies themselves defy understanding—an example being the qwerty phenomenon. Why is that the order of the keys on typewriters, and now computer keyboards? More efficient arrangements have been invented, but qwerty remains. Sometimes being there first creates habits and investments built upon by subsequent developments. Economists agree that local metered service is really the only efficient method of telephone pricing and would solve most of the deregulation issues raised by the 1996 Act. But fixed-charge, unlimited-use telephone technology was here first, and entire industries grew up around it. The definition of universal service embodied in the 1996 Act is, compared to past policies, weak. Most citizens will not like paying more for local telephone service. When members of Congress said services would become cheaper, they meant business and new specialized services.

Politicians are subject to the same ambiguities faced by companies. The Clinton administration's early enthusiasm for technology policy contained many guesses about the future of telecommunications, but the legislative process boiled these down into issues readily understood by the interested parties. The process was influenced by generally accepted ideas, and actors in the process had very limited power to deliberately change these ideas.

Part of the limited leadership ability of public officials has to do with the role of the news media in keeping the public informed of pending legislation. Some issues garnered more attention than others. Media stories on the legislative process leading to the 1996 Act placed particular emphasis on the procompetitive policies that were expected to deliver cheaper services, and on the social or cultural policies embedded in the legislation. The V-Chip and the Communications Decency Act made for good press because they pitted committed foes against each other in areas that dealt with sex and violence. From the standpoint of political economy, these issues are minor. The V-Chip was not a sign of a market approach to regulating the content of television. It was rather a Clinton administration attempt to take a position on one of the cultural issues expected to be used by Republicans in the upcoming elections. The lack of a coherent approach to these issues enables opposing sides to make any claim they wish and provides an opportunity for the opposing political parties to argue over largely symbolic issues. The CDA went even further to elevate cultural issues above constitutional limits on Congress. This is the topic of a section in the next chapter.

The procompetitive provisions in the 1996 Act are subject to similar ambiguities. Many interpretations of the act are possible. At one extreme is the notion that the bill is about deregulation and that attempts to reregulate at the federal level are contrary to the will of Congress.[63] But it is also possible to read into the 1996 Act a strong role for government regulators, and that is the interpretation taken by the FCC. Both Republican and Democratic members of Congress disagreed on whether the proregulation stance of the FCC was an appropriate interpretation of the 1996 Act.[64]

For example, the 1996 Act goes into some detail about the need to quickly establish ground rules for interconnection, so that RBOCs and long-distance carriers can compete in one another's business. Yet after a lengthy section on RBOC entry into long distance, the act contains the following statement: "Nothing in this subsection shall be construed to limit the authority of the FCC under any other section of this Act to prescribe safeguards consistent with the public interest, convenience, and necessity."[65] The FCC, with some justification, took this and similar provisos to mean that its rules for the shift to competition should involve procedures for ongoing regulation to define and protect the public interest.

In a related section, the 1996 Act states that "no State or local statute or regulation, or other State or local legal requirement, may prohibit or have the effect of prohibiting the ability of any entity to provide any interstate or intrastate telecommunications service."[66] The very next section says that "nothing in this section shall affect the ability of a State to impose, on a competitively neutral basis . . . requirements necessary to preserve and advance universal service, protect the public safety and welfare, ensure the continued quality of telecommunications services, and safeguard the rights of consumers." It is not too difficult to find instances where the two admonitions collide. Universal service implies subsidies, and subsidies, even if administered through a central fund, distort prices and leave open the possibility of companies designing a service geared to make money off the difference between cost and price in regulated services. Moreover, it is clear that a state commission has power to deny applications for service if it wants to: "Any interconnection agreement adopted by negotiation or arbitration shall be submitted for approval to the State commission. A State commission to which an agreement is submitted shall approve or reject the agreement, with written findings as to any deficiencies."[67]

These provisions were the result of legislative compromises among officials with very different views on the desired direction for policy. The result was to introduce ambiguities that ensured that clear policies would not emerge from the legislation. In the midst of a procompetitive bill were clear statements of a continuing role for the FCC and state commissions in the regulation of telecommunications.

These ambiguities in the act meant that, in the years immediately after passage, policy was never strictly defined in telephone regulation. General directions were identified, but exceptions and new developments always produced perverse incentives in the system. Legislators constructed an institutional framework for setting policies rather than setting policy themselves. The economic incentives for big payers to leave the universal service framework, for example, were too powerful for the weak regulatory structure organized under the FCC. Courts, state regulators, and resourceful new companies found ways to amend the FCC policies. The intellectual tools for understanding these policy issues, the consensus needed to set consistent policies, and the institutions needed to enforce them simply did not exist.

Ideas and the Policy Process

The attempt in the previous section to apply a strict definition of policy quickly turned into a list of reasons why careful consideration of policy was difficult leading to the 1996 Act. But it did serve the purpose of pointing out that people in the policy process justify their actions and desires with ideas. The ideas that are popular at a given time appear to have an important effect on policy.

A focus on the role of ideas in the policymaking process requires some account of the relation between ideas and interests. We can imagine a range of possible relations, from a Hegelian concept of an idea unfolding through history and humans—in a sense, chasing the idea—to a flat denial that ideas are important. It is possible, after all, that ideas are merely the rationalizations interested parties attach to their material designs.

Frank Baumgartner and Bryan Jones offer a middle ground.[68] Their research focused on the periods of instability in policy, those times when long-term relationships among institutions and interests change, sometimes in dramatic fashion. New policy arrangements can arise quickly. The many political venues in the United States—different levels of governments, regulatory agencies, courts, Congress and its many committees—constitute opportunities for people who want policy change. Battles for change revolve around what they call a "policy image,"[69] the set of ideas that constitute the way people understand and discuss a policy. Slack resources in the political system can be quickly mobilized following a redefinition of the policy image.[70]

They argue that policy changes lead swings in the public mood, rather than the converse. Here they rely on James Stimson's account of public opinion,[71] which has an equilibrium model of change in public ideas. It goes like this: If government continues to increase its spending, the public becomes more conservative about government spending habits. When the public perceives that government is doing too little, it supports more active engagement and higher spending. Yet Baumgartner and Jones conclude that the major institutional actors change their views before the public mood swings. Elite-level politics leads the way in redefinitions of policy images.[72] Yet without the broad support that comes with endorsement on the part of nonelites, the change in policy image is not complete, and rapid policy change does not happen.

Steven Kelman finds that ideas are important in policymaking but that their effects are slow in coming.[73] Ideas, and the ability to persuade others on the merits of ideas, are one of many sources of political power. The policy process works well when the policies produced address problems, when the problems are alleviated in some form by the policy, and when there is broad support for the policy. He finds that policymaking processes in the United States do not work very well if people follow a strictly self-interested approach. Instead, policymaking works well when participants show a high level of public spirit. Kelman describes public spirit as "an inclination to make an honest effort to achieve good public policy." The public-spirited political figure shares societal ideas about right and wrong and shows some concern for others as well as the self.[74]

If ideas do have an effect on the policy process independent of material interests, could we see it? Kelman points out that the real test of the claim that ideas matter in the policy process is "the ability of ideas to overcome interests in determining political choices."[75] He sees both the general growth of government in the 1960s and the limitation of growth in the 1980s as examples of the power of ideas as compared to that of interests. The various interests in the country were not remarkably different, but the ability of one set of groups or another to persuade elites and the general public did change. Specific examples of changes in ideas are not hard to find: the organization Mothers Against Drunk Drivers (MADD) was highly effective, as were the economists mentioned above in the field of regulation. Gary Orren offers the example of the Voting Rights Act, impossible to pass in 1962 but running over the opposition three years later.[76]

Keynesian economic ideas are another example of the power of ideas in the policy process. Peter Hall concludes that "Keynesian ideas did not simply reflect group interests or material conditions. They had the power to change the perceptions a group had of its own interests, and they made possible new courses of action that changed the material world itself. . . . [The ideas] had a good deal of independent force over circumstances."[77]

Deregulation offers an example of the importance of ideas in the policy process. Robert Horwitz argues that the irony of regulatory reform is that the regulated interests that desired continued regulation were the ones who got deregulation.[78] Telecommunications may be a better policy arena for investigating deregulation than some other possibilities because the conflict was drawn out and fought in arenas, such as the Congress, open to investigation. For example, Martha Derthick and Paul Quirk compare airline, trucking, and telecommunications deregulation.[79] The latter was the exception to a general pattern in that, as of the mid-1980s, Congress was slow to adopt more competitive policies.[80] Discussions of deregulation commonly choose the purest cases of the airline, trucking, and natural gas industries because they demonstrate the clarity of the economic case while avoiding the decades-long delay in deregulation in the case of telecommunications.[81]

Examples from telecommunications policy demonstrate at least an occasional triumph of ideas over interests. Consider the following:

- During the 1970s, AT&T's leadership was actively resistant to trends toward more open competition in long distance and the changing definition of the public interest in monopoly regulation. The mistake cost them a good deal of influence in Congress and left others to redefine the regulatory agenda.

- The RBOCs endorsed competition, particularly during the 103rd Congress when legislation less to their liking nearly passed, knowing full well that in a competitive situation they had, by far, the most to lose.
- Telecommunications companies gave a general endorsement to competitive policies. A decade before, they were not ready for it, but in that time a new management ethos had penetrated their ranks. The new expectations were for bold moves by audacious and risk-taking leaders.[82]

Regulation, technology, and economic pressures interact constantly, and businesses build strategies at their turbulent collision point. The 1996 Act introduced greater uncertainty for most businesses. No one was sure where the trends would lead, and so businesses used convenient signposts to make their calculations. What mattered were the ideas of business leaders. To say they pursue material interests without regard to ideas disregards the way their perceptions of the world are in large part shaped by the society they are in. They are, in this respect, citizens.

Ideas mattered in the 1996 Act. The influence of ideas varies with the stage of the policy process. During the problem-definition stage, a host of ideas are at stake. In telecommunications issues, the quality of democracy, the need to redefine the public interest in a more competitive environment, and different models for delivering what might be considered socially important services were all part of the material circulating among the telecommunications policy community.[83] The main function of the ideas is to educate, to enable people to try out ideas and see which ones gain support and which are rejected. For several years, the literature on the future of telecommunications technology prominently featured the idea of a resurgent democratic spirit and new electronic opportunities for participation.[84] Early characterizations of the wonders of the NII were based on hope more than on solid knowledge. In this sense, the vision of a wired future was largely symbolic politics.

In the time leading up to passage of the 1996 Act, a complicated set of benefits was at stake in the 103rd and 104th Congresses. The election of 1994 is one obvious change, and the changing leadership on floor management of the bills reflected this. The corporate interests had an additional year to sort out their assessments of future business. The politics changed, the companies changed, the technologies changed—and, for a brief period, the goals of many large businesses and of many elected officials coincided.

Ten years earlier, the idea was still widespread that unleashing AT&T or other large communications companies would lead to predation. Fewer people, certainly fewer public officials, believed that in 1995.

Telecommunications and the Politics of Technical Change

So far this chapter has described a complicated route by which ideas grow in the political stream. Technical inventions, company perceptions of economic pressures, elections, and the stock of public ideas each play a role in the growing legitimacy of an idea like deregulation. Technological issues have significant features that merit attention. Chapter 1 presented three guidelines for understanding the politics of technological issues. The remainder of this section discusses what has emerged in light of these guidelines.

All Technical Choices Carry Political Consequences

Perhaps the main feature of telecommunications policymaking was that the policy area includes a collection of technical issues that average citizens do not understand. For most issues that garner attention in elections of the last generation—the state of the economy, taxes, education, the size of the annual budget deficit, abortion, anticommunism—citizens have found it easy to take positions. But not so with telecommunications issues. Most citizens as recently as 1995 believed that AT&T was still their local telephone company and thought the 1980s breakup of AT&T was a mistake.[85] The policy issues targeted by the 1996 Act almost completely eluded the attention of the general public. Surely this is not a cause to fault the mass of citizens. As it turned out, most businesspeople don't understand the issues either. The uncertainty of the emerging telecommunications markets gave rise to false starts on mergers and wild promises and forecasts about the speed with which new technologies would be adopted. Industry and government officials alluded to connections to a wide range of social and technical systems that would change in the near future. These instances point to a lack of reliable knowledge about a new industry. In a few years we will look back and say who saw the future clearly—but right now we are unable to do so.

Supporters of the 1996 Act embraced a market metaphor to understand the technical choices involved and the institutional means for making them. A market metaphor imposes a dichotomy of public versus private concerns. Belief in the superiority of market choices supports an emphasis on an enlarged private realm and a smaller public realm. This did not mean that technical issues had no political consequences—it only meant that many significant issues were not debated in policymaking.

For example, some people in the policy stream argued that the quality of democracy was at stake in telecommunications policy.[86] Once the process moved to institutional agendas, this point was almost completely ignored. An emphasis on this issue became an important standard for defining what it meant to be a crackpot.[87] The administration, major corporate interests, and a few public interest groups that could garner the attention of congressional leaders set the agenda. Here are examples of groups that claimed democracy was at stake in telecommunications reform.[88]

- *Computer Professionals for Social Responsibility* is a group of computer scientists concerned about the effects of computer technology on society. They wish to use their technical expertise as a political resource in public debates about policies involving computer technology. In particular, they are interested in involving the public in technology debates, debunking myths about technologies, and using information technology to improve the quality of life. Their main concern in the debates over the 1996 Act was that sufficient public subsidies be included to encourage development of new models for giving citizens access to information about government and politics. They call themselves a "democratically organized membership organization."
- *The Benton Foundation* promotes public interest values and noncommercial services for the NII. Their mission statement says that the many possible public interest benefits of the new technologies are not guaranteed in a system built by commercial interests. They publish analyses about universal service, diversity, free speech, democratic participation, and noncommercial access and attempt to organize the nonprofit sector to lobby for these values. While endorsing competition in telecommunications, they too lobbied for substantial public subsidies to support access to information technologies, particularly for poorer citizens.
- *The Electronic Frontier Foundation* has the singular goal of ensuring that civil liberties are protected during the development and application of new communications technologies. They were, in the first years of implementation of the 1996 Act, among the top ten "linked" web sites on the Internet—the professional community that constructs web sites find them interesting and relevant to whatever else they do there.

These and related organizations argued that the technical choices at stake in telecommunications policy had political consequences. Yet as constituencies they were not powerful in the legislative process.

All Rules About the Costs of Technologies Are Political Rules

The 1996 Act set rules for the costs of technologies. For example:

- States are not allowed to continue the regulatory regimen under the MFJ, even if most citizens in the state want it. A long-standing constitutional doctrine granting federal preeminence in interstate commerce makes this obvious, but only if it makes sense to have a new national policy about issues like universal service.

• Some of the costs of the technologies are not adequately accounted for in the procompetition model used by policymakers. Free markets are inhabited by, among other beings, sovereign consumers. The assumption in the free market model is that individual tastes are a given, and that it is snobbery (at best) for others to attempt to influence consumers' tastes and behavior. That would be an imposition on consumer freedom. But the model pays inadequate attention to other values. Cellular radio and microwave towers are, in the minds of many residents, unsightly things. The towers have to be on high ground because of the line-of-sight nature of their transmissions. The technology can be ugly. Yet a community cannot say, for instance, that views are sufficiently obstructed with the towers already in use, because that would constitute discrimination in favor of the firms that first erected towers. Communities cannot even get around this by going into the business as public providers, because the local parts of national networks would still need to be accommodated. The nondiscrimination rules in the 1996 Act—that is, once a community allows one firm to put up a tower, it has to allow any firm to do the same—work against a clarification of property rights of people who live close to public rights-of-way that become host to the towers. The rules actually rely on poorly defined property rights to lower the costs to the technology companies.

• In Chapter 1, the issue of separations and settlements was mentioned as one example of how politics affected the costs of technologies. The problem does not end with competition. Under the old universal service rules, the subsidy from one to another type of service, across several organizations, made the separations and settlements process necessary to allocate revenues. Under full implementation of the 1996 Act, the companies will negotiate appropriate shares of revenue without standards set by a state commission. This position relies on the assumption that no bottleneck exists. Will there be a second telephone wire into houses? Will the costs of the contending telephone technologies—twisted pairs of wires like the current telephone, coaxial cable like cable television, fiber-optic wires, or wireless telephones—be sufficiently close and available so that customers actually have a choice? Their prospective development constitutes an important assumption in the implementation of the 1996 Act. If it does not actually happen, to some extent the local bottleneck will exist and the bargaining situation among competing companies will generate economic rents.

Some types of users will probably be able to bypass the local telephone company, and some will not. The lower-income customers are likely to have less access to the higher-end services that will build on the newer technologies. The rules about the costs of technologies may well serve to divide people by economic class.

These possibilities were not part of the act. Indeed, the market metaphor explicitly denies the importance of such questions. The FCC may choose to get involved in their administration, as discussed in Chapter 5. But many officials in Congress will consider it a violation of the competitive spirit of the 1996 Act if they do.

One Technology Is Chosen over Another by Political Criteria

Part of this derives from the second principle: the costs of technologies are influenced by politics. Some are given an advantage pure markets would not confer.

Market-oriented values serve as an important background to telecommunications policymaking in the 1990s. The entire field was defined by officials as part of a larger issue of the role of the U.S. economy in the world. The language of competitiveness seemed to answer complicated questions to lawmakers' satisfaction. This is a sufficiently large part of our economy—as large as automobile manufacturing—to make it unquestionably a public issue. Yet what kind of issue should it be?

Market metaphors include a theory of desert: stockholders deserve whatever earnings are due them because they own the company, and ownership confers the right to use and benefit from property. Nonowners should compensate owners if the former limit the uses of the property—or at least the owners should have recourse to public power to protect their property. The competing metaphor is democracy, in which citizens come together to make the rules (including those about property) that we will live by. In the classical origins of both metaphors, they were combined in the Athenian agora. It was a marketplace, but it was also the location of public assemblies. The notion that the market comes first, and should not be influenced by the public assembly, is a modern one.[89]

Under a market metaphor, citizens do not share much of anything beyond an interest in the rule of law. Users of services should pay for them. The 1996 Act embodies this value. The limited attention to universal service promises price relief to the deserving few—most public, education, and government users, with some attention to poor and handicapped users—but not the blanket coverage, such as the subsidy to households, of the previous regulatory era.

The Clinton/Gore technology initiatives explicitly tied telecommunications policy to economic policy. Competition seemed like such a good idea because it appeared, for a time, that all things were possible. Businesses appeared ready to make huge investments, markets seemed to be demanding sophisticated new services and new machines, and U.S. companies seemed poised to dominate the international markets. Widely shared positive images of technology and competition helped political officials see the positive possibilities and hide the costs of the new rules.

* * *

The 1996 Act can be seen as the outcome of an idea whose time had come. Ideas about deregulation had influence beyond what we could expect from a calculus of consent among interested parties. It occurred at the confluence of the business plans of corporations, the expected (or feared) outcomes of technological change, and the approaches to policy popular among elected officials. Legislators shared some goals with corporate officials, and consensus was possible. Elite opinion mattered. The telecommunications field embraced deregulation gingerly, and when it did appear on the legislative agenda, fundamental changes occurred quickly. Interests and officials endorsed competition, but for different reasons.

A review of the development of deregulation policies shows that this was not entirely accidental—business forces organized to be more effective in politics, and an important part of that organization was their success in ideological contests. But the development of deregulation policies was not planned either. The confluence of favorable elections, coalitions demonstrating the political appeal of deregulation, and regulatory and court decisions that supported the eventual legislative compromises were part of a largely chaotic process. Of course, corporate interests came out well in the political contest. But that is very different from saying corporations drive or control the political process.

Passage of the 1996 Act did not end the policy story. Substantial issues were left for implementation, the subject of Chapter 5.

Notes

1. The model is depicted in Figure 1.1.

2. Wireless telephones do not have to be digital, and the shift to digital technology came into full swing only in the mid-1990s. The special contribution of digital technology to wireless transmissions is in the reduced cost of switching and the expanded abilities to move virtually any type of information between members of a network.

3. A similar comparison can be made with digital watch technology. The first commercial digital watches were expensive, on the order of hundreds of dollars, and simply told time. Thirty-five years later a watch that contains several alarms, a stopwatch, a lap-timer, and a lighted face, and that will work 300 feet underwater, is available for about twenty dollars. Yet the social changes wrought by digital watches are, at most, subtle.

4. This prediction looked particularly solid if regular telephone service became competitively priced. In that case, the RBOCs would be able to "reapportion"

costs and perhaps double the cost of basic monthly service. Cellular service would in that case be immediately competitive with regular telephone service.

5. These include Netscape, Microsoft, publishers, and telephone companies that offer Internet services.

6. See White House, Executive Order 12864; White House, "Technology for Economic Growth"; Newton L. Gingrich, Speech to Republican National Committee, Friday, January 20, 1995 (expressing confidence that a communications revolution will change the way we all live); Gingrich, Speaker's Address to the Nation, April 7, 1995; Gingrich, Speaker-Elect Acceptance Speech to the House Republican Conference, December 5, 1994.

7. Perhaps the most significant example of this was the merger of MCI with British Telecom (BT), announced on November 2, 1996. MCI understood that its advantage in regulated markets was about to disappear, and it needed the worldwide network and access to more customers available through BT.

8. Chapter 5 contains a brief discussion of this issue, including ISDN services, in the section on federalism.

9. See Landler, "New Weapons, New Rivals." A sense of the rapid growth expected in wireless services during legislative consideration of the 1996 Act can be seen in "Wireless Industry Outlook," *New York Times*, February 9, 1994, p. C5; and Gibbs, "When Cells Divide." Compare later estimates in the five articles, "Special Report: Wireless Technologies," *Scientific American,* April 1998, pp. 69–96.

10. From MCI's point of view, these added costs of struggling against an industry giant were a central theme of the company ethos. See the sympathetic account of MCI in Cantelon, *History of MCI.*

11. A comparison of U.S., European, and Japanese styles of technology policy in telecommunications is presented by McKnight and Neuman, "Technology Policy."

12. WEFA Group, *Economic Impact*.

13. This does not mean that half the messages contained sexual or pornographic material. A digital file containing one screen-size picture consists of approximately 250,000–300,000 bytes, or bits of information. That is roughly twice the size of each chapter in this book, including footnotes and formating information. If we assumed the average nonphotographic message sent through the Internet contained 250 words of text, and a little over one-half of 1 percent of the messages were digitized screen-size photographs, the volume of bytes from photographs would roughly equal the volume of bytes from text messages. Since the early 1990s, the spread of graphic user-interface Internet software, such as Netscape Communicator, has altered these proportions.

14. The effects on popular culture are widespread. Film versions of digital adventures have been popular for years, including *Colossus: The Forbin Project* (1970), *Tron* (1982), *Wargames* (1983), and *The Web* (1997). During the mid-1990s, the popular comic strip *Dilbert* chronicled farcical lives of workers in a computerized organization. Most large-circulation magazines carry sections on information technology and multimedia publications.

15. See Crandall, *After the Breakup,* pp. 14–15.

16. See Derthick and Quirk, *Politics*, p. 36. A supportive summary of the new orthodoxy is Wiedenbaum, *Business and Government,* pp. 174–177. A careful analysis that weighs the strengths and limitations of the mainstream economic beliefs is Rhoads, *Economist's View of the World.*

17. Ronald Coase won a Nobel Prize for demonstrating that externalities, such as pollution, can be efficiently handled in bargaining situations in which property

rights are clearly assigned. His idea provided support for policies that attempt to produce outcomes that would have occurred under market conditions, rather than policies that focus on setting standards for proper behavior. The Coase Theorem is described in Viscusi, Vernon, and Harrington, *Economics of Regulation,* chap. 21. Coase's original article was "The Problem of Social Cost," *Journal of Law and Economics* 3 (1960):1–44. The story of how market-oriented concepts in antitrust and economic regulation have given rise to new approaches to regulation is told in Bardarch and Kagan, *Going by the Book.*

18. This is one of the main points in Horwitz, *Irony*. The businesses that were deregulated in the late 1970s were generally those that did not want deregulation.

19. For an example of the optimism of the time, see Reagan, *Managed Economy*.

20. Derthick and Quirk, *Politics*, pp. 36–41, briefly trace the story of the Ford Foundation encouraging the Brookings Institution to conduct more studies of regulation and they link this to the politics of airline deregulation.

21. In addition to Derthick and Quirk, *Politics*, the most complete history is Blumenthal, *The Rise;* see also Dorrien, *Neoconservative;* and Pertschuck, *Revolt*.

22. Blumenthal, *The Rise*.

23. Ibid., pp. 182–194. See Wanniski, *The Way the World Works,* which was influential in conservative circles. David Stockman, President Ronald Reagan's first budget director, credits Wanniski's book for spreading ideas that became policy. The Stockman story is told in William Grieder, "Education of David Stockman."

24. To make this comparison I counted editorials criticizing the role and size of government that appeared in the *Wall Street Journal* for the years 1965–1995. I estimated the total number of stories about government using the *Wall Street Journal Index* for the years 1965–1995. I was sensitive to the problem of changes in the indexing system and checked the various categories against microfiche copies of selected editions of the *Journal*. Although the number of stories about government is roughly steady for the entire period, the topic selection and point of view within the articles took a decided antigovernment turn during the periods studied. After 1971, a larger proportion of stories focused on the folly of government programs and regulations, although such stories did appear prior to that. This judgment might be countered with the argument that government began engaging in more stupid activities in about 1971 and has continued this pattern up to the present. I doubt it, and I know of no study that has measured the ratio, over time, of wise to stupid government activities.

25. See Blumenthal, *The Rise;* and Dorrien, *Neoconservative.* See also Hodgson, *World Turned Rightside Up*.

26. Neoconservatives have by no means been allied with the actions of either of the two political parties. Indeed, their point was that the contending sides in policy debates need to be disciplined by a respect for national values and a regard for our limited capabilities.

27. For example, Wiedenbaum, *Business and Government*, especially chap. 8.

28. Bardarch and Kagan, *Going by the Book*. These conditions of unreasonableness are listed on p. xviii.

29. The expanding influence of W. Brian Arthur's ideas are one possible basis for such a shift. See Arthur, "Competing Technologies"; and Arthur, *Increasing Returns.*

30. For example, ATT, MCI, U S West, TCI, NYNEX, and ABC.

31. The most thorough discussion of this redefinition is von Auw, *Heritage and Destiny.*

32. Compare the letters by AT&T board chair Robert E. Allen in AT&T annual reports during the period 1991–1996. The decisive one was the 1996 report, which explained the separation of AT&T, Lucent Technologies, and NCR into separate companies. Some of the developments leading to this are alluded to in the 1995 report (see especially pp. 24–25), but the decision to separate as a way of shedding costs through layoffs and focusing parts of the companies on growing markets came only with the passage of legislation in the 104th Congress.

33. Cantelon, *History of MCI.*

34. Ibid. For early development of microwave technology, see Millman, *History*, pp. 207–235.

35. This guess is from NII 200 Steering Committee.

36. Horwitz, *Irony*.

37. This conclusion is shared by many, including Horwitz, *Irony*, pp. 238–239; Derthick and Quirk, *Politics*, p. 101; and Brock, *Telecommunications*, p. 294.

38. Chapter 5 contains a discussion of the 1996 Act's implications for local governments, in the section on federalism.

39. Persons, *The Making*.

40. LeLoup and Shull, *Congress and the President.*

41. Gosling, *Budgetary Politics,* pp. 112–129, provides a rich description of this dynamic.

42. The Democratic Leadership Council can be visited online at http://www.dlcppi.org. See, for example, "The New American Choice," resolutions adopted at the DLC Convention in Cleveland, Ohio, May 1991; and "The Politics of Evasion: Democrats and the Presidency," by William Galston and Elaine Ciulla Kamarck (DLC, September 1989).

43. The archives of the Commerce Department and the Office of the Vice-President can be visited at www.whitehouse.gov, and www.ntia.doc.gov.

44. Waldman, *The Bill*, pp. 245–247, describes the subterfuge involved as Clinton's belief in mixing members of social classes through the program at the same time he refused to openly acknowledge this direct and highly unpopular strategy of social engineering.

45. The failure of the 103rd Congress to pass the legislation is described in Chapter 3.

46. Perhaps the big exception was the Communications Decency Act, added during the 104th Congress. The regional Bell companies probably were more pleased with the legislation of the 104th Congress.

47. These are borrowed from James Q. Wilson's typology of policy areas, described in his essay "The Politics of Regulation," in Wilson, *Politics of Regulation,* pp. 357–394.

48. See Hofstadter, *Age of Reform*, pp. 164–173.

49. See Waldman, *The Bill*, pp. 249–251.

50. Wyatt, "Stocks Rise."

51. See Barboza, "Another Year."

52. See note 6.

53. WEFA Group, *Economic Impact*, p. 36, predicted that deregulation would cause cable rates to drop by 25 percent over five years and would "help keep local rates affordable," although it is not clear whether that meant rates would not double. For an example of the discussions telephone companies had with regulators, see Washington Utilities and Transportation Commission, U S West Rate Case–970766. U S West argued that it needed to double basic residential charges to realistically recover depreciated costs of its network. State regulators refused (and

were upheld by the state supreme court) on the grounds that recovery through rates should be applied to future investments, not recovering existing investments. Since passage of the 1996 Act, cable and telephone rates have risen, not dropped. See Landler, "F.C.C. Is Urged"; and Karr, "Cable Rates."

54. WEFA Group, *Economic Impact*, predicted employment gains but did not address salary levels or distribution impacts. Policymakers were likely aware of trends in the industry, described in such sources as Bryant, "Along Digital Path"; Tomasko, *Rethinking the Corporation;* and Gates with Myhrvold and Rinearson, *The Road Ahead,* excerpts of which were published prior to passage of the 1996 Act, such as in *Newsweek,* November 27, 1995. Reports of job cuts by telecommunications companies occurred almost weekly while legislation was pending. They continued for at least two years after passage of the 1996 Act, as well.

55. See Mills, "Phone Firms." See also Chapter 5, section on federalism.

56. This is an industry group representing local telephone companies, including the regional Bell companies. The press release in this example was issued May 7, 1996, 3:30 p.m., from their Washington, D.C., office.

57. See Hofstadter, *Age of Reform*, pp. 204, 316–317.

58. See Rivkin, "Electric Utilities Will Build"; Rivkin, "If Competition Won't Build"; and Rivkin, "Positioning the Electric Utility." The argument in this paragraph relies on his analysis.

59. The Antitrust Division's scrutiny of Microsoft is discussed in Cassidy, "Force of an Idea."

60. The model is depicted in Figure 1.2.

61. Wenders, *Economics of Telecommunications,* p. 218, emphasizes that market outcomes are largely beyond the control or even clear understanding of individual firms.

62. Some examples are told in Cauley, "Phone Giants."

63. See the argument by John J. DiIulio Jr., "How Bureaucrats Rewrite Laws," *Wall Street Journal*, October 2, 1996, p. A 16.

64. *Amici Curiae* briefs filed by members of Congress in the Eighth Circuit Court's review of *Iowa Public Utilities Board v. FCC* reveal that Republicans and Democrats who authored the legislation are found on each side of this question. See the tabular summary of their views in Delitte & Touche Consulting Group, "FCC's Local Competition Rules"; and Lavelle, "Baby Bells."

65. Section 271 (b) 3.

66. Section 253 (a).

67. Section 252 (e) 1.

68. Baumgartner and Jones, *Agendas.*

69. Ibid., p. 25.

70. Ibid., p. 239.

71. Stimson, *Public Opinion in America.*

72. Baumgartner and Jones, *Agendas*, p. 248.

73. Kelman, *Making Public Policy,* p. 9.

74. See Kelman, "Why Public Ideas Matter." The relation between legitimate government—in which citizens believe officials have the right and the ability to wield authority, and generally trust them—and effective government is described in Kelman and investigated extensively in the case of Italy by Putnam, *Making Democracy Work.*

75. Kelman, "Why Public Ideas Matter," p. 39.

76. Orren, "Beyond Self-Interest," p. 28.

77. Hall, *Political Power of Economic Ideas,* p. 369.

78. Horwitz, *Irony*.

79. Derthick and Quirk, *Politics*.

80. Horwitz, *Irony*, noted the same pattern. He compared the airline, trucking, railroad, telecommunications, banking, oil, and natural gas industries.

81. One of the best treatments is from one of the originators of the idea of deregulation—Wiedenbaum, *Business and Government,* chap. 8.

82. The new dynamism is described in such management literature as Peters and Waterman, *In Search of Excellence*.

83. U.S. Congress, *Critical Connections*; Ronfeldt, "Cyberocracy."

84. These sorts of predictions are not new. Similar arguments accompanied the growth of the telephone, television, and cable television.

85. "Washington's Wake-up Call," *The Economist*, January 20, 1996, p. 61.

86. This is taken up as a concluding theme in Chapter 6.

87. Vigdor Schriebman, whose news service, FINS (Federal Information News Service), was distributed electronically and by mail, raised these issues regularly—and had his press credentials denied ostensibly on the grounds that he was not a full-time or serious journalist, which meant he could not gain entry into the halls and meeting rooms of Congress through the special procedures arranged for journalists. The denial did not withstand close scrutiny, and he won back his credentials. Personal communications, December 16–17, 1996.

88. The organizations are simple to contact. Their electronic addresses are www.cpsr.org; www.benton.org; www.eff.org. Each contains links to many other organizations with similar interests.

89. This is a contentious issue in liberal political theory. For an emphasis on the virtue of market outcomes, see Hayek, *Constitution of Liberty;* for an emphasis on the virtues of democratically produced outcomes, see Arendt, *Human Condition;* an attempt to balance them is Dworkin, *A Matter of Principle*.

5 The New Playing Field After the 1996 Act

This chapter describes the new regulatory regime created under the 1996 Act. Implementation issues accompany any major legislation, perhaps particularly so when the legislation embodies new direction for policy or new institutional roles. From the perspective of the analytical model, implementation is evidence of how well the legislation made policy. As it turns out, the 1996 Act was ambiguous on several important issues. It did not set a clear direction for policy and in analytical terms was a disappointment. Particularly for procompetitive policy experts, the near-term outcomes of the act were perverse. From the perspective of the political model, active disagreements remained among political actors who pursued their goals through administrative agencies and courts. Several of the bill's authors disagreed about its intent. Federal and state regulators disagreed on the meaning of key sections of the law, and federal court decisions during the first years of implementation made it clear that it will be years before we can understand what the legislation requires.

Chapter 4 made a case that a significant feature of the 1996 Act was the degree to which some powerful interests were unable to protect their turf. Compared with the earlier telecommunications legal framework that favored some corporate players, the new framework compounded the problems of knowing where one's interests lie. Important interests endorsed competing and conflicting visions of the future. Large companies slowed their investments in new telecommunications technologies, most likely because of the uncertainties produced under the postact regulatory regime. In retrospect, the rhetoric of procompetitive policies was shared by virtually all interests that influenced the legislation, and they failed to predict that the act would not significantly unleash competitive forces. In this situation, ideas appear to have had important effects.

The period during which new routines are established is recognized by interested parties as the time to act, plead, and apply pressure before appropriate institutions. Unresolved issues in the act imply that the policy community can expect more, not fewer, court cases. The enormous list of changes required from the FCC meant that the agency's role would, if anything, expand in the near term and perhaps endure for some time. By setting down rules for competition for the entire nation, the national government forces major changes in state and local governments. The 1996 Act's unknown effects on industry concentration should lead us to expect more activity by the Department of Justice's Antitrust Division.

THE ROLE OF THE FCC

The 1996 Act required the FCC to initiate approximately ninety separate proceedings to make rules, set rates, and monitor implementation.[1] Analysis and documentation required by the agency is extensive.[2] The intensive involvement of the agency in implementation of the act puts it at the center of telecommunications politics.

Was the FCC put under tremendous pressure deliberately? Agency personnel told journalists about rumors to the effect that conservative legislators wanted them to get their implementation business done and then abolish the agency. The FCC had been ordered to move to a new building in 1996, but given the usual time required for the General Services Administration to relocate agencies, it is unlikely the move was for policy reasons.

One of the ways the FCC coped with the time constraints was to shorten the public comment periods for proposed rule making. Normally, files on proposed rules are open for inspection and comment for one to three months. Under the accelerated implementation schedule, only the most technical and time-consuming issues were open for a month. Most were open for one to two weeks. This has the practical effect of opening the process only to organized groups that already monitor FCC actions. In formal terms, this appears to have diminished the openness of federal rule making. It lent itself to a simple quantification: half the time for participation means democratic access was cut in half. The actual effects were probably small, however. Organized groups are usually the only participants in such procedures, and at least one study of the FCC comment process found that comments by nonindustry participants actually enhance the success of industry positions before the agency.[3]

The most anxiously awaited FCC ruling under the 1996 Act were the rules about local telephone competition and interconnection.[4] The sheer volume of the rules—500 pages of text, supported by 200 pages of analysis—suggests that the FCC intended to keep an important role in the regulation of local telephone markets. The RBOCs had argued before the FCC that costs and conditions of local telephone service vary across states, and so state regulators should be granted substantial authority to interpret broad rules about competition. Rival long-distance carriers desired a heavier national presence in policy, for several reasons. The long-distance carriers like AT&T and MCI operated national networks. They did not want to have dozens of regulatory proceedings stand in the way of their offering local telephone service. Their perspective was national instead of regional. RBOCs had not only substantial expertise working with state utility commissions but also, their critics feared, influence with those same commissions. In the midst of these concerns about political influence, the FCC issued detailed rules about the costs and technology of interconnections, rather than opening the issues to market forces. What does it cost to acquire access to a regional network? Should historical or future costs (or both) of maintaining the network be included? When looking at reasonable costs over time, what discount rate should be applied to future estimates? The FCC asserted that its role was to provide answers to these kinds of questions. In the minds of commissioners, there was no contradiction between imposing extensive rules and encouraging competition. FCC chairman Reed E. Hundt said of the 700 pages of rules and analysis about local competition, "This order is the most pro-competitive action of government since the break-up of the Standard Oil Trust."

The interconnection rules offer a window on the approach to policy questions taken by the FCC and illustrate the nature of policymaking in the nation's capital. An agency like the FCC acts as a broker among interests, subject to the broad rules laid down in legislation, budget and time constraints, and the ideological bent of commission members. The interconnection rules attracted the attention of a wide variety of interests, whose entry into the process was through the docket and through discussions with commission members.[5] It is too simple to say that the agency simply splits the difference between rival industry interpretations of legislation. But the image of an agency interpreting legislation—parsing rival claims with care to avoid the appearance of siding with one interest or another—is not misleading. As one FCC bureau chief put it, "We're not going to put our thumb on the scale one way or another."[6]

The FCC chose not to simply balance interests but instead to provide policy leadership. Although it sounds like a contradiction, the FCC chose to expertly administer a transition to competition. From one angle, conservative legislators subscribed to a vision of creating a new competitive era in which the heavy hand of regulation was abolished. Congress produced no consensus on the future role of the agency, which constitutes a direct threat to future agency budgets. The act placed the agency in the center of a complicated web of interests facing an uncertain future—so uncertain that between the signing of the act and the issuance of interconnection rules six months later, regional Bell company stocks dropped in value by nearly 12 percent. If the agency creates a reasonable framework for the interests, it has recreated a constituency for a continuing policy role. FCC commissioners understood this. After his speech announcing the new interconnection rules, Hundt held a meeting for securities analysts to explain the rules. He told one reporter that the "ultimate judge of our competition policy is the capital markets," that "if they don't invest in competition, we won't get competition."[7] The 700 pages of rules and analysis issued over the interconnection issue are a strong sign the agency intended to remain at the center of telecommunications policymaking.[8]

Quandaries of rule making were illustrated in the need to interpret section 713 of the act. In this section, Congress stated that closed captioning, a service that enables viewers to read a display of television dialogue, is required in regulated services. Exemptions are permitted according to the law, under guidelines to be set and enforced by the FCC. At least two problems arise for the FCC. First, what is closed captioning? Existing practices may not exhaust the possibilities. Should all video programming be affected, or just that of major networks? Should all hours be covered, or just prime-time and selected daytime hours? Should old movies be included? Should presidential debates be included? Second, what conditions should warrant an exception? Is this requirement to be enforced regardless of cost? What constitutes a reasonable limit to the cost a program maker or broadcaster should carry? The Clinton administration argued that the widest possible interpretation of section 713 is appropriate and consistent with the will of Congress. Broadcasters wanted a narrower interpretation similar to existing practices.[9]

This pattern is typical for rule making after legislation, but that is the point: the 1996 Act was not a significantly new way of doing business in telecommunications. If the authors of the legislation did not intend a traditional role for the FCC, they failed to say so directly. While the agency intended a more competitive approach to telecommunications policy, it pursued such ends in a traditional fashion.

During implementation of the 1996 Act, the FCC was active in making other policies that affected telecommunications companies. Complications among policy areas support arguments for a traditional and continuing FCC role in telecommunications. For example, in early 1996, the cable company TCI wanted to expand its direct broadcasting satellite (DBS) television service.[10] In DBS, a customer uses a small receiving dish, about 18 inches in diameter, to pick up transmissions from a satellite. Transmissions are scrambled, and the receiver pays a monthly fee for the equipment and codes to unscramble the signal. DBS services are limited by the available slots for stationary satellites above the United States. International treaties allocate the available slots. In early 1996, the last U.S. slot in space was licensed to News Corporation and MCI. TCI had to negotiate with those companies in order to gain access to the slot. News Corporation and MCI were planning a rival service but had to wait a year for delivery of a new satellite. TCI owned a satellite but had no place to put it. Negotiations between the companies did not produce an agreement, so TCI began discussions with Canadian companies that controlled another satellite slot. Most U.S. markets could be reached from the Canadian satellite. But the United States and Canada did not have an agreement on cross-border satellite markets. U.S. negotiators in the Office of the U.S. Trade Representative emphasized the need for free and equal trade across borders. The Canadian position was that U.S. broadcasting into Canada had to be limited so that Canadian culture would not be crushed by products from the wealthier U.S. media companies, supported by their larger domestic markets. The FCC received the petition of TCI to broadcast from the Canadian satellite and had to make a decision. During the comment period, critics of the plan raised the issue of unreasonable media concentration if the TCI request was approved. But the FCC denied the request based on the lack of an international agreement on satellite broadcasts.

Another area of FCC activity not covered by the 1996 Act was its continuing policy of auctions of available electromagnetic spectrum to achieve a variety of goals, including increasing federal revenues, encouraging competition in wireless telecommunications markets, encouraging development of wireless technologies, increasing the number of minority-owned businesses in telecommunications markets, and supporting small businesses.[11] The spectrum auctions seemed like a policy with many interests. Some of the goals were achieved more easily than others. Federal revenues were generated to the tune of more than $50 billion over a period of two years. Minority set-aside rules may have made the spectrum auctions the largest affirmative action program, measured in dollars, ever undertaken by the government. Standards for qualifying as a minority firm were rather loose, suggesting that partial ownership by minorities was good enough, and many small businesses able to purchase the licenses were conduits for large foreign conglomerates.[12] Auction administration illustrated two trends within the FCC during its months of working on the implementation of the 1996 Act: the agency was focusing on procompetitive policies, and its policies were highly technical and financially complex, attracting the interest of a very small proportion of citizens and elected officials.

The relatively successful experience with spectrum auctions led the FCC to apply its principles in rules made under the 1996 Act. The spectrum flexibility provisions[13] could have been interpreted in different ways, each with significantly different costs to the nation's broadcasters and the U.S. Treasury. The FCC sought broad political support through the principle that private users should pay for their use of the public resource. The language of competition cut both ways for telecommunications companies.

Occasionally an issue comes before the FCC that displays an unusual side of the relation between regulatory, technological, and economic issues.[14] As suggested in Chapter 1, politics is often at the heart of technical choice. In March 1996, Netscape, which at the time held 85 percent of the market for graphic user-interface Internet software, announced that it planned to include voice software into an upgrade of its product later in the year. The voice software compressed an audio signal and sent it over the Internet, enabling a person with the same software at the message destination to hear the audio message—essentially the same operation performed by a telephone. The Netscape software delivered a sound quality far below that of a telephone, but long-distance telephone conversations were possible. From the standpoint of Netscape, this was one more feature that made it likely people would use its software whenever they turned on personal computers. For the Netscape user, this technology made possible a telephone call to Japan for no more expense than the incremental cost of staying on the Internet. For many users, that cost was from zero to three dollars per hour.

From the point of view of long-distance telephone companies, this feature had potentially serious economic consequences. If 25 to 30 million personal computer users (to use Netscape's estimate of the likely users within a year of issue) are willing to accept lower quality for dramatically reduced cost, telephone company revenues were sure to suffer. The technological innovation posed a threat to the long-distance companies. Just as the RBOCs were concerned with the possibility of local loop bypass a few years earlier, this technological innovation hinted at the possibility of a significant number of customers bypassing long-distance companies.

The long-distance companies protested the proposed technology. The America's Carriers Telecommunication Association petitioned the FCC to disallow this "misuse" of the Internet.[15] The cost of Internet traffic is heavily subsidized by other network users. The subsidies make calls sent via the voice software cheap—but since the prices of different types of telephone services were not based on costs, no one knew the actual cost of the new service. It appeared to be free. As suggested in Chapter 1, the cost of the technology was a function of political rules.

The Netscape example is an extreme version of a common class of policy problems that come before the FCC. A controversy surrounding open video systems (OVS) is more typical of the class. OVS is a term for a regulatory arrangement under which a telephone company offers video services, earlier called "video dialtone." Cable television companies have traditionally been under fairly close state and local regulation as to who may offer services to the cable company customers. The cable company, in effect, has editorial control over content. This is why the regulators have required what are called "must carry" channels, such as public-access channels, educational channels, local-airwaves channels, and "leased-access" channels (channels available for lease to outside companies). Telephone companies have operated as common carriers and do not have control over content. When they enter video services as well, do telephone companies face the same regulatory restrictions as cable companies?

The example suggests the makers of regulatory boundaries seldom anticipate technological changes. New technologies test the boundaries. In the OVS case, the FCC ruled that carriers must operate under the same access rules applied to competing cable companies in a local area.[16] Although this seems like an obvious solution, it points to a continuing role for the FCC. There will be more innovations that leap regulatory boundaries, and companies will complain of the unfair advantage given to the new creation. It is unreasonable to expect courts to maintain the expertise and experience for sorting out the technical and economic issues involved in such cases. Unless the prices of telecommunications services are based on costs, the FCC, or something that can fulfill the regulatory role, will be needed to adjudicate these claims.

ANTITRUST

The FCC is not the only active regulator in the telecommunications field. The FTC has jurisdiction over proposed mergers.[17] The agency has paid particular attention to whether a merger results in product extension (when the merging companies sell noncompeting products but will rely on products made by each other) and market extensions (when the merging companies sell potentially competing products in geographically separate markets). The 1996 Act did not directly change the jurisdiction of the FTC.[18] The agency can, on its own initiative or responding to a complaint, investigate proposed telecommunications mergers. It is common for informal negotiations between FTC staff and company officials to result in compromises on the structure of companies. This happened in the case of a proposed merger between Time Warner and Turner Broadcasting System.[19] The proposed merger of the industry giants would have been worth $7.5 billion, and the resulting corporation would have produced about 40 percent of all cable television programming in the United States. Turner had long provided cable programming to the other large cable TV company, TCI, and TCI owned about one-fifth of Time Warner stock. The FTC alleged that the merger would enable the new company to raise prices unilaterally and to restrict programming choices. Unless rival cable television companies had access to the programming at the same prices, the FTC feared, competition would suffer.

Nowhere did the FTC allege that the company had committed these anticompetitive acts. They claimed the merger would create the power to do so. The companies signed an agreement with the FTC with the following terms, aimed at establishing the conditions for access by rival companies:

- TCI agreed to turn its interests in Time Warner over to an independent company or to limit itself to a much smaller percentage of voting stock in the company.
- TCI, Turner, and Time Warner agreed to cancel their long-term carriage agreements.
- Time Warner agreed to not discriminate by price or content among purchasers of its programming.
- Time Warner cable was required to carry a rival to CNN, the news network.

The consent decree enabled the FTC to influence company officials without the time-consuming processes of courts and enabled company officials to get on with their business. FTC policy is inherently unstable because of the turnover of appointed officials, but these informal procedures enable it to set policy.

The main antitrust agency of the national government is the DOJ's Antitrust Division.[20] Its duties overlap with those of the FTC, and in some cases the Antitrust Division will pick up a case after the FTC declines. The division's relationship with Microsoft, the software company, began in earnest when the FTC decided to not pursue complaints against Microsoft's marketing practices. The division picked up the case and settled in 1994 in what most analysts regarded as a victory for the company.[21] The division regarded Microsoft as the industry giant—its operating software was installed on more than 80 percent of personal computers sold—whose power against rivals was automatically an issue. The relationship became a telecommunications issue when the division launched an investigation based on a complaint by Netscape, the maker of popular Internet software. Netscape's software was installed on more than 80 percent of the machines that employed such software, but the danger of Microsoft's power became the issue. Netscape and Antitrust Division staff were concerned that Microsoft could "bundle" its Internet software with its operating system on new computers, thus giving them an advantage over competitors like Netscape. It was a replay of the 1994 issue.

As the example suggests, the Antitrust Division plays an important role in policymaking. If it believes a merger or marketing arrangement constitutes a move away from competition, it can initiate an investigation that will cost the alleged offender time and money and possibly go to trial with its costs and delays. Since there are no precise standards for what constitutes an affront to competitive forces, the discretion and leadership of the division matter.

Anne Bingaman, who served as the head of the Antitrust Division during the first Clinton administration, spoke often about the need for a vigorous approach to antitrust.[22] Her position was somewhat at odds with the direction taken in the 103rd and 104th Congresses, to rely more on markets to determine outcomes. The conflict hinges on how long one is willing to wait for competition to affect the structure of an industry. During the 1980s, for instance, the Antitrust Division pursued a suit against IBM for its alleged abuse of dominant power in the computer industry. But IBM lost its prominent position because rivals were able to make cheaper and better personal computers. The Antitrust Division dropped the suit. Yet the division did not seem to think the same thing would happen to Microsoft. The company appeared able to dominate some segments of the software industry, and DOJ continuously monitored it. But it is not bigness per se that motivated the antitrust investigation. The mergers that happened in the years before and after the 1996 Act have not attracted the same level of division scrutiny. How will regulators approach the issue? The situation two years after passage of the 1996 Act suggests that antitrust is a significant part of telecommunications policy but that it was not clarified in the act.[23]

Federalism at Stake

The 1996 Act asserted federal authority over a host of issues traditionally reserved to state regulatory commissions, yet a substantial state role remains. State and local governments are quickly moving to a new approach to regulation and are learning about limits to what they may choose to do.

The National Conference of State Legislatures (NCSL) asserts a "sovereign right and responsibility" to regulate telecommunications within states and proposes a cooperative approach where jurisdictions overlap with the national government.[24] Their chief concerns are to preserve state powers to forbid telecommunications companies from using revenues from one line of business to subsidize other investments, to promote transparency in corporate accounting, and to make price rather than "corporate affiliation" the determinant of who gets services and products. Another important issue is PEG access, which the NCSL argues should be left to individual states and regions to decide what mix of subsidies and technologies work best. They also want to avoid federal preemption in regulating such new services as caller identification, which involves a balancing act between the safety and privacy interests of customers, and in limiting child access to sexually explicit material.

The NCSL did not get its way in most instances. A national market needs a national marketplace. While states may still create barriers to entry if the barriers are neutral with regard to competition and are pursued to ensure such values as universal service and consumer protection, the FCC may be able to preempt states after a notice and comment period.[25] State efforts to go beyond the federal minimums for providing universal service are preempted by the FCC if they "burden" federal universal-service policies. That might mean federal courts would find that a special state fee or tax earmarked for PEG uses violates the law. Local governments may not impose taxes on direct-to-home satellite services. By October 1996, the FCC was preempting local government denials of telephone franchises under section 253 of the 1996 Act. Deregulation meant the opposite of decentralization.

The 1996 Act did authorize the Joint Federal-State Board on Universal Service, charged with studying and recommending to the FCC ways to define and fund universal service. Yet the FCC's implementation schedule makes it clear that the board makes recommendations, and the FCC makes rules.[26]

The FCC met its deadline for appointment of the Joint Board (March 1996) and the board in turn met its original deadline (November 1996) for making recommendations. The FCC review process produced rules that fall short for advocates who wanted the large companies to heavily subsidize access to PEG users and low-income groups, but it did open the issues of subsidies to schools based on need. The emerging concept of universal service will apparently mean that those who can afford to purchase access will do so, with subsidies included for schools and some community groups.[27] What did the 1996 Act intend with regard to universal service? Can it be consistent with the rhetoric of competition embraced by the 104th Congress and the Clinton administration?

From the perspective of the political model, the 1996 Act contained references to universal service and empowered an institution—a board—to announce a policy recommendation. Legislators should have expected that board members from the FCC and state regulatory commissions would be sympathetic to public requests for subsidies for low-income, PEG access, and rural customers.[28] In the United States, universal service has been a synonym for subsidized residential rates—a constituency of at least 60 million households that would likely want low monthly rates to continue. The procompetition rhetoric of the legislation became vague when legislators approached the topic of universal service. Once an institution is created, it will do its work. The FCC ended up considering universal service not only with regard to basic telecommunications services but also for advanced services, such as Internet connection.[29] This principle was not endorsed by Congresses of the same period. The idea of universal service was rejected for health care in 1993 and was not seriously considered for other apparently vital goods and services such as housing, education, and food.[30]

Under the 1996 Act, states do retain authority to approve or reject interconnection agreements, although the state role is arbitrator among negotiating private carriers. The act contains procedures and criteria state commissions should follow in their review of agreements. They may also designate which carriers qualify for federal universal service support.

In most regulatory matters where the state retains a role, the FCC position is that it is still the primary rule maker. Issues like universal service, rates to be charged in rural and high-cost areas, number portability, PEG access for advanced services, RBOC entry into interLATA services, policies protecting information about consumers, and identification of market entry barriers are governed by FCC standards. Two months after the act became law, the FCC issued a statement on a notice to make rules about interconnection, an area controlled by the states under section 251. The National Association of Regulatory Utility Commissioners (NARUC) announced their displeasure with the FCC's approach, which in effect proposed one set of requirements for all states, with little local discretion.[31] The state commissions were to become implementers of FCC rules. State officials were not pleased when FCC's Hundt put the issue this way:

> Are we going to set a pro-competition policy in our rules that is uniform across the country, or will we bless 50 different state variations? . . . Will we write specific rules that can be easily enforced, or will we issue general guidelines that can be debated and litigated in tough interconnection battles for years to come?[32]

For most state utility commissions, this is a startling increase in workload. On passage of the 1996 Act, state legislatures were urged to expand the resources and authority of the commissions and to work through their congressional delegations to put pressure on the FCC to recognize state implementation progress.[33]

During the first two years of implementation, the 1996 Act actually increased telecommunications regulations.[34] For example, under what conditions may a local exchange carrier (LEC) purchase or otherwise acquire a cable operator providing service within the LEC's area?[35] The act says the LEC may not own more than a 10 percent stake in such companies. Joint operating agreements are also prohibited. Yet there are exceptions for rural areas. If the cable operator serves no more than 35,000 people outside urban areas, an exception is granted. The LEC may acquire "the use of that part of the transmission facilities of a cable system which extends from the last multi-user terminal to the premises of the end user."[36] Another exception can be granted if the cable system is not owned by the fifty largest cable operators (measured by number of customers), operates outside of the top twenty-five television markets, and operates where there is competition for cable service. Still another exists for cable systems with 17,000 or fewer customers, with about half of their subscribers in urban areas. And another exemption exists if the LEC buys a cable operator with no more than 20,000 customers if 12,000 or fewer live in an urbanized area. And, "in addition to the exceptions, there are waivers from the general prohibition."[37]

A similar exemption process affects so-called rural telephone companies. Telephone companies serving fewer than 50,000 lines, or fewer than 2 percent of the nation's phone lines, may ask state regulatory commissions for exemptions to rules that foster competition, such as the requirement that local phone companies sell lines to rivals at a discount.[38] Several companies with more than $1 billion in annual revenues qualify for the exemptions under the 2 percent rule. It is an example of a lack of congressional scrutiny of the many details in the act.

During a transition to competition, states retain many rate-setting responsibilities. In Washington state, for example, the Utilities and Transportation Commission (WUTC) entertained a proposal by U S West to roughly double residential line rates and lower business rates in a move the company called "rate rebalancing."[39] The argument offered by the regional Bell company was that long-distance rates had historically subsidized local rates, and in the emerging competitive industries the subsidy had to stop. In a reprise of the separations debates of the previous decades, the company included depreciation costs in its calculation of the cost of services.[40] The WUTC commissioners did not accept the argument. The company was engaging in many businesses, attempting to expand by acquiring a cable television company and adding new wireless services. It appeared to the commission that the company was attempting to build a larger network in part by acquiring the capital from residential rate payers. Strictly speaking, the commission was correct. Yet U S West officials saw that its ability to compete and maintain its customer base depended on acquiring the additional capital. It had not been granted a residential line rate increase in more than a decade. In the absence of competition for residential line service, the state commissioners felt they had to ignore the system costs of U S West and focus on the marginal costs of serving another residential customer.[41]

The same issues emerge in many states over ISDN pricing. RBOCs saw a large emerging market for ISDN lines, as Internet and on-line service software applications, which were increasingly transmitting pictures, were requiring more bits of information. By early 1997, virtually no competition existed for ISDN services, so the telephone companies were subject to the politics of rate setting before state utility commissions. Advocates of low-cost ISDN pricing pointed out that virtually all users of the service were installing second telephone lines on wires that already existed. Some new equipment needs to be installed in the place of existing analog circuit boards, and the marginal costs of a new line was quite low. Several RBOCs estimated the true cost of monthly service for 100 hours of use at close to $200, while some critics put the cost at under $10.[42] The issue was active before more than twenty state commissions in early 1997.

Similar issues are bound to arise in ADSL technology offered by telephone companies.[43] Should the companies be allowed to charge what users are willing to pay for the service? That is how markets are supposed to work. But as long as some price regulations remain on telephone companies, rate regulators will be sensitive to the argument that the companies use profits from such services to finance other operations—the same issue that has always faced regulated telephone companies.

One possibility unleashed by the 1996 Act was that publicly held utilities, and private utilities, could provide telecommunications services. Utilities have certain advantages over other new entrants into various businesses: they already control rights-of-way, they currently reach more homes than cable television or even telephone companies, they are generally well liked by customers (a stark contrast to the situation with cable companies), they are experts at financing and building conduits to homes, and communications technologies would help them conduct their gas or electric businesses more efficiently. Some utilities have installed coaxial cable into homes, and most have sophisticated communications capabilities along their main lines to allow them to control various parts of their networks.[44]

Congress, aware of this possibility, wanted to promote competition among telecommunications companies rather than encourage acquisition or sharing of assets between existing telecommunications companies and utilities. The 1996 Act went into some detail amending the Public Utilities Holding Company Act of 1935[45] to prohibit such combinations. It is possible that utilities could use their customer base to build competing services.

The Bonneville Power Administration (BPA), for example, already had a high-quality internal fiber-optic system it employed to manage its electricity. Once the 103rd Congress made it clear that some kind of legislation was going to pass, officials within the BPA began to investigate the possibility of expanding their communications network to include entering telecommunications markets. The private telecommunications companies knew where to stop the BPA's planning in its tracks—by having a congressional budget committee cut the research and development funds that were to be used to study the idea.

Local public utilities may also seek to enter these markets. For example, in early 1997, Tacoma Public Utilities, in the state of Washington, was studying the feasibility of upgrading their information network.[46] In the previous two years several things had happened that caused utility officials to inject telecommunications into their strategic planning. Some private companies had contacted them with proposals to have the utility build and the company manage a communications network. The expected technology convergence that would enable telephone and cable TV companies to consider one another's markets caught the attention of utilities as well. Then the Federal Energy Regulatory Commission issued a proposal to make rules that would deregulate utility systems and subject them to nondiscrimination rules similar to those found in the 1996 Act.[47] Federal regulators announced their intention to require "open-access" rates for a wholesale electric energy market, accept service from competitors under the new rates (including "ancillary" services, which might include telecommunications systems run by utilities), and refocus regulation to deal with the problems of transition to competitive markets.[48] Tacoma officials hired a consultant to help them plan to adjust to the new regulatory regime, set up a planning process to hear from interested parties, and began looking for ways to finance a new network.

The experience was repeated in local governments all across the United States.[49] The 1996 Act seems to have set in motion a general response among local government—but a response to what? Congressional debate about deregulation was certainly a catalyst for injecting telecommunications into their planning, but it also depended on the convergence of technologies, an evolving internal need to provide better control of their resources and serve customers, and economic changes in the utilities industries. The ideas driving the 1996 Act affected other government regulators at about the same time and served to bring public utilities into the politics of telecommunications policy. State and local governments have their own institutions and points of view and have generally not been as procompetitive as has the national government. As Robert Crandall describes state regulatory practices, "old ideas die hard."[50]

The Courts and Implementation

As Alexis de Tocqueville wrote in his classic work *Democracy in America,* "Scarcely any political question arises in the United States that is not resolved sooner or later into a judicial question." This is due in part to the power of judicial review, in which courts declare unconstitution acts of legislatures, executives, and administrative agencies. Courts derive some of their power when the vagueness of legislation invites litigious disagreement. The U.S. federal system, in which state and federal courts exercise powers, enables political actors to use courts to influence policy. The 1996 Act quickly brought courts into action.

Title V of the 1996 Act was also called the Communications Decency Act of 1996, which prohibited obscene or harassing communications,[51] prohibited making obscene communications available, and prohibited making indecent communications available to minors. The prohibition applied to both foreign and domestic sources and applied to terms patently offensive "as measured by contemporary community standards." The measure's sponsor, Senator James Exon, argued that the standards in the act would meet the scrutiny of courts because indecency has been prohibited or controlled with court approval in broadcasting and on cable television. Children can be screened out of offending programming by the use of personal identification numbers, for example.[52]

The CDA is an example of how telecommunications technologies challenge ideas about government rules on cultural issues. Public opinion about pornography is divided in the United States, but First Amendment doctrine is fairly well defined. In *Miller v. California,* the Supreme Court said that obscenity is defined by local community standards: "People in different States vary in their tastes and attitudes, and this diversity is not to be strangled by the absolutism of imposed uniformity."[53] Strict standards can apply to some media, such as broadcasting, as the court found in *FCC v. Pacifica Foundation*.[54] Although the standard does not apply beyond broadcasting, material that is not obscene but merely indecent by community standards (citizens in a particular community might find material to be "patently offensive") can be prohibited because of the presumption that broadcasts are easily accessible by children.

The prohibitions and limits to government regulation can be confused by new technologies. Consider a recent case based on the laws that served as a model for the CDA. A federal appeals court found in *U.S. v. Thomas*[55] that the *Miller v. California* standard of community standards can apply even if the accused never entered the community whose standards were offended. Thomas is a man who, with his wife, ran a subscription-only electronic bulletin board in California that sold graphic images of sexual conduct, some quite bizarre. A Tennessee postal inspector subscribed to the service and downloaded some of their pictures.[56] These were presented to a federal grand jury in Tennessee, which found violations of local community standards. After their California house was raided by federal officials, the Thomases were put on trial, and they were convicted of transporting obscene materials in interstate commerce. They received prison sentences, which were upheld on appeal.

Should communities be able to politically control their cultural surroundings, even when it involves the regulation of speech and images?[57] The Supreme Court has long held that states may not forbid individuals from keeping obscene materials in the privacy of their own homes.[58] It has also held that notions of morality are the basis of law, and some states might find that, for example, homosexual sodomy is "immoral and unacceptable."[59] In an important case that guided the author of the CDA, the Supreme Court ruled that Congress could ban telephone pornography services.[60] If a state's community standards find some material repugnant, the seller of the service can tailor its content to avoid violations. As the Thomas case suggests, legal doctrines may have to take into account the special nature of cyberspace. To receive prohibited images, a person in Tennessee has to take the active step of soliciting or acquiring the material, and software to keep children from doing this is readily available.

The CDA did include some exemptions intended to protect Internet access companies that provide conduits to services like those offered by the Thomases, but the people who actually sell pornography to adults could be jailed and fined for offending community standards.[61] The CDA clearly asserted that borders of states and communities are basic elements of telecommunications policy. Proponents of the act argued that the law should be construed narrowly, aimed at whether producers of pornography could be asked to take steps to ensure their product does not find its way into the hands of children.[62]

Is pornography a special case that requires less protection than other types of speech in telecommunications? An argument can be made that it does constitute a special type of speech, with harmful effects on many citizens,[63] but courts have not been able to draw that line without intruding on artistic and political expression.[64] Courts too are presented with a challenge by the nongeographic nature of telecommunications. This is not just about the Internet. A raunchy California bulletin board can be contacted through the Internet or through a telephone line. The CDA authors' position would have a court apply the most restrictive community's standards—for example, a town in eastern Tennessee—to the entire global communications network.

A federal district court found that the CDA was unduly restrictive.[65] The Justice Department decided to appeal the case, and the Supreme Court agreed to hear the case during its 1997 term. The U.S. Supreme Court found the CDA was a violation of the First Amendment protections of speech, for several reasons.[66]

The CDA did not bother to define indecency. It did not allow parents to control their children's access to prohibited material; it relied on the state to do so. If someone transmits prohibited material for free, rather than sells it, that person would still violate the law. Courts had held that "patently offensive" material may be protected if it had some social redeeming value, but the CDA did not allow this. While in the case of broadcasting a government agency limits prohibitions to certain times of the day and evaluates standards of indecency, the CDA did not provide for these limits to regulation. The CDA intended to protect children by prohibiting a large amount of material intended for adults.

The two sides pushed competing metaphors of how to think of cyberspace—the new technology challenged boundaries of policy categories. The government, arguing in favor of the CDA, asserted that the Internet was like broadcast technology, and courts had found it acceptable for the state to limit the time and place of obscene broadcasts.[67] CDA opponents successfully pressed a different metaphor, one endorsed by federal courts:

> The Internet may fairly be regarded as a never-ending worldwide conversation. The Government may not, through the CDA, interrupt that conversation. As the most participatory form of mass speech yet developed, the Internet deserves the highest protection from governmental intrusion.[68]

Thus the federal courts invalidated the CDA.

Another federal court amended important parts of the FCC local competition order.[69] The FCC had required state regulatory commissions to use a single method to determine pricing for some telephone services, follow a national rule for conditions under which new local telephone companies could buy services from existing companies, and follow FCC price guidelines for interconnection. NARUC sued in federal court. In July 1997, the U.S. Court of Appeals for the Eighth Circuit invalidated the FCC requirements.

The court rejected FCC arguments that the rules were needed for a new national regulatory regime. The FCC envisioned a wide variety of state conditions that would discourage competition. Political choices had to be made in the administered path to more competitive policies, and the FCC did not want the states to make them. The court noted that sections 251 and 252 of the act, which guide pricing policies, had the clear intention of leaving those powers in state hands. Policy delegated to the FCC in other areas of the act—such as setting rules for systems of telephone numbers, regulating cellular telephone rates, and imposing rules that prohibit sellers of telephone services from discriminating against companies that resell their services—were left intact.

The decision pointed to a central feature of the 1996 Act that complicated smooth implementation. First, the act was not consistent in its vision of what would be federal and what would be state responsibilities. The court found clear statements about state responsibilities in some sections, but not in others; clear statements about FCC responsibilities in some sections, but not in others. The authors of the act faced a conflict between competing values that emerged at the point of having to define jurisdictions in a federal system. Members of Congress valued deregulation and competition. They also valued decentralization. What did they want in those cases where state regulatory commissions would go their own way and confound national policymakers? They had not answered that question in the legislation. *Amici* briefs before the court revealed disagreements crossed party lines.[70] FCC attempts to implement the act ran into a roadblock, created by competing jurisdictions in a federal system, courts making policy, and a drawn-out time frame for implementation. This might sound like a description of the federal policy system from the perspective of the political model. From the analytical model perspective, it means that the act did not set policy and did not clearly set up a regulatory regime that would set policy.

A decision that symbolizes how important the courts can be was issued in federal district court on the last day of 1997.[71] Judge Joe Kendall agreed with SBC (formerly Southwest Bell) that the 1996 Act and FCC rules that kept it and the other RBOCs from offering long-distance service were unlawful. The judge wrote that the RBOCs were being made to pay for the "sins of their father," the prebreakup AT&T, and should not be restricted from entering the long-distance business unless it had been proved they had done something illegal. The RBOC long-distance restriction was the decisive compromise made in Congress to pass the 1996 Act.[72]

The decision was on appeal at the time of this publication, but it suggests that even the most basic and central ideas that Congress puts into legislation can be amended in the federal courts. Courts are likely to remain involved in the implementation of the 1996 Act.

The Internet and the National Information Infrastructure

As the momentum for telecommunications legislation picked up in 1993, government officials argued that the central task before them was the creation of a national information infrastructure. The term was a concept rather than a plan, a set of hopes for what might be accomplished through digital information technologies. Computer networks (the Internet with its World Wide Web, in addition to private and governmental networks), new machines and services, software, and possibly the people that operate and use the machines, would be woven together in a network of networks.[73] Examples of the new NII possibilities for work and play cited by administration officials were drawn mainly from Internet usage, but the entire telecommunications sector consists of about one-sixth of the U.S. economy, which at the time of the signing of the 1996 Act was about $1.2 trillion per year. Elected officials claimed this would be the most dynamic part of the economy.

The language of the NII was used to legitimize the procompetitive policies called for in the 1996 Act. But on the way to legislation, the rhetoric of the NII became disconnected from the visions of a future on the Internet. What happened?

Internet usage changed too rapidly to serve as a model for policymakers. One way to measure the shift in thinking is to recall a commercial deal between Microsoft, the software giant, and TCI, the cable television giant. In December 1994, the two agreed to a partnership in creating the Microsoft Network, or MSN. MSN was created as a commercial alternative to the Internet where virtually anything transmissible could be read, viewed, bought, and sold, including orders for goods and services. MSN was to be a sort of credit card worldwide shopping network. Low-cost access to such commercial networks was the wave of the future, according to the plans of the two companies.[74]

But the Internet grew at a surprising rate. By late 1996, Microsoft and TCI agreed to call off their deal because customers did not want a proprietary network. Users wanted the variety available over the Internet, with a flat-fee structure that makes additional time on the Internet free or low cost to individual users. Each company moved toward a different model of on-line services, called a "value-added" carrier. This means they would offer access to the Internet, as well as provide other features consumers might be willing to purchase. These might include encyclopedias; software; quick access to news, sports, and other information; interviews with celebrities; and other services.

The vision encapsulated in the Clinton administration's NII policy initiative was based on a snapshot of the Internet in 1994. All they knew were the stories and hype offered by industry visionaries and the news media. The beliefs of futurists made their claims of building a new economy and education system seem possible.[75] But many people were wrong about the Internet. Microsoft believed as late as mid-1994 that the Internet would evolve quickly into a commercial model dominated by whomever offered the best graphic on-line service, much as its Windows operating program won the race for the standard in desktop computers. It had to abruptly change in 1995 and recast its view of the Internet.[76] No one really knew how many people were using it.[77]

The Congress heard from a variety of interests in its drive for telecommunications legislation, but few companies spoke directly for the Internet. Instead, the discussions were almost exclusively focused on the problems confronting large communications companies. The debate before Congress turned into two debates. The first, and most important for the Congress, was among the large companies that dominated telephone and cable television services. The second was among groups interested in what was called the distributed network, the connections various classes of users—businesses, households, schools, the poor, community groups, and so on—would have to the NII.[78] There is a reason for that: the internet is pieced together through assets held by a variety of companies. At the time of the legislation, there was no consensus on what would become of it and how companies could make money off of it. The prevailing idea among legislators and telecommunications companies was that a private competitive model would open up whatever opportunities the Internet had to offer.

How might the Internet be affected by the 1996 Act? One can pursue the question by looking at the economics of the Internet.[79] The discussion will be in three sections. First, voice telephone services and Internet services are in competition with each other. Second, distinct pieces of the Internet may require a mix of cooperation and competition that defies central policymaking. Third, commercial possibilities are constrained by policies on issues such as encryption of messages.

The Telephone and the Internet

When people make long-distance telephone calls in the United States, they are charged a rate, based roughly on the distance called, multiplied by minutes used. The longer the call, the more the charge—the call is metered. Local telephone calls are not metered. Instead, a customer pays a flat rate for unlimited service. Why the difference? As noted in Chapter 2, flat-rate unmetered local service is a tradition in the United States. Telephone service began that way, and citizens expect it. Most other nations have metered local calls.

Internet use is more like unmetered local service. Individual users need an access provider—the organization or person that maintains a node, or computer—that can be called through a modem. The node is connected to a regional telephone network via a leased line—again, a flat rate as opposed to a metered fee. The regional lines of access providers are connected to "backbone" lines, or high-capacity, long-distance lines leased by regional telephone companies from long-distance companies. This hierarchy of lease fees is based on the purchase of capacity and not actual usage. Once the line from one carrier to another is leased, the incremental cost of adding one more user to the system is close to zero.

This places regional and long-distance telephone companies in a difficult situation. A growing proportion of their business consists of leased lines, which provide monthly fees. They also lease lines to small companies that provide competitive long-distance telephone usage, to pay phones, data services, and so on. At the same time, they handle long-distance calls, which are charged by the minute. The companies that handle the pieces of a long-distance call—say, the two regional Bell companies at either end of a cross-country call carried by AT&T, or a regional Bell company and a foreign telephone company at both ends of a call carried by Sprint—have a system of payments to each other based on use.[80] For almost all Internet users, access is a local call; it is not metered.

Long-distance and regional companies carry many more bits of information on their leased lines than through their metered calls. Although difficult to estimate, the Internet may carry as much traffic as do voice calls. In early 1997, the proportion of telephone company revenue from leased services was somewhere between 40 and 50 percent, with the probability of increasing to more than 60 percent within a decade. These revenues include private lines leased to companies with far-flung installations. The metered calls might be considered to be grossly overpriced. But such calls eat up capacity by monopolizing a circuit, while an Internet message uses packet-switching technology to use network resources more efficiently.

Unless the telephone companies lower the price of voice calls and charge more of the system costs to leased lines, the pricing distortion will leave incentives of the type illustrated by Netscape's voice software.[81] If that is so, why don't telecommunications companies simply "rebalance" rates and charge each type of user something that more closely approximates the actual cost of providing a service? Part of the answer is simple: a transition from one form of pricing to another will anger some customers, who will look for cheaper ways to achieve their ends. They will find those opportunities on carriers that linger with the old pricing system. One legacy of the regulated era of telephones is price distortion. An example of the problem arose when AT&T announced its Internet access program in early 1996. Under existing regulations, AT&T had to pay access charges to the RBOCs for the use of their circuits. But computer lines were exempt from the charges, an FCC relic from the formative years of the Internet.[82] The FCC was aware of the issue, but by the time the regional Bells complained about the regulation, substantial numbers of Internet users were able to complain and stay the FCC's hand. Beyond the distortions of regulation, part of the answer has to do with the decentralized nature of the Internet and the resulting mix of cooperation and competition.

The Pieces of the Internet

The Internet is more a collection of things than a thing itself. It grew during the late 1960s and early 1970s as universities and government agencies set up computer nodes—one by one, local network by local network—connected to the high-speed backbone line.[83] The only centralization was an agreement on technical standards so that the computers on the Internet could exchange information. The original Defense Department backbone was replaced by one set up by the National Science Foundation in 1990. It, in turn, was replaced in 1994 and 1995 by a consortium of private companies, including MCI and Sprint. This privatization of the Internet backbone[84] followed closely on the heels of the invention of the World Wide Web (the www in many Internet destinations) and browser point-and-click technology. Together they contributed to geometric rates of growth—

roughly doubling every nine months—as companies and organizations of all types put a page on the Web, government agencies established sites, and thousands of small Internet providers competed for their business. Internet growth has always been decentralized, and that gives it its special character.

A typical Internet customer acquires service through a provider for a monthly fee. Most people in the United States can choose among several national firms (such as America Online, Prodigy, and Microsoft Network), public access through a county library, or access through one of several small local firms. They all try to generate revenue by charging a monthly fee, which ranges from about $10 to almost $50 for basic services. The small providers lease telephone lines from the regional Bell company, whose fees vary according to the capacity of the line. Big Internet clients like major universities and Microsoft Network lease high-capacity lines that connect them to the backbone. MCI, Sprint, and some of the other backbone operators charge thousands of dollars for such access. Each level faces a challenge in getting enough revenue to periodically upgrade to better equipment and larger capacity as usage continues to expand. The companies that sell access to individual customers may provide several hours of connection at a flat fee, and metered rates after that. During 1997 and 1998 the common practice was to offer unlimited use for a flat fee of around $20 per month. Further up the pipeline the connections are purchased by capacity, not by usage. The different parts of the network agree to carry each other's messages without charging by volume of use.

This means that the organizations and people at each piece of the Internet have an incentive to minimize their costs and use capacity purchased by others. The decentralized nature of the Internet allows them to do this. Computers called routers connect the various components of the Internet, and not every company upgrades to handle the increasing volume of bits. Large access providers that have high-capacity switches find that providers with less capacity send them messages as soon as possible. The smaller-capacity users simply cannot carry the message volume very far. In effect, the large backbone providers and regional networks that install the latest technology offer a subsidy to the other carriers. The problem is magnified when foreign Internet providers, such as telephone companies, want to link to the Internet. They may have to lease expensive telephone lines to hook up to lines in the United States. A line that spans the Pacific Ocean can cost ten times as much as one that traverses the United States. A quick look at a globe reveals the reason: most Internet usage is generated in the mainland United States, and to connect to it, carriers in New Zealand or Singapore must purchase lines that are as long as the cross-country lines in the United States—and the lines have to withstand being installed on the ocean floor. Users in New Zealand may feel they subsidize the U.S. users, who get worldwide access at lower costs.

Much of the congestion has to do with the Internet's method of sending messages. Packet-switching technology breaks up individual messages into "packets," or pieces, of the message, each marked with an address so that it can be relayed by a decentralized network to its ultimate destination and there be reassembled into the message. Each switch a message passes through is called a router, a computer that compares the address on each packet to a table listing delivery instructions. A typical Internet message can pass through ten routers on its way to a destination. As more users get on the Internet, the tables get larger, and searching the tables takes more and more time, slowing network traffic. And the work and equipment to handle the added traffic costs money.

While an Internet provider has an incentive to be a "free rider," it also feels an incentive to keep up with customer demands. For at least the first two years after the 1996 Act, the contending pressures have led, however unevenly, to sufficient investment to keep the Internet from collapsing from overuse.[85] But the uneven incentives to provide the extra capacity may lead to refinements in pricing. For example, a company that builds a very high capacity line and switching equipment may charge extra for access to the better route. It may require that users attach some indication of priority to their message, and higher-priority use results in additional charges. Within two years of passage of the 1996 Act, several universities and companies have begun to build an Internet II. The research universities that helped form the original Internet want to have a network dedicated to noncommercial and research-oriented messages.

If past experience is a reliable guide, these pricing and traffic problems will be solved through a decentralized and largely unpredictable negotiations process among business and government organizations interested in developing the Internet. Policy was not set by the 1996 Act.

Encryption Policy

One very important political problem is the need for a policy toward encryption of Internet and related network communications. Most of the companies who wish to make money from building and operating part of an NII encounter a simple fact: electronic commerce, both retail and commercial, requires security. For example, electronic commerce will need to safely transmit credit card numbers. The number of electronic sales over the Internet is rising steeply, from roughly $40 million in 1995 to more than a quarter billion dollars in 1996 and is expected to reach over $35 billion by 2002.[86] It is possible to purchase virtually anything over the Internet, from compact discs to automobiles. Yet protection against fraud is a problem. Wireless communications make it simpler for thieves to tap into data. Corporations with several locations, often across international borders, need to guard proprietary information. State regulators in the offices of attorneys general are not equipped to handle false advertising and outright scams that so easily cross state and national borders. The FTC has limited resources and tends to focus on big cases that affect many citizens rather than on small examples of fraud.[87] Software makers, such as Microsoft and Netscape, claim their encryption methods guard against fraud and theft of credit card numbers. But a full-fledged Internet economy awaits consumer confidence and standards of behavior that present a reasonable level of security.[88] Law enforcement officials and organized criminals are interested in the same issues: how are ill-gotten gains laundered and moved across borders, and how secure are those means? Some basic aspects of modern life rely on encryption, such as the banking system, the electric power grid, the public-switched telecommunications network, and the air traffic control system. The 1996 Act failed to address perhaps the key Internet issue that faced Congress during the years that followed: what form of encryption is possible, and what policies are appropriate for an international technology?

The Clinton administration urged the adoption of "key escrow" style encryption and a prohibition on exports of encryption technology.[89] Key encryption is a system of coding messages so that the key to unlock the code can be given to a third party, who holds it in "escrow." The Clinton administration wanted government to hold that key in situations where wiretaps and spying are necessary for national security. For example, if a drug cartel is using the Internet to control drug shipments and to launder its ill-gotten gains, the government would be able to unlock its coded messages and collect evidence to support criminal charges. When civil liberties groups successfully convinced lawmakers that government could not always be trusted to safeguard the keys to codes, the Clinton administration proposed that "trusted third parties" would hold keys to allow deciphering messages if warranted by law.[90]

Export controls on encryption technology are a way the government seeks to protect state secrets and prevent commercial spying. The Clinton administration believed it could stop undesirable foreigners from acquiring the technology by controlling exports.

The Internet community, including software makers who wish to sell programs outside the United States, believed that the administration was unnecessarily restrictive. Export controls should be case sensitive, they argued, since the technology of encryption is rapidly changing. Moreover, unless treaties provide for uniform rules for international trade in software, U.S. companies are at a disadvantage if their government restricts sales more than other governments do. These opposing voices found support for their case in a report by the committee on cryptography of the National Research Council (NRC).[91] In the report, the committee chair wrote that "the committee could not even find a clear written statement of national cryptography policy that went beyond some very general statements."

Policy depends on the ideas officials use to understand a problem. For example, the Clinton administration wanted to preserve the ability of law enforcement officials to tap into communications of organized criminals. This was perhaps the main concern behind their "Clipper" and key escrow proposals. Yet unrestrained markets in encryption will deliver to corporations and individuals constantly improved encryption technology that protects them from espionage and criminal acts. Where should the balance be?[92]

Most of the NRC suggestions were incorporated into an executive order[93] that transferred jurisdiction over the export of encryption technology from the State Department to the Commerce Department and appointed a special envoy for cryptography, who at the time was also the U.S. permanent representative to the Organization for Economic Cooperation and Development.

While the complaints and the NRC report influenced the content of administration policy, the president and his advisers wanted to keep control of the policy process. Congress had demonstrated an increasing conservatism in foreign affairs, and the executive order was signed during preparations for treaty negotiations on related subjects with the European Union. Yet by retaining control of the policy process by avoiding Congress, the administration adopted a policy that failed to satisfy most Internet policy experts.[94] Perhaps the greatest source of disagreement centered on the value of personal freedom in the new technology. Opponents noted that telecommunications are now international, and that a U.S. corporation with sites in Washington and Paris would be open to snooping under the rules of both countries. With so many unresolved issues at stake, encryption policy was left out of the 1996 Act and did not appear ready for congressional or administration resolution before the end of 1998.[95] Instead, policymakers and the interested policy community were moving toward self-policing, although regulators expressed a willingness to pursue issues that fit into their existing practices, such as pursuing fraud.[96]

International Issues in Telecommunications Policy

Supporters of the 1996 Act believed they were freeing the pent-up competitive forces that would drive U.S. telecommunications companies to invest and lead the world in sales of new services. But they did not speak to international affairs.[97] Implementation of the act takes place in a world where borders do not mean what they used to.

The ideas of government officials have not yet caught up with the world situation. The nation-state is fundamentally territorial.[98] The world economy may be crossing borders more frequently, but a nation-state is still the fundamental political organization. It monopolizes the ultimate authority within its geographic boundaries and, in the case of world powers like the United States, projects its power overseas through military and economic influence. Nation-states make laws to define the limits of appropriate behavior for their citizens. The laws define sanctions to be applied to people and organizations that break the laws. Citizens are obligated to follow the laws of their country because of the practical application of power and the legitimacy of government—citizens believe governments have the right and the ability to wield such authority. The status of a citizen in the world begins with his or her nation-state.

But modern telecommunications organizations and technologies do not follow borders. The Internet, for example, is literally a world institution. Borders are almost completely insignificant to its operation and to the experience of users. Multinational corporations draw upon international assets and serve international markets. They can wield power beyond the reach of organizations that are limited to their nation's borders, or to even smaller geographic entities. The merger between British Telecommunications PLC and MCI Communications Corporation is an example of the global nature of telecommunications industries.[99] Analysts may differ on the likely future of nation-states in economic affairs, but there is general agreement that the nation-state is fundamentally challenged by the developing international character of industries like telecommunications.[100]

Are national laws and international treaties the appropriate or most likely models for Internet governance? Will telecommunications corporations be governed according to rules for national corporations or for multinational corporations, or by some new model? If some means of communications like the Internet defies control by traditional laws and rules, is there an alternative method of making rules for appropriate conduct by providers and users worldwide?

These are difficult questions, and because the technologies are new, there is little accumulated experience to turn to for answers.[101] It is likely that some economic trends are similar for many industries. In trademark rules, for example, there used to be little danger of infringement before brands and store names became regional and national. Now many trademarks are recognized in international markets, and treaties and other international agreements are evolving to protect them. In other areas, telecommunications technologies present novel situations. In the case of trademarks, borders are important: a business has to have a presence in two countries—someone has to make and move a product, or sell a service within the borders of the host country. But telecommunications services can link people and data without regard to borders. This book could be put on my web page and be read or reproduced by people in Argentina and

China. What happens to any local controls they may have on publishing procedures or content? What protects the author's and publisher's rights to control their product?

Judging by experience with the Internet up to 1998, participants will be able to establish rules that support an open and active network. Among the issues that have implications for rights and behavior are the control and ownership of domain names, standards for fair use of copyright materials, and a norm to resist territorial states' attempts to restrict content on the Internet.

One example of the role of nation-states in regulating communications networks arose in late 1996 in a meeting of the World Intellectual Property Organization (WIPO). Diplomats from many developed countries met in Geneva to discuss a proposed treaty to deal with the content of telecommunications that cross borders.[102] Existing international law has recognized copyrights and extended them to the rights of reproduction and communication. These copyrights enable authors, for example, to control the reprinting and broadcasting of their work. The proposed WIPO treaty included a third right, the right of distribution, to apply to the use of copyrighted material. Distribution is an issue, for example, in the preceding note. If you contact those sites and download or print the proposed treaty to your screen, you have taken part in distribution of the work. Have you infringed on the rights of the author(s)?[103]

The proposed treaty was ambiguous. Part of the difficulty lies with the nature of the nation-state: WIPO was based on a model of copyright laws in individual states and the international treaties for respecting such rights. Treaties cannot spell out the details in every case to which it will eventually apply, and national and international courts must interpret them. Some opponents raised the issue that many "facts" that people presently consider in the public domain are actually intellectual work produced by someone who retains a right to them. Professional sports leagues contract with an organization to hire scorers to keep official statistics on play. It was possible that the treaty would imply a right to every use of earned-run averages in major league baseball or sacks in professional football.

Political forces supporting U.S. participation in the proposed treaty included film and recording industries, computer firms like IBM and Microsoft, and the U.S. commissioner of patents and trademarks (in the Commerce Department). Opponents included most of the Internet policy community, library groups, telecommunications companies, and the Library of Congress. It was unusual for an administration to proceed on a divisive issue like this prior to extensive debates before the Congress, as has been the case in earlier copyright law changes.[104] This did happen at a time when the Clinton administration foreign policy team was in disarray in the process of changes following the 1996 election, but it shows that officials supporting the treaty did not do their political homework. In the face of mounting opposition, the U.S. diplomatic team agreed to not agree to the treaty.

Clearly, nation-states are and will continue to be strong participants in the international system and will influence the rules governing communications networks. Communications technologies are contributing to the growth of plural authority structures that present challenges to nation-states.[105]

Business Trends

Two months after passage of the 1996 Act, Vice-President Gore delivered a speech that illustrated what the bill did and did not do.[106] He praised the new direction in policy but found it necessary to exhort companies to take additional risks and invest where the rewards are uncertain. In particular, he wanted cable companies to take the lead in offering competitive services by providing the so-called second wire to almost all homes in the country. Apparently the vice-president understood just how difficult it is going to be.

The cable companies can offer services on the second wire only if they have the money to build and market them. They will get that money through higher consumer charges, borrowing, or lower profits, which will trouble stockholders. At the time of the vice-president's speech, it was apparent that cable companies were interested in either higher consumer charges or in mergers with telephone companies—the ones the vice-president had hoped they would compete with.

Contrasts between large and small businesses help to explain the dynamism of telecommunications. New entrants into business lines tend to be smaller, with low costs and less bureaucracy. Their workers are less likely to be unionized, and they are less likely to have substantial commitments to their surrounding communities. As a former official of McCaw Cellular put it, "You could run a hell of a business just on what the Bells spend on golf tournaments."[107] As it became clear to the leaders of the large telephone and cable companies that competition would increase, they cut their workforces.

Gore noted that the compromises in the legislation that passed the 104th Congress were perhaps heaviest on the part of the cable companies. The race for deregulation had a momentum of its own, and they were caught up in it against their better judgment. The trend since then has been toward consolidation of both phone companies and cable companies. It seems that the predictions accepted by corporate executives focus on big companies with lots of capital and customers, not on new ideas and innovations. The companies were searching for ready applications of existing technologies, in configurations that could make money right now. Rapid growth occurred in wireless services, in part because the expensive right-of-way concerns were smaller. The newest and biggest entries into the wireless market in the year after passage of the 1996 Act were the RBOCs, which had the capital to rapidly build their networks.

What would they do with all their capital? Two years after passage of the 1996 Act, the main financial activity of the large companies was to merge with others, to assure the new, larger organizations of a secure customer base—some that AT&T gave up in the 1982 company breakup. The mergers were accompanied by new ways of organizing the companies, however. For example, an RBOC has an incentive to be less than cooperative in sharing its network with companies that wish to compete for its customer base. To deal with this problem, Southern New England Telephone divided itself into retail and wholesale businesses, so that each part of the new organization would be in the thick of competition. At the same time, it pursued mergers with other large companies.[108] It was arrangements like these that policymakers hoped for, but could not predict, when they pursued deregulation.

It is difficult if not impossible to make the predictions needed for a consistent industrial policy. The march to legislation was accompanied by many mergers, and mergers occurred at a record pace the year after passage of the 1996 Act. Surely a new regulatory regime had something to do with this, but business leaders respond to many things. Some of the merger activity was spurred by a search for economies of scale—and among other things, that means layoffs in the new larger firms. In general, mergers among telecommunications firms within the United States have been vertical rather than horizontal, which enables firms to offer new services to an existing base of customers. The international mergers have been aimed at business customers to provide one-stop shopping for communications services.[109]

The new technologies affect business practices in other ways. Attorneys are licensed to practice law in single states and may petition to practice in states that have reciprocal licensing agreements. When an attorney in one state responds to an e-mail from another state, has the practice of law crossed state lines? Must the contents of a web page follow the restrictions on advising content and advertising of the most restrictive state? The issues prompted professional associations to discuss and issue new rules.[110]

* * *

This summary of implementation issues highlights the difficulties in making policy in a field with rapid technical change that affects a significant proportion of businesses and citizens. Implementation brought forth conflicts between values the 1996 Act did not adequately reconcile. For example, deregulation does not mean decentralization, and the act was particularly vague on how the new regulatory regime was to fit in with federalism. The Congress wanted more competition in telecommunications but could not abandon the anticompetitive notion of universal service. Communications technologies evolve for reasons not controlled by lawmakers, and the boundaries of policy are frequently tested by new developments. Although the 1996 Act initiated a great deal of administrative rule making, it cannot be said to have closely guided policy. Significant contributions by regulators, courts, and states helped shape the new regulatory regime.

Notes

1. FCC implementation tasks are described in "Draft FCC Implementation Schedule for S 652, The Telecommunications Act of 1996," on March 25, 1996. The document is periodically updated by the agency. A brief summary of the implementation schedule is "Telecommunications Act of 1996: Timeline for Implementation," available from the Benton Foundation, www.benton.org.

2. For example, its notice of proposed rule making for dialing parity and other local competition access issues runs to ninety-nine single-spaced pages. See FCC, "Notice of Proposed Rulemaking."

3. Persons, *The Making*.

4. The rules for interconnection are described in FCC, News Report no. DC 96-75, CC Docket no. 96-98, August 1, 1996.

5. Arguments submitted to the FCC can be read in their archives under CC Docket no. 96-98, available through the Internet at http://www.fcc.gov/Bureaus/Common_Carrier/Comments.

6. Regina Keeney, chief of the common carrier bureau, quoted in Karr and Gruley, "FCC Rules."

7. Landler, "Sigh of Relief."

8. The point was suggested also in Landler, "F.C.C. Ready."

9. See the release from the Department of Commerce, National Telecommunications and Information Administration, "On Anniversary of Americans with Disabilities Act, NTIA Urges FCC to Make Video Programming More Accessible," Washington, D.C., July 26, 1996.

10. Landler, "Ruling on Satellite Service." The concentration argument was made in a letter to FCC chair Reed Hundt from James Love and Todd J. Paglia of the Consumer Project on Technology, April 16, 1996, reprinted in TAP-INFO, Information Policy Note, Washington, D.C., April 16, 1996.

11. Federal Communications Commission, "Broadband PCS Auctions"; Federal Communications Commission, "Bidder's Seminar"; Federal Communications Commission, "Auctions Fact Sheet."

12. Andrews, "Big Bidders."

13. Spectrum flexibility refers to broadcasters' use of spectrum freed up by more efficient use of their broadcast channels, described in Chapter 3. See Karr, "FCC's Digital Plan."

14. This point is discussed in more detail with attention to economic issues in the section on the Internet in this chapter. See Fisher, "Long-Distance." This story was about technology from Motorola, using Vocalnet software. Fisher quoted a Motorola price of $250 for its modem that included the voice capability.

15. The long-distance telephone industry position on Internet voice software is contained in their petition to the FCC, "Petition of America's Carriers Telecommunication Association for Declaratory Ruling, Special Relief, and Institution of Rulemaking," RM-8775. For an opposing interpretation of the controversy, see Newsletter of the Internet Users Consortium, Northstar #13, March 17, 1996. A summary of the legal conflicts over the issue is Blakeley, "No Bliss."

16. Federal Communications Commission: "Open Video Systems," "Commission Adopts Open Video Systemsorder," "Second Report and Order."

17. The Federal Trade Commission Act of 1914 created the agency and gave it power to investigate and adjudicate antitrust issues and to pursue "unfair methods of competition." Its reputation has varied over the years from a captured agency to a vigorous investigator of corporate abuses of power. See Katzmann, *Regulatory Bureaucracy;* and Pertschuck, *Revolt*, p. 54.

18. This does not preclude courts from finding that the procompetitive provisions of the act restrict the agency. The 1996 Act says: "Sec. 601. Applicability Of Consent Decrees And Other Law. (A) Applicability Of Amendments To Future Conduct. . . . (B) Antitrust Laws-. . . . (1) Savings Clause-Except as provided in paragraphs (2) and (3), nothing in this Act or the amendments made by this Act shall be construed to modify, impair, or supersede the applicability of any of the antitrust laws. . . . (e) (4) Antitrust Laws-The term 'antitrust laws' has the meaning given it in subsection (a) of the first section of the Clayton Act (15 U.S.C. 12[a]), except that such term includes the Act of June 19, 1936 (49 Stat. 1526; 15 U.S.C. 13 et seq.), commonly known as the Robinson-Patman Act, and section 5 of the Federal Trade Commission Act (15 U.S.C. 45) to the extent that such section 5 applies to unfair methods of competition."

19. U.S. Federal Trade Commission, "For Release: September 12, 1996, FTC Requires Restructuring of Time Warner/Turner Deal: Settlement Resolves Charges That Deal Would Reduce Cable Industry Competition"; U.S. Federal Trade Commission, September 12, 1996, File No. 961-0004, "In the Matter of Time Warner, Inc.; Turner Broadcasting System, Inc.; Tele-Communications, Inc.; and Liberty Media Corporation, Consent Package Including Separate Statement and Dissenting Statements." See also Landler, "Time Warner-Turner Deal."

20. The role of the DOJ Antitrust Division in 1956 and 1982 settlements with AT&T is described in Chapters 2 and 3. The division is indirectly mentioned in the 1996 Act in reference to consent decrees in two cases involving AT&T and with regard to antitrust laws. The act did not alter antitrust laws.

21. See the position in Virgin, "Mild Rebuke."

22. See the speech by Anne K. Bingaman, "Promoting Competition in Telecommunications," National Press Club, Washington, D.C., February 28, 1995; and the portrayal accompanying the announcement of her resignation by Simpson and Felsenthal, "Bingaman Will Leave."

23. Presidential appointments appear to be important to antitrust policy. During the Reagan administrations, Antitrust Division appointees were notably less concerned than their predecessors with bigness per se, and companies read this as permission to pursue mergers. The Clinton Justice Department appeared willing to pursue Microsoft for its business practices, and that appears to have encouraged complaints against the company. See Cassidy, "Force of an Idea"; extensive anti-

Microsoft material is found at NetAction's web site, http://www.netaction.org/msoft/index.html.

24. National Conference of State Legislatures, Committee on Commerce and Communications, "Policy Statements on Telecommunications," expiring July 1996, distributed May 9, 1996, at NCSL Telecommunications Reform Summit Washington, D.C.

25. Telecommunications Act of 1996, section 253. An excellent description is in "State Telecommunications Issues Following Passage of the Telecommunications Act of 1996," National Conference of State Legislatures, March 7, 1996.

26. Federal Communications Commission, "Draft FCC Implementation Schedule." The draft schedule clearly states it is the FCC staff's then current plan and may be changed without notice. For many issues, like interconnection agreements, the FCC planned to do much of its work within six months of passage of the bill. The joint federal-state board was constituted within one month of passage of the act and presented its recommendations nine months later.

27. The documents set before the FCC in the universal-service process can be obtained at http://www.fcc.gov/bureaus/common_carrier/www/universal_service. See, in particular, "Report and Order in the Matter of Federal-State Joint Board on Universal Service," Federal Communications Commission, 97-157, CC Docket No. 96-45.

28. See "The New Definition of Universal Service and the Role for Public Interest Advocates to Make Federal Telecommunications Policy Work in Your State," Benton Foundation, 1997, available at www.benton.org/Update/summary.html.

29. The FCC schedule for implementation described a notice of inquiry due in August 1998, on the availability of advanced telecommunications services to all Americans. The commission expected to conduct regular proceedings on this issue after that time, a process that would probably take well over a year. The provision suggested that implementation of universal-service policies would not be complete for at least four years after passage of the 1996 Act.

30. The irony is pointed out in Crandall, "Are We Deregulating?"

31. National Association of Regulatory Utility Commissioners, "NARUC Responds to FCC Interconnection Rulemaking," press release no. 23-96, May 2, 1996, Washington, D.C. NARUC successfully sued the FCC and, before the Eighth Circuit Federal Court of Appeals, won recognition of significant state independence in regulatory rule making. The case is described in the next section of this chapter.

32. Address to the Town Hall Meeting, Los Angeles, May 1, 1996, on the role of FCC in rule making to implement section 251 of the Telecommunications Act of 1996.

33. James Bradford Ramsay, deputy assistant general counsel, National Association of Regulatory Utility Commissioners, presentation to National Conference of State Legislatures Assembly on Federal Issues, May 9, 1996, Washington, D.C.

34. See Crandall, "Are We Deregulating?"

35. The example is taken from OPASTO (Organization for the Protection and Advancement of Small Telephone Companies), *On The Record* 3, no. 2 (March 1996).

36. Ibid., p. 4.

37. Ibid., p. 5.

38. 1996 Act, section 251 (f) f; Title VI, section 3 (47) B. See also Cauley, "Phone Rivals."

39. See Erickson, "U S West Seeks Big Rise"; and Erickson, "U S West Told to Cut." The WUTC findings on the case, issued after passage of the 1996 Act, can be read at http://www.washington.edu/wutc/#agency.

40. For a defense of the argument, see Pascall, "Depreciation Sound Basis."

41. Most other states make more generous depreciation allowances than does Washington. Partly as a result, in the mid-1990s, Northwest rates for regular telephone service were among the lowest in the nation.

42. See the testimony of Dr. Scott Rafferty before the Delaware Public Service Commission, March 13, 1996, for a statement of this position. It is available through the archives at the Taxpayers' Assets Project, http://www.essential.org/listproc/tap-info/. See also the Consumer Project on Technology archives at http://www.essential.org/cpt.

43. ADSL stands for Asymetrical Digital Subscriber Line. It is a way of sending digital signals over regular telephone lines that is much faster than even ISDN. One virtue of ADSL is that it costs less to buy the equipment needed to upgrade telephone lines.

44. See Bill Richards, "Trojan Horse?"; Rivkin, "Electric Utilities"; Rivkin, "Competition"; Rivkin, "Positioning the Electric Utility."

45. The Public Utility Holding Company Act of 1935 (15 U.S.C. 79) was amended in section 103 of the 1996 Act; the amendment was entitled Exempt Telecommunications Companies.

46. I am grateful to John Athow of Tacoma Public Utilities for helping me understand Tacoma's situation.

47. U.S. Federal Energy Regulatory Commission, "Promoting Wholesale Competition." This is usually referred to as the "mega-noper" because it was the largest and farthest-reaching utility regulatory policy change in more than a generation.

48. The main issue was "stranded costs," when the embedded costs of a utility were more than could be recovered through competitive markets. In the Washington case, the costs could not be recovered because the state regulatory commission tightly limited U S West's depreciation claims.

49. In Oregon, for example, the search for a state approach to regulation included debates about oligopoly and distribution issues. See Oregon Telecommunications Forum Council, http://www.das.state.or.us/OTF/otfc-col.htm.

50. Crandall, "Waves of the Future," p. 28.

51. Section 502.

52. Press release and statement from Senator Exon, June 12, 1996, "Exon Issues Statement on Court Ruling." The Senator also described his reasoning at a press conference, with transcript available from the Citizen Internet Empowerment Coalition.

53. 413 U.S. 15 (1973).

54. 438 U.S. 726 (1978).

55. 96 C.D.O.S. 609 (1996).

56. As discussed in the previous section, the technologies leap over our categories of thinking. Did the Thomases send something to Tennessee, did the postal inspector go to California to get something, or did the transactions take place somewhere else?

57. Issues in this paragraph were discussed by Schweber, "Invisible Community." The political rhetoric can become divisive and obscure the issues; see Berkman, "Medium Is Message."

58. *Stanley v. Georgia.*

59. *Bowers, Attorney General of Georgia v. Hardwick, et al.*

60. *Sable Communications of California, Inc. v. Federal Communications Commission et al.*

61. The 1996 Act, section 502 (2) e. (1).

62. See *Reno v. ACLU,* Brief of Members of Congress as *Amici Curiae* in Support of Appellants (available also from National Law Center, Washington, D.C.,

and Family Research Council for Children and Families, Fairfax, Va.). In their brief, the *amici* argued that "this Court must decide whether the provider of such patently offensive material should be relieved of all burden of making any good faith effort to restrict his indecency from children, in light of the compelling interest that government and all of society have in protecting minor children from premature exposure to patently offensive pornography."

63. MacKinnon, *Only Words*.

64. See Dworkin's review of MacKinnon's *Only Words*, "Only Words." The evolving legal doctrines at stake are reported through, among other sources, the Voters Telecommunications Watch, available at www.vtwctr.org/casewatch/.

65. *ACLU v. Reno,* no. 96-963 (E.D. Pa., February 8, 1996); a temporary restraining order was issued on February 15, 1996.

66. Supreme Court of the United States, *Reno v. American Civil Liberties Union,* Appeal from the United States District Court for the Eastern District of Pennsylvania, no. 96-511. Argued March 19, 1997; decided June 26, 1997

67. *Reno v. ACLU,* Brief for the Appellants, Walter Dellinger, Acting Solicitor General, et al., Summary Part B.

68. U.S. District Court for the Eastern District of Pennsylvania, *ACLU v. Reno,* no. 96-963, and *American Library Association v. United States Dep't of Justice,* no. 96-1458, Part E, Conclusion. The U.S. Supreme Court, op. cit., p. 40, agreed.

69. *Iowa Public Utilities Board v. FCC,* On Petitions for Review of an Order of the Federal Communications Commission. The FCC rules are described in FCC, News Report no. DC 96-75, CC Docket no. 96-98, August 1, 1996.

70. Deloitte & Touche, "FCC's Local Competition Rules."

71. Judge Joe Kendall, United States District Court in Dallas, December 31, 1997.

72. The head of the FCC and several non-RBOC experts responded to journalists' inquiries about the decision in uniformly negative terms. Some called it "looney" and "bizarre." Schiesel, "Judge Strikes Down."

73. Different definitions of the NII are discussed in Drake, "Turning Point."

74. On the difficulties of predicting such business trends, in particular on Microsoft not seeing the potetial of the Internet, see Auletta, "Annals of Communication."

75. For an example of books popular at the time see Rheingold, *Virtual Community.* Popular media stories emphasized the growing commercial and other possibilities. See the September 1991 special issue of *Scientific American* on communications, computers, and networks, subtitled "How to Work, Play, and Thrive in Cyberspace"; "End of the Line," a survey of telecommunications appearing in *The Economist,* October 23, 1993; and Corr, "ads-new@Internet.now."

76. Erickson, "Internet Poses Real Threat."

77. Lewis, "Doubts Are Raised"; Loht, "An Estimated 5.8 Million Log Internet Time in U.S."; Wilson, "24 Million on Net, Surveys Says"; Lewis, "Report of High Internet Use"; Lewis, "Most Go On Line."

78. The distinction between the debates concerning oligopolistic companies and distributed-oriented groups is made in Drake, *New Information.*

79. This section is based on MacKie-Mason and Varian, "Economic FAQs"; Gibbs, "Cyber View"; Bailey and McKnight, "Internet Economics"; "Too Cheap to Meter," *The Economist*, October 19, 1996, pp. 23–27; Ziegler, "Slow Crawl on the Internet"; and White House, Office of the Vice-President, "Internet II."

80. It appears the industry is moving toward a system where the sender, such as a regional Bell company, keeps the entire fee from the call.

81. Blakeley, "No Bliss Yet."
82. Markoff, "Bell Companies."
83. The story of the creation of the Internet is told in Hafner and Lyon, *Where Wizards Stay Up Late*.
84. The term *privatization* is widely used but is perhaps misleading. As Bailey and McKnight, "Internet Economics," point out, the NSF paid for less than 10 percent of the cost of the network.
85. Periodic warnings that the Internet infrastructure will overload have so far been wrong. See Lewis, "Traffic Jam"; and Bajak, "Hackers." A balanced discussion of the issues is in Gibbs, "Cyber View."
86. Gotts and Fry, "Danger May Await"; Jupiter Communications, "Jupiter Says Holiday Season Means 44 Percent of $2.6 Billion in Online Sales in '97," press release, December 10, 1997, New York.
87. Cases undertaken by the FTC can be viewed on their web site, www.ftc.gov.
88. Problems exist with physical exchange of credit card numbers. How many cardholders have waited at a restaurant table while a young minimum-wage employee they don't know from Adam takes their card to an unseen location for processing the bill? A similar comparison can be made with check fraud. There is little accumulated experience on whether the Internet will be better or worse at calling forth the everyday sort of honorable behavior on which a civilization depends.
89. The encryption issue caught the interest of a large portion of the Internet community and many members of Congress. Detailed discussion of policy issues is available at www.crypto.com.
90. Encryption issues are described in Abelson, et. al., "The Risks of Key Recovery"; and Flamm, "Deciphering the Cryptography Debate."
91. Dam and Lin, "Cryptography's Role."
92. See hearings on S.1726, the Promotion of Commerce On-Line in the Digital Era (Pro-CODE) Act of 1996 (submitted by Senator Conrad Burns [R-MT]) Before the Committee on Commerce, Science, and Transportation, United States Senate, July 25, 1996. The contending judgments are espressed in "Statement of Louis J. Freeh, Director, Federal Bureau of Investigation," and "Testimony of Ambassador Michael Skol, Senior Vice President of Diplomatic Resolutions, Inc." Flamm, "Deciphering," suggests outlines of a policy.
93. White House, "Administration of Export Control"; White House, "Presidential Memorandum."
94. Objections to the Clinton executive order are described in *EPIC Alert*, Electronic Privacy Information Center, November 21, 1996; *CDT Policy Post* 2, no. 38 (November 18, 1996), from the Center for Democracy and Technology; Billwatch no. 66, November 18, 1996, from the Voters Telecommunications Watch.
95. Representative Bob Goodlatte (R-VA), chief author of the bill considered by Congress in 1996 and 1997, made the prediction. Reported in Aaron Pressman, "Encryption Bill Not Likely Until '98, Author Says," Reuters News Service, September 26, 1997, available at http://www.crypto.com/reuters/show.cgi?article=875310388.
96. Wilson, "New Noises"; Morrison and Lehrburger, "FTC."
97. The only exceptions are a brief acknowledgment that the Internet is international in scope and that foreign communications are included in the prohibited acts under the Communications Decency Act.
98. See the argument in Luttwak, "From Geopolitics to Geo-Economics."

99. See the analysis in Keller, "BT-MCI Merger."

100. For views on the significance of the trend, see Weidenbaum, "Shifting Roles"; and Carlisle, "Is the World Ready?"

101. See David R. Johnson and David G. Post, "By Law and Borders—The Rise of Law in Cyberspace," forthcoming in *Stanford Law Review;* and Miller, *Civilizing Cyberspace."*

102. On the WIPO treaty issue, see USIS Geneva Daily Bulletin, www.itu.ch/missions/us, especially Lubetkin, "New Treaties"; and Love, "A Primer." The proposed treaty, which was not accepted at the December 1996 WIPO meeting, can be read with accompanying analysis at www.public-domain.org/database/database.html.

103. Personal computers using graphic user-interface Internet software, such as Netscape, automatically make copies of images. This reduces the amount of information that needs to pass through the network. In effect, the personal computer does the same thing as a user who, wanting to copy an image that appears on the screen, hits the "print screen" key. The proposed treaty language could be construed to outlaw this incidental distribution of material. Computer professionals were astounded that the WIPO treaty negotiators apparently did not understand this.

104. James Love reports a discussion he had with a State Department official who was standing in front of a photocopy machine. The official was making copies of a copyrighted article about the treaty, a normal process in informing members of the discussion team about issues. The implications of the proposed treaty for everyday behavior had apparently not been carefully thought out. Taxpayers Asset Project, *Info Policy Notes*, December 5, 1996.

105. The growth and implications of many nonstate souces of authority are discussed in Held, "Democracy, the Nation-State, and the Global System." See also Ganley and Ganley, *To Inform or to Control?* They argue that economies are becoming global, that economies based on traditional national-oriented industries and management concepts are beginning to collapse, and that for some time the power to make policies will reside in states.

106. Gore spoke on April 29 to a cable company national conference. Accounts of the speech were in "Gore, Hundt Blow Cable Kisses," *Multichannel News Digest* (formerly *Cable Regulation Digest*) 3, no. 19 (May 16, 1996); and Landler, "Gore Urges."

107. Wayne Perry, quoted in Cairncross, "A Connected World," p. 9.

108. Cairncross, "A Connected World," p. 15; Ane MacClintock, SNET vice-president of Public Policy and Regulatory Affairs, statement on June 5, 1997, "SNET Responds to DPUC Decision on Corporate Restructure"; "Southern New England Communications to Merge with SBC Communications," press release from SBC, San Antonio, Tex., January 5, 1998.

109. Long and Spinks, *International Telecoms Review '97;* Pitsch, "Innovation Age."

110. Beckman and Hirsch, "Rules of the Road"; Kuester, "Attorney Sites."

6 Conclusions

What did the 104th Congress produce in telecommunications policy? This chapter presents an answer to that question, beginning with a discussion of the sources of continuity and change in telecommunications policy. The second section is an appraisal of the first two years of implementation, which includes a comparison of what the political and analytical models each help us understand. A final section offers an appraisal of the possibilities for wider participation in the making of telecommunications policy.

Continuity and Change in Policy

The many sources of continuity and of change in telecommunications policy identified in previous chapters are used here to further explain the 1996 Act and its implementation and to generate expectations for the future.

Sources of Continuity

Six sources of continuity are discussed here: the lawmaking functions of Congress, the presence of large corporations that dominate key parts of telecommunications businesses, FCC regulatory powers and expertise, the U.S. constitutional framework, a policy community that substantially agrees on a preferred direction, and a large constituency for universal service.

Congress is a lawmaking institution that exhibits considerable continuity in the way it takes on and decides issues. Its leadership is likely to find continuing interest in telecommunications if only for the fact that it constitutes one-sixth of the economy; but we need to keep in mind how often this interest translates into policy change. Congress has been able to generate agreement on new directions in telecommunications policy only twice—in the 1934 and 1996 laws—both times in response to substantial consensus in the industry that Congress needed to act.

Congress divides its labor among its committees. Legislators usually win reelection and tend to develop careers based on expertise in one or a small number of policy areas. In other words, Congress is likely, at a given time, to have just a few members with considerable expertise in telecommunications. The leadership is likely to assign bills to committees on which these members serve—bills likely to be introduced by these congressional experts. The 1996 Act came out of Congresses where policy experts, for all their disagreements, were united on the need for new legislation and were able to convince colleagues that reasonable compromises were possible. One key feature of this process was committee hearings, which demonstrated widespread support for ideas like deregulation, a transition to competition, and universal service.

This also suggests that Congress is responsive to some kinds of claims and not to others. Its members know that policy disputes are iterative. Losers of a debate are not likely to lose everything, and they can come back the next year to test laws for which there is weak support. Supporters of legislation should demonstrate that significant interests—such as large companies that dominate an industry, or the majority of large blocks of interested citizens—support a particular course of action. For most policy areas this happens episodically, if at all. Given these features of the lawmaking functions of Congress, we should recognize the 1996 Act as an event that seldom occurs in telecommunications policy. Large swings in policy are unlikely to emerge from Congress in the near future.

A second source of continuity in policy stems from the structure of telecommunications businesses. Most of the industry is dominated by giants. Three long-distance companies, a handful of regional telephone companies, a few cellular companies, and several broadcast and cable companies own most of the assets, serve most of the customers, and employ most of the workers in telecommunications industries. As we saw in Chapter 3, for example, the RBOCs were most likely to suffer from rules that would cause a sudden opening of local service to competition, and they presented a strong voice in Congress against such rules. Similarly, AT&T stood to lose the most if long-distance services were immediately opened to competition, and they made a convincing case against such a rule to the Congress. The pattern of these petitions to Congress is likely to be as stable as is industry structure.

In addition to the large companies there are thousands of smaller companies that include resellers (they buy access to telephone networks from other companies and resell it), software and equipment companies, companies that serve isolated communities, and so on. These are highly unlikely to build competing networks that serve telephone customers. The "second wire" into households, which would signify basic competition for communications services, is likely to be built, if at all, in the late 1990s by cable television companies. But that development has been much slower in coming than was expected during passage of the 1996 Act. Over the next decade, that second wire might come through some kind of wireless connection, but at this point such technical guesses are not at the center of policy.

Perhaps new institutional arrangements can change the structure of parts of the telecommunications industry. The idea of breaking up an RBOC into a wholesale telephone company that runs the network and a customer service organization that competes with other resellers opens up the possibility of significantly reducing the reluctance of regional telephone companies to cooperate with possible competitors.[1] Changes like these will probably emerge slowly and be tested before widespread adoption.

At the top of any list of large recent changes in the industry are the two breakups of AT&T, the first as a result of the antitrust agreement in 1982 and the second as a result of the voluntary split of the company after passage of the 1996 Act. Yet to most customers this was not a large change, and to government regulators the industry was still highly concentrated into a few large companies. Telecommunications companies may split apart, merge, and create new services, but the policy problems have been consistent for many years. Experience suggests that rapid and unexpected shifts in industry structure, and the resulting demands on policymakers, are unlikely.

A third source of policy continuity is the regulatory authority and expertise of the FCC.[2] The agency is an institution that employs policy experts that devote full-time attention to their duties. During the hearings on legislation that became the 1996 Act, FCC officials presented authoritative arguments. The agency, by law and with some skill, has mobilized public support during its hearings, leading to rules issued under the new legislation. The FCC has little expert competition in the U.S. government on matters of telecommunications policy, except when the administration designates a policy initiative that involves, for example, cabinet secretaries who wish to be active. Ron Brown and Larry Irving of the Commerce Department were Clinton administration officials who regularly issued analyses and opinions about legislative proposals that led to the 1996 Act. In the history of the FCC, this competition is unusual. The FCC found the 1996 Act to be ambiguous in several ways and successfully asserted a significant agency role in policymaking. Although the agency acknowledged a shift from regulating monopolies to encouraging competition, the first two years of implementation suggest that the FCC is unlikely to initiate sudden or surprising shifts in policy. The agency is mainly a force for continuity in policy.

A fourth source of policy continuity is the U.S. constitutional framework. On some matters, the Constitution is rather clear, such as the First Amendment admonition that "Congress shall make no law . . . abridging the freedom of speech." That language was applied by federal courts that found the Communications Decency Act, or Title V of the 1996 Act, to be unconstitutional. RBOCs have argued that the restrictions on their offering long-distance service, without evidence that they have violated any law, constituted an impermissible seizure of their property under the Fifth Amendment to the Constitution. Constitutional provisions regularly provide the basis for judicial checks on the actions of legislatures and administrative agencies.

The constitutional framework includes federalism, which in the first years following the 1996 Act has slowed the move to a more competitive telephone industry. State regulatory commissions have a history of supporting universal-service policies that keep basic telephone service inexpensive, and an association of state officials successfully sued to avoid the constraints of FCC policies. Federalism is weakening as a constraint on national policymaking,[3] but in telecommunications policy it is likely to remain important. Courts have recognized their authority in regulating businesses, and states are home to large numbers of constituents who want low monthly bills for basic telephone service. Unless there is a remarkable ideological shift in Congress, the values of decentralization and devolution of authority to states will continue to find a sympathetic ear among policymakers in the nation's capital.

A fifth source of policy continuity is the policy community that takes an interest in telecommunications issues. The ideas of deregulation and the benefits of competition appear to be durable and enjoy considerable institutional support. Organizations such as the American Enterprise Institute and the Brookings Institution house scholars with a remarkable degree of agreement on communications policies. Twenty years before, the former was regarded as politically conservative and the latter politically liberal, but at the end of the 1990s, both appear to be mainstream think tanks on these issues. This is not surprising given the substantial consensus on deregulation among academic economists. The policy studies organizations, and the universities are the largest nonbusiness recruiting grounds for political appointments in the national government. If experience is a guide here, we should expect such a broad agreement on policy perspective to take a generation to change.

A sixth source of policy continuity was briefly mentioned with regard to federalism. The constituency for universal service numbers around 60 million households. State regulatory commissions and members of Congress have demonstrated a willingness to listen to groups that claim to represent these people and to include rule-making provisions that give states a voice in making policy. Consumer groups have found it easy to organize around a threatened doubling of basic monthly telephone rates. The largest price distortions from market conditions have been products of universal-service policies, and proponents of competition have insisted the subsidies should, except in a very few cases, be dropped. Unless these citizens agree that the benefits of competition outweigh their low monthly telephone bills, or unless policymakers pay less attention to their claims, universal service is likely to be a part of telecommunications policy in the United States.

Sources of Change

Congress did pass the 1996 Act, which indicates the factors that support continuity of policy are balanced by others that support change. Four sources of change are discussed here: the digital revolution in telecommunications, elections, shifting ideas, and the relation between telecommunications policy and budgetary politics.

Emerging digital telecommunications technologies test the boundaries of regulatory policies. The old idea of a regulated monopoly telephone company required customers that were satisfied with basic telephone service and a web of subsidies flowing from one type of user to another. Businesses became more information intensive, and higher-capacity communications devices made it feasible for new firms to find a home in niche markets and make money outside the older, tightly regulated services. At first the services were private—insurance companies and banks sending data from one office to another. But companies that paid a lot for long-distance telephone service between their own offices could benefit from the new technologies as well. Soon wireless telephones created similar markets between the boundaries of regulations. The Internet used lines developed in telephone systems but used switches that were based on digital technologies; and it more efficiently used the network shared with telephones. Regulators could not fit the new services into the pricing schemes developed for plain old telephone service. It was digital information technologies—and the money-making opportunities made possible through them—that undid the old regulatory framework.

The new technologies did not simply pit business interests against those of household telephone users. For example, homeowners could make local and long-distance telephone calls on their cellular telephones and send faxes through their personal computers without buying service from a local telephone company. Would it not then be fair to allow the local telephone company to compete in long distance service? The long-distance company might object that, until it had access to the local telephones on the same conditions as did the local telephone company, competition in long distance would be unfair. This conflict of interests, central to the 1996 Act, started with the invention and marketing of digital switching technologies.

The digital technologies show no signs of standing still. Improved switches, connecting lines, and wireless connections—and new communications devices—promise continued decrease in the cost of moving information and a continued increase in the capacity of telecommunications networks. That will enable communications companies to sell more and newer services to business and residential customers. Regulations that control prices of services that might be bundled into the new technologies will be difficult to apply.

Global business developments might present even more of a challenge than the mainly domestic forces that figured so prominently in the debates over the 1996 Act. Companies with international operations, citizens that travel frequently, and customers of companies that sell through the Internet or similar networks may provide strong incentives for communications companies to develop one-stop shopping for international communications. Will regulated domestic businesses fit neatly into global markets? Based on past experience, U.S. firms will need to be flexible and enter into business arrangements with foreign firms. Regulatory assumptions about who offers what services to domestic customers will present challenges to policymakers.

A second source of change discussed in the earlier chapters is elections. Republicans became more successful at winning seats in Congress and in state legislatures, and Democrats became more conservative in economic policy. Elections turn out to be part of a web of political changes that include the public mood about governmental performance, ideological distribution of members of Congress, policies advocated by pressure group campaigns, and ideas about the proper role of government. In spite of the overlap among these forces, we can say that without the election of a president (and vice-president) who emphasized technology issues, and of a Congress that was reliably in favor of regulatory policies that moved more toward competition, Congress would not have passed the 1996 Act. It is impossible to predict whether the next few national elections will bring to Washington elected officials—and their appointees—who wish to make their mark by introducing reforms in telecommunications policy. But this has been a precipitant of change in the past and remains as a volatile source of change.

A third force for change lies in ideas. Chapter 4 included a discussion of the relations between ideas and interests and suggested that there is an independent effect of ideas on the policy process. The mid-1990s was a time when ideas about deregulation, competition, and limited functions for national government were very popular and influential in several policy areas.[4] How volatile are ideas about policy? In the preceding section, the consensus among academic economists and scholars in policy organizations was described as a source of policy continuity. Earlier chapters described examples of ideas changing rapidly because of three types of actors: leaders of influential business organizations, pressure groups, and elected officials. Like elections, these sources of change are impossible to predict. They have proved significant in the past, and may do so again. New academic ideas appear, although they spread slowly.[5] It is not far-fetched to imagine a leader of a major telecommunications or computer company proposing a new relationship between business and government, or among businesses. Some pressure groups that advocate more state and local control of policy were energized by the 1996 Act, and it is possible they would have greater political success in policy processes.[6]

The last source of policy change discussed here is the relation between telecommunications policy and budgetary politics. For many policy areas, budget constraints severely limit presidents and members of Congress. This was not true of telecommunications during passage of the 1996 Act. The budget of the FCC at the time was well under $1 billion—about seven-tenths of 1 percent of the budget—which oversaw most regulation of one-sixth of the economy. Elected leaders encouraged support for regulatory reform with estimates of as many as 10 million new jobs. From a budgetary perspective, the reform policies were nearly costless. Congress and the president spent considerable time during the legislative process, but the budget restraints on policy change were few.

* * *

These sources of continuity and change in telecommunications policy appear to balance on the side of continuity. Does this make sense historically? The major changes in telecommunications policy can be listed quickly: the quest early in the century by AT&T to become a monopoly; the 1912 shift of AT&T goals to be a regulated monopoly with public responsibilities, culminating in post–World War I acceptance by Congress; the 1934 Act, which mainly formalized the status of AT&T as a regulated monopoly; the post–World War II antitrust actions, culminating in the 1956 decree; the opening of some lines of business, like equipment manufacture and long-distance service, to competitors in the 1960s and 1970s; the antitrust action that resulted in the breakup of AT&T in 1982; and the processes that led to the 1996 Act. A simple count of the record suggests that during the twentieth century, fairly major changes occur about every fifteen years, and that some major event leading to one of the changes is going on during every decade. While this may not be extraordinary for national policymaking, it gives pause to any hope that a regulatory regime has been created that can take us very far into the twenty-first century. On balance, we should expect change, but slowly.

The forces that lead to changes may not be well understood or controllable by public officials and pressure groups. Can future digital technology developments be accurately predicted? The record of guesses that helped feed enthusiasm for the 1996 Act is poor. Investments in competitive technologies since passage of the act have slowed, with some exceptions. Can electoral outcomes be predicted, particularly with respect to specific policy preferences of winning candidates? Again, the track record of experts is poor. Is commitment to ideas flexible enough so that pressure groups, elected officials, and others can set goals and realistically have a chance of changing the minds of key policymakers? This is simply a guess, but as difficult as it sounds, it seems the most promising avenue for those who wish to pursue a different course of policy. Policy change appears to be driven by forces that are not well understood and are not controlled by interested parties. Some features, such as the prevailing stock of ideas about the proper role of government, change with consequences for policy, but these usually seem to shift for reasons outside the control of institutions and individuals interested in change.[7]

Implementation

Was the 1996 Act important legislation? Was it good policy? Did it meet the objectives of policymakers? This section approaches these questions by way of the two models described in Chapter 1. Each perspective raises its own concerns about the policy process and the content of policies.

The Political Model

The political model suggests we focus attention on a wide array of events, institutions, and actors, as depicted in Figure 1.1. Briefly, the model says that if all of those things point in the same direction, a "policy window" opens and a new set of policies, such as those embodied in legislation, can receive institutional approval. The narrative in the first two chapters attempted to account for major shifts in policy through the concepts in the political model. Chapter 4 focused on the role of ideas, and some of the problems that arise from such a focus, which occupies a prominent place in the model.

One of the clearest lessons from telecommunications policy is how difficult it is for policy windows to open. The previous section of this chapter suggested that major changes occur every fifteen or so years. That does not mean that interested political actors or leaders can control or guide the process. Had the heads of major telephone companies agreed to the need for major legislation but an election or two had gone a different way, the outcomes of major interest group involvement may well have been very different. The following example is not so far-fetched: Were it not for the Iranian revolution, Jimmy Carter might have won the 1980 presidential election. Would the idea of deregulation have spread so far and wide without the Reagan presidency? Or, George Bush appeared to be headed for certain reelection a year before he lost the 1992 race to Bill Clinton. Had Dan Quayle been vice-president instead of Al Gore, would the administration have worked as vigorously with the 103rd and 104th Congresses to pass a telecommunications bill? These questions are completely speculative, but they suggest how many of the elements in the political model are parts of the world that are difficult to predict, let alone control.

From this perspective, the policy process looks something like a rambunctious and unruly family: it gets together occasionally, if at all; its members share few long-term commitments and represent different values and walks of life; and gatherings are successful only if several key members adopt a temporary mission to cooperate in spite of desires to be doing something else.

A second insight from the political model is the importance of interest groups in the policy process. This is a slightly redundant claim, since the model was constructed with that expectation in mind. Nevertheless, interest groups were active and aggressive in the march to legislation and in court contests over implementation issues. In telecommunications policy, a case can be made that interest groups should be the main focus of studies of the policy process, more so than Congress or executive branch officials. For example, reform legislation was attempted in the late 1970s but failed because of opposition by AT&T. Major telephone companies may have differed on the desired content of legislation leading to the 1996 Act, but they agreed on the need for legislation. After the commercial interests, the most influential groups in the telecommunications policy process appear to be associations of state and local government officials, such as NARUC and NCSL. One sign of the depth of interest group involvement in the legislative process was the "volunteer" policy specialist working in the Speaker of the House's office during the 104th Congress.[8] The major federal court cases that have affected implementation of the 1996 Act, discussed in Chapter 5, were pressed by interest groups. It is simply impossible to understand the policy process in America without a significant focus on interest groups.

It could hardly be otherwise. The legislation considered by the 103rd and 104th Congresses involved significant economic assets and income opportunities that, while regulated by government institutions, were almost wholly owned by private interests. Nationalization of the telephone and related communications systems was seriously considered only briefly in our history, and the question was essentially settled by 1921. The regulations made by public officials have huge financial consequences for telecommunications companies. The private owners include large, wealthy corporations that can afford to employ legal and policy experts to express their interests to public officials. And our constitutional framework was constructed with an eye to limiting possible abuses of governmental authority. The policy process has many procedural limitations on the exercise of power—two houses of Congress, a separate executive, opportunities for involvement in administrative rule making, independent courts in national and state governments, frequent elections—that offer opportunities for organized interests to exert influence.

The groups involved in the telecommunications policy process were, with some exceptions, narrowly focused on commercial and regulatory questions. The process did not catch the attention of large numbers of citizens. Citizens are much less likely to become politically involved when the policy area is highly technical.[9] Some groups attempted to speak for broader citizen interests but did so without much contact with the mass of the population.[10] All of them face the problem of how to mobilize and communicate with large numbers of citizens who are unsure about why telecommunications policy affects them. There are different possible models for such broad-based associations. Some associations are more influential than others, particularly if membership is distributed over many congressional districts,[11] as in the case of the National Education Association; and some groups' members have ready access to their own representatives, such as associations of local government officials.[12]

The most likely explanation for low participation is the unequal distribution of politically important resources. The time, money, and skills available to an individual are due to luck at birth, job choices, family, and involvement in organizations.[13] Is it likely that an increase in electronic participation will change this? It might depend on the form of particulation. Equal consideration of all citizens might be more possible through surveys, which may provide a way of giving officials more than the opinions of the active and wealthy.[14] People who participate in politics are not representative of the general population and, according to one study, differ in "their personal circumstances and dependence upon government benefits, in their priorities for government action, and in what they say when they get involved."[15]

News media cannot be blamed for any lack of citizen involvement in the making of the 1996 Act. Some hearings were carried on C-Span, and major newspapers such as the *New York Times* and the *Wall Street Journal,* and news weeklies, featured regular coverage. Specialized magazines such as *Business Week* featured a regular column on developments in politics and technology and occasional major supplements. Coverage by network news teams was by comparison sporadic and brief. An interested citizen willing to spend a short time reading and watching such news coverage could learn about the developing legislation in some detail. Anyone connected to the Internet could subscribe to several listserves and receive twenty messages daily about congressional committee developments, analyses commissioned by protagonists, and discussion groups devoted exclusively to issues surrounding the legislation. Many of the groups organized petitions and letter-writing campaigns so that citizens could take part in arguments put before legislators at each stage of the legislative process. An interested citizen could easily spend an hour each day reading about the issues.

Why weren't citizens interested in the largest economic policy of the decade to pass Congress? The technical nature of the issues, and the sheer number of details involved in changing from regulated to competitive services, were formidable. The substantial portion of the population that thought AT&T was still their local telephone company are perhaps not candidates for intense involvement. But many other citizens have the skills and can develop the habits to prepare themselves for some type of participation in the policy process.

Citizens who wish to become more involved face a difficult problem, discussed in earlier chapters. When the legislation was introduced in the 103rd Congress, the claims of interested parties were often uncertain and fantastic. There was no way to find out if the claims were reliable. One vice-president of a major software company said that regular telephone service would be such a minor part of telecommunications in the near future that the service would be free.[16] Many industry people told congressional committees that 500-channel interactive video services were right around the corner, if only the market would be allowed to work. Several gave testimony to the effect that the television set and the personal computer would merge in a home communications system that could manage shopping, bills, household appliances, investments, and entertainment. Vice-President Gore led the administration's efforts to generate support for the legislation, and he did so through references to these technical developments—he is credited with the creation of the term *information superhighway*. The selling points for supporters of legislation suggested that technical progress is absolute, or that undesirable side effects are not worth consideration.[17] While such policy claims may not be unusual, citizens have a particularly difficult time making sense of them when the technologies involved are complicated, or even not yet invented.[18]

A third insight from the political model is that ideas are important in the policy process. Organized interests pursue their objectives in a context of ideas. Ideas such as competition, smaller government, and an information superhighway were among the powerful images that figured in the making of telecommunications policy. Competition would have been better served by a clear priority that included an estimate of the target population that still needs a subsidy of some type, the way a policy should affect individuals, and the amount of resources needed to bring about the effect. Because demands for smaller government have been effective in winning national elections for almost a generation, they are likely to be used more, not less. The concept of an information superhighway obscures more than it clarifies. It literally offers as example something we do not understand, praises it and declares it inevitable, and deflects concerns about undesirable side effects. With ideas like this dominating the policy discussions, we have reason to ask whether we are satisfied with the quality of democratic control of policy.

Groups that attempt to generate support for positions at odds with those of property owners run into a very powerful idea: market outcomes are connected to freedom. Government-regulated outcomes are connected to limits on freedom.

This simple idea helps to decipher the context of recent telecommunications policymaking. It was part of a late-twentieth-century political movement to restrain government restrictions on property. What was the compelling logic in the case for deregulation? Here is a list of the ideas used at the inception of legislation.

- Boundaries—between countries and between industries that traffic in information—are falling rapidly. Telephone companies are increasingly competing with cable companies, cable companies with broadcast companies, broadcast companies with wireless communications companies, wireless with telephone, and so on. Services are increasingly crossing borders; and emerging markets, both in developing countries and for new services in rich countries, are highly competitive. We increasingly refer to these trends as "globalization."
- The regulatory structures existing prior to 1996 limited the ability of U.S. companies to compete in this emerging global competition.
- A new regulatory scheme that relies more on markets will enable U.S. companies to lead global telecommunications markets.
- Consumers will benefit from the new deregulation policies. More services will be available, and the costs of basic services will decrease.
- The country will become stronger. If the leading telecommunications companies are ours, we will have stronger economic growth. The nation will be more competitive. That translates into more jobs and wealth for our citizens.

It was not necessary for policymakers in Congress or in the administration to pose these as questions or propositions. The answers were provided by confidence in the ability of markets to provide desirable outcomes. The idea was shared by both leaders of major political parties. Public officials armed with such ideas were visited frequently by representatives of corporations and interest groups that knew what they wanted from government and couched their entreaties in the language of competition. These ideas were so influential because they had no effective competitors. As argued in Chapter 4, even the major public-oriented interest groups used the language of competition. One who went outside the consensus ran the risk of being labeled as irrelevant, or as a crackpot.

A less enthusiastic appraisal of the free market vision might borrow some concepts from the analytical model and raise questions about the actual outcomes of policies, such as the following:

- The impulse to deregulate telecommunications is part of a larger trend to rely more on markets and less on government to make decisions about investment, production, and employment. Proposals to change policy should explain how these dimensions of life are affected for specific individuals. How will each be affected by legislation?
- Claims about global competitiveness need to be disciplined by real experience of the effects on human lives. The telecommunications industries are leading, not following, a trend toward global markets. Subjecting the myriad information-based services in the United States to global competition may have social consequences as our high-wage and high-benefit jobs come to compete with cheaper labor overseas.
- It is true that the good-paying jobs of the future will be increasingly based on higher skills and more education. Those are mostly available to young and future workers. Will today's displaced workers find employment at or near their accustomed level? Should we consider this a transition cost of the new policies? Should these workers be assisted through public policies? If so, how?

These are questions, not answers, but they are examples of remembering a simple truth about policies: economic development always comes at a cost. With all the talk of benefits to come from policy reform, what are the expected costs? The context of ideas surrounding the 1996 Act appears to have obscured these trade-offs.

Horwitz concluded his late 1980s study of deregulation with concern about the trade-off between state and markets.[19] A retreat from regulation means backing away from policies that had been accepted as pursuing the public interest—at least, it involves a redefinition of the public interest.

In the bargain that promises fewer regulatory inefficiencies, we get less democratic access. It is possible that the political forces that created the regulatory structures in the first place—such as demands for universal service—will respond to this bargain with pressure for renewed regulation.

Given the experience with ideas surrounding the 1996 Act, it is possible to conduct a thought experiment: What would have to occur in order to reverse the procompetitive trend in policy? The context of ideas would have to change, which would involve significant steps, such as the following:

- Consensus in the field of economics would have to be changed. Most of a generation of economists believe the benefits of government regulation outweigh the costs. A change would need to be supported by years of research that demonstrates why that proposition is faulty.
- Proregulation ideas would have to get out of universities and into the policy stream. Leaders of think tanks like the Brookings Institution and the American Enterprise Institute would have to support scholars with the new ideas. The ideas would have to be accompanied by phrases that are widely taken up in political dialogue and that help officials defend favorable policy positions.
- Key elites in government would have to support the ideas. New administrations would have to fill key appointments with people who hold the new ideas.
- The ideas would have to spread among industrial interests. Business associations would need to give at least lip service to the new values of regulation.
- At that point, the policy, problem, and political streams would have to come together. There is no assurance that the events that lead to the opening of a policy window would occur, but if the above conditions were met, at least the context of ideas would not stop it.

The list is intimidating. Policy discussions take place in a context of widely shared ideas; durable roles for citizens, interest groups, and the media; and uncertainty about the future. The best intentioned legislators working on highly technical and rapidly changing issues such as telecommunications deregulation will find it exceedingly difficult to find citizen voices that challenge plausible claims by business groups. Money was at the heart of deregulation, and the groups pursuing the money were the ones that mattered in constructing the 1996 Act. A faith in market outcomes and hopes for rapid economic growth went a long way toward justifying policy changes designed to help businesses pursue the money at stake in telecommunications markets. Occasionally, widely shared ideas lured business leaders into advocating positions against their interests and allowed legislators to endorse language that led to surprising directions in implementation. It is a powerful force for political consensus when agreements reached by business interests are consistent with widely held ideas.

The Analytical Model

The analytical model examines policy by asking questions about the extent to which policy is based on knowledge. As described in Chapter 1, the approach is a way to make sense of the content of policies and, by extrapolation, the policymaking process. So far the summary in this chapter suggests that the main influences on policy were (1) perceived self-interest of organized, mainly business groups; (2) a context of ideas that endorses deregulation and procompetitive policies; and (3) events outside the control or understanding of policymakers. The justification process for policies is representative within a system that limits power and observes the rights of organized property owners.

In Chapter 1, the analytical model had the following requirements for knowledge-based policymaking: projecting two or more outcomes on the future; constructing arguments for preferring one outcome to another; generalizing the preference into a priority system that covers the range of decisions under consideration; constructing policies that apply the priority system to specific cases; and refining the entire analytical project through experience. How does passage and implementation of the 1996 Act fare by this standard?

In the policymaking process, the first three steps are not distinct. No one is responsible for conducting such activities; rather, priorities for policies are expected to emerge from any number of institutions and actors. In the case of the 1996 Act, the vice-president appears to be the earliest public figure predicting a procompetitive, high-technology future that would include robust economic growth and other national objectives. As far as the policymaking community was concerned, congressional hearings were important in testing the waters for a consensus about legislation. The hearings produced reasons for going forward, rather than revealing significant differences in views of a desirable future. Chapter 4 and a previous section in this chapter characterized this consensus as an article of faith, one that enabled policymakers to proceed without seriously questioning its central claims. Very reputable experts advocated actions that had the same descriptors as early versions of legislation—deregulation, competition, NII—even though the legislation called for rules that did not satisfy the expert opinion.[20] Rather than explicitly do the work of constructing priorities, Congress, in particular, relies on a working consensus emerging through a political process. It can be argued that when an arm of Congress does engage in analysis of priorities, it loses support of legislators, as in the case of the Office of Technical Assessment.

From an analytical perspective, the loose emergence of a consensus on direction for policy has unfortunate effects. If a direction is vague, many rules can be consistent with it. Under such conditions, few expectations are attached to policies, and officials have a very loose sense of whether policies achieve desired outcomes. Indeed, under the definitions presented in the analytical model, these are not policies. A policy is a rule, applied in a specified situation, that is expected to produce an outcome measurable in terms of the quality of individual lives. Vague expectations for outcomes—more competition, more economic growth, lower prices for services, fewer restrictions on telecommunications businesses—are insufficient bases for this tight definition of "policy."

Vague priorities lead to a further problem at the fourth step of the analytical process. As described in Chapter 5, the 1996 Act did not closely direct the actions of government officials. Ignoring the implementation difficulties presented by court cases, the act's directions to the FCC were open to different interpretations. Its local competition order surprised several of the act's authors, although some of the authors expressed support for the order. The creation of the joint board on universal service was not a policy at all. It was instead an order to the FCC to create a process that would produce priorities and, eventually, policies. So it appears that the study of policy in this case should not focus so much on legislation as on the rules adopted by the FCC. The rules issued pursuant to the 1996 Act will take several years to complete, although some were issued within the first years of implementation. Given the FCC implementation schedule, a fairly complete picture of telecommunications policy can be assembled by 2002 or 2003.

If steps one through four of the analytical approach were not adequately constructed, it does not make much sense to discuss the fifth step. A loose and disjointed policy process might just as well be assessed through a loose and disjointed approach to analysis. Neither Congress nor the administration shows a tendency to commission and follow the recommendations of panels of impartial knowledgeable persons in policy matters.[21] Yet from an analytical perspective, policy knowledge needs to be developed. The confounding and surprising results that follow attempts to set policy are a sign of this need. Reliable knowledge about telecommunications policy is possible,[22] but that does not mean the policymaking institutions will follow it. It is beyond this study to explain how to increase the knowledge base for policy. Progress along those lines would probably involve think tanks that can eschew partisanship, develop a knowledge base open to policymakers and citizens, and develop connections to democratic citizen organizations and educational institutions.[23]

A broader reason for encouraging more knowledge in the policy process stems from interest in the justice produced by the policy process.

As Theodore Lowi suggests, a government that refuses to specify ends and instead delegates rule making to administrative agencies has put itself out of the justice business.[24] It has adopted no general standards by which a rule can be evaluated. It is not for ends—it is for means. This is perhaps an inevitable outcome of compromises on the scale involved in the 1996 Act, but it is a regrettable one. Compromise might work on decisions that threaten to destroy a society, but, as Meehan puts it, "It is a recipe for moral stagnation when applied to every issue in society."[25]

This is not to say that politics is without intellectual integrity. It is rather a description of the current balance in U.S. politics. The political and analytical models help show that the load is imbalanced, there is far too little knowledge about policy outcomes, and there is far too much change for reasons unrelated to whether policy is good or bad, however we would define those terms through politics. More analytical rigor is possible and defensible.[26] Whether it is consistent with democratic institutions is an important theoretical and practical question.

Conclusion

I want to conclude by returning to the theme of citizen participation in the policy process. As noted, able citizens are unlikely to participate in politics when issues are highly technical, though there were groups that attempted to encourage more widespread participation in the process surrounding passage and implementation of the 1996 Act. I do not pretend to evaluate their efforts but rather to use them as a starting point for asking questions about the future of telecommunications policy. I begin by asserting a double-barreled value: It would be a better world if more citizens were informed about policy issues and took the time to participate in the formation of policy.

Some people claim that the Internet is a technology that can encourage wider knowledge and greater participation—that it is a place, albeit a virtual one; that it contains a community; and that the community can do politics.[27] Community-without-traditional-space is new to our political thinking, in much the same way that the Internet presents a challenge to the concepts of public and private that underlie the regulation of obscenity. As we saw in the discussion of the CDA, the virtual space available through advanced telecommunications might be always somewhere else—not exactly private, not exactly public. Can it serve as a model for political action?[28] The two-way quality of the Internet, and its many-to-many connections (compared to the one-to-one of regular telephone service) enables a person to ask questions of many people at once, tell interesting things to people with similar interests, and track down answers to questions. In principle, if citizens are able to meet and discuss shared interests, it might be possible to organize meetings—and then it starts to sound like a tool that supports democratic participation.[29]

Models for community organization on the Internet include FIDOnet and TINCAN. FIDOnet consists of tens of thousands of independently operated electronic bulletin boards operated as local discussion groups for rural areas and gateways to commercial services.[30] It works essentially like a community radio station, only it is interactive. TINCAN is a regional network in the inland Northwest that supports rural Internet connections, community discussions that tie in with local radio and television public affairs programming, and on-line information presented by local groups and institutions.[31] Members of the network emphasize training citizens to use advanced telecommunications to take part in community civic associations and political meetings.

Although e-mail and virtual discussion groups will never take the place of lobbyists in the Congress, perhaps they can serve as a middle ground in a civic association, somewhere between groups with regular physical meetings and groups whose only contact with members is receiving their checks and sending them newsletters. Perhaps the technologies can be a way to have much more active participation in interest groups. Citizens who know more can be more influential in politics.[32]

Electronic discussions seem like a small part of the puzzle of low participation. Citizens need to make sense of policy proposals. In the case of the 1996 Act, the technical and economic issues have occupied hundreds of analysts in national and state regulatory bodies for decades. Some of the complications were described in Chapters 2 and 3. Citizens are going to need trustworthy and competent contacts that will reliably explain the trade-offs involved in policy. Is this possible? One way to conceive of this is as a professional responsibility of engineers and other experts who understand the business of telecommunications.[33] Computer Professionals for Social Responsibility was one group that attempted to fill this role in the politics of the 1996 Act. The record of professional associations in other fields, such as medicine, law, the civil service, and the military, is mixed on this score.[34] Professional groups tend to stake a territory in which they seek to control entry and education standards, employment in organizations, and career systems. If professional groups do take on more responsibility for informing interested citizens, these guild-oriented behaviors present an obstacle to citizen trust.

Another model for expert guidance is in openly partisan groups. The Taxpayers Asset Project and other Ralph Nader–style groups are suspicious of corporate power in the United States.[35] Staff members tend to be dedicated policy professionals who share the Naderite values. They do not pretend to be neutral on policy questions.

Market metaphors for policy issues do not leave much of a public role for businesses beyond that of a politically active self-interested property holder. The notion that businesses have a social responsibility grew rapidly during the Progressive Era and was implicit in many New Deal institutions.[36] Today the main theme on the social responsibility of corporations is the management of public and political affairs that affect communities and consumers, such as advance notification of plant closings or involvement in philanthropy.[37] It is possible to argue that businesses have no social responsibility to shareholders beyond those. An asocial stance seems inconsistent with the history of ideas about citizenship in the United States. Business leaders have changed civic orientations in the past and may do so again in ways that enable citizens to better understand technical policy issues.

Robert Putnam's work on civic engagement offers some lessons about relations between citizens and government.[38] Citizens who are less involved in civic organizations, clubs, and voluntary associations are less likely to trust and participate in political groups and events. Putnam refers to the shared norms and expectations that are part of a rich associational life as "social capital." Over the past forty years, social capital has decreased. People just are not joining the groups as often as their parents did. When Putnam sought an explanation for the decreased participation, he eliminated hypotheses based on changes in the economy, the family, the evolving roles of women, and the growth of the welfare state. The strongest remaining hypothesis was the growth of television. People might be watching television instead of doing more social activities.

Television likely isolates citizens from one another, although citizens who regularly watch public affairs programming may use the information to participate in politics.[39] The argument raises questions about the content of television. Should broadcasters and cable companies be responsible for more public affairs programming? If more public affairs programming was on television, would citizens watch it? If they watched more of it, would they understand technical policy issues better and participate more in politics?

The Internet model for telecommunications might serve as a catalyst for increased public affairs interest. Yet it is possible that interactive television will be even more isolating. Participation in electronic public forums might actually encourage hostile and downright uncivil behavior.[40] A good deal of the participation might take the form of polling, which because of the self-selection of subjects is not likely to give a meaningful account of citizen ideas. The community is inherently unstable, since membership does not involve moving to another house or even moving one's person. Electronic community advocates need to understand that the concept is experimental and that some experiments will fail.

If citizens are to become more interested in and knowledgeable about technically sophisticated policies, it will likely result from a lot of things.[41] Part of it may include access to reliable information about policies. Part of it might be a greater willingness of elected officials to actually make policy and to value widespread citizen participation in the process. Part of it might be more publicly responsible technical professionals and business leaders. A major force behind such a shift would have to be a change of heart among large numbers of citizens that such education and participation is an important responsibility.[42]

Public ideas have gone through changes like this before, and they will probably do so again. It is for historians of the future to write about the strength and duration of the current trend toward more-market-oriented approaches in the midst of a large state, and about whether digital communications technologies played a decisive role in changing them. Perhaps they will write about a widespread democratization of policymaking along the lines just mentioned.

New technological wonders in telecommunications are touted by political and business leaders as wonderful new gadgets that make life better and are the engines of economic growth. Citizens interested in policy should say, "Not so fast." All developments involve important design issues, all have costs, and all have political consequences. Choices will be made by someone—probably experts and top officials in the organizations that imagine and build a national information infrastructure. Citizens interested in democratic control of policy may just have to get used to working a bit harder at it.

Notes

1. An example of this was discussed at the end of Chapter 5.

2. A discussion of the sources of administrative power is in Schuman and Olufs, *Public Administration*.

3. Peterson, *Price of Federalism,* p. 13, argues that where Congress is willing to spend money, states have "no independent sovereignty." Tribe, *American Constitutional Law*, uses the metaphor of the states as "islands in the stream" of federal power.

4. Skocpol, *Social Policy,* pp. 297–310, describes a conflict of ideas and organizational strategies to support them; Gosling, *Budgetary Politics,* pp. 99–124, describes institutional features that affect the abilities of members of Congress and the president to affect policy.

5. For example, Arthur, "Competing Technologies," and Arthur, *Increasing Returns*.

6. For example, see the Alliance for Community Media's *Public Policy Update* for March 13, 1997, which describes model state legislation for putting state

and local governments in more control of right-of-way issues. It is available at http://www.alliancecm.org.

7. Kelman, *Making Public Policy;* Kelman, "Why Public Ideas Matter."

8. The adviser, Donald Jones, was reported to have written a memo to business partners about his role in the Speaker's office. He wrote that the content of legislation is the "the subject of daily negotiations involving the Speaker, committee chairmen, and a constant parade of TelCo CEOs," and that his role was to interpret and analyze such meetings for the Speaker. See Elperin, "'Informal' Gingrich Adviser."

9. A wide ranging discussion of the issue is in Benveniste, *Politics of Expertise.* See also Latour, "*The Prince* for Machines."

10. Examples of public interest groups described in Chapter 3 include the Benton Foundation, the Taxpayers Assets Project, the Alliance for Community Media, and the Electronic Freedom Foundation.

11. Smith, "Advocacy, Interpretation, and Influence."

12. Salisbury, "Interest Representation."

13. Brady, Verba, and Schlozman, "Beyond SES."

14. A sobering discussion of this is Verba, "The Citizen As Respondent."

15. Verba, Schlozman, Brady, and Nie, "Citizen Activity."

16. During the 1950s, I watched a television documentary that made the same claim about nuclear power. A narrator said that atomic power would be too cheap to meter and so would be free.

17. Hills, *Democracy Gap,* calls this the "technology push" argument, in which government officials believe that if they endorse a technology, it will in turn cause social progress.

18. U.S. history offers many examples of the belief that technology gives us progress, improvement is absolute, and progress is virtuous. See Kaason, *Civilizing the Machine.* Karl Polanyi, writing at mid-century, argued that liberal dreams of a market society, where all social value is subject to competitive forces, was utopian. He expected a reaction to policies derived from the ideology to provoke "the self-protection of society," a reaction by citizens who often bear the undesirable side effects. See Polanyi, *The Great Transformation.*

19. Horwitz, *Irony*, p. 284.

20. Several examples are found in Chapter 3. See Crandall, "Waves of the Future," for an example of recommendations that competitive policies be enacted. The Congress said it wanted competition but did not include some of the important provisions for including it—such as a known date for expiration of the period of transition to competition.

21. Formidable barriers stand in the way of designating and training informed and competent persons who can develop the judgments applied in policy processes. Meehan, *Ethics for Policymaking*, pp. 133–136, discusses the problems.

22. See, for example, Cairncross, *Death of Distance.* Cairncross includes a good deal of speculation about the consequences of digital technologies, but the heart of the book is a summary of what experience in different countries and with different institutional arrangements can teach us. She describes a consensus among the policy community for procompetitive policies, enacted by a set date, that include a managed transition to competition, a continuing but limited role for universal service, and a restructuring of industry to make self-interest coincide with public purposes.

23. For an attempt to teach the approach to high school and college students, see Meehan, *Thinking Game.*

24. Lowi, *End of Liberalism,* pp. 126, 296.

25. Meehan, *Quality of Federal Policymaking,* p. 209.

26. See, for example, Cairncross, *Death of Distance*; and Neuman, McKnight, and Solomon, *Gordian Knot.*

27. This is distinct from using work organizations as conduits to some wider political network. Even universities are uneasy about political uses of their resources. See letter to Princeton University president Harold Shapiro from the American Civil Liberties Union, August 15, 1996; and release from American Civil Liberties Union, August 23, 1996, "ACLU Responds to Princeton 'Clarification' of Internet Censorship Policy: End It, Don't Mend It," both available at www.aclu.org.

28. The most enthusiastic endorsement of this concept is Rheingold, *Virtual Community*. He has been the editor of the *Whole Earth Review*. See also Abramson, Arterton, and Orren, *Electronic Commonwealth.*

29. Miller, *Civilizing Cyberspace*, especially pp. 212–215, describes electronic meetings as one tool in a broader program to get more citizens involved in political life.

30. Jack Crawford, "FIDO/K12Net: Dirt Cheap Gateway to the Global Village for the Rural Masses," Wayne–Finger Lakes Area Teacher Resource Center, jack@rochgte.fidonet.org, 1995.

31. The TINCAN Civic Discourse Project, the Inland Northwest Community Access Network (telnet: tincan.tincan.org; URL: http://www.tincan.org).

32. Dahl, *Modern Political Analysis,* lists expertise as one of the key political resources; money is the first.

33. Arguments about the possible responsibilities of professionals and businesses are found in Wenk, *Making Waves.*

34. See Larson, *The Rise of Professionalism;* Mosher, "Professionals in Public Service"; and Noble, *America.*

35. Nader's book royalties, beginning with his *Unsafe at Any Speed,* and his speaking fees have gone into the creation of Public Citizen, Public Interest Research Groups (PIRGs), and consumer-oriented groups. Together these groups have been models for successfully influencing policy. The Taxpayers Asset Project, begun by Nader to monitor the management of government property, includes federal information policy. It can be visited at www.tap.org.

36. In Chapter 2, Theodore Vail of AT&T is described as an important figure in this regard. For Progressive Era ideals on the social responsibility of business, see Croly, *Marcus Alonzo Hanna,* especially pp. 402–407. Hofstadter, in *The Age of Reform*, pp. 234–237, describes the concept as a business strategy for disciplining their most outrageous members while they bargained their differences with government and other groups.

37. See the discussion in Weidenbaum, *Business and Government*, chap. 17.

38. Putnam, *Making Democracy Work*. This book focused on Italian politics. See also his "Tuning In, Tuning Out."

39. The possibility is discussed in Norris, "Does Television Erode Social Capital?"

40. This might be a wider problem, not limited to electronic forums. For an account that describes how town meetings have become less pleasant in one town, see Gross, "Political Poison."

41. Pagels, *The Dreams of Reason,* points out there is much we do not understand about how art, religion, and science fit into our society; we really know very

little about human psychology; our ability to use reason to build social institutions is very limited.

42. Miller, *Civilizing Cyberspace*, p. 217, argues that an NII can contribute to a more vibrant democracy if policies support universal service, preserve substantial noncommercial activity, protect First Amendment freedoms in cyberspace, and experiment with ways to use telecommunications to support civic organizations.

Bibliography

Books and Articles

Abelson, Hal et al., "The Risks of Key Recovery, Key Escrow, and Trusted Third-Party Encryption," Final Report, May 27, 1997. Also available at http://www.crypto.com/key_study/report.shtml.

Abramson, Jeffrey B., F. Christopher Arterton, and Gary R. Orren, *The Electronic Commonwealth: The Impact of New Media Technologies on Democratic Politics* (New York: Basic Books, 1988).

Andrews, Edmund L., "Accord Is Reached for Sweeping Bill on Communication," *New York Times,* December 21, 1995, p. A1.

———, "Bell Atlantic to Drop AT&T as Builder of Video Network," *New York Times,* February 16, 1995, p. C1.

———, "Big Bidders Win Auction for the Small," *New York Times,* May 7, 1996, p. C1.

———, "Cable Price Freeze Is Extended," *New York Times,* February 9, 1994, p. C1.

———, "Clinton and Technology: Some Policies Clash," *New York Times,* April 11, 1994, p. C1.

———, "Clinton Enters Battle over Telecom Bill," *New York Times,* October 28, 1995, p. 17.

———, "Conference Accord on Communication Faces House Snag," *New York Times,* December 22, 1995, p. A1.

———, "Digital TV, Dollars, and Dissent," *New York Times,* March 18, 1996, p. C1.

———, "F.C.C. Approves New Rate Rises for Cable TV," *New York Times,* November 11, 1994, p. C1.

———, "A Free-for-All in Communications," *New York Times,* February 4, 1994, p. C1.

———, "In Twist, Consumer Group and F.C.C. Back Cable-TV," *New York Times,* May 12, 1994, p. C1.

———, "Phone-Bill Lobbyists Wear Out Welcome," *New York Times,* March 20, 1995, p. C1; *Telecom Post,* August 6, 1995.

———, "The Phone-Law Static," *New York Times,* September 26, 1994, p. C1.

———, "Sweeping Revision in Communication Is on the Horizon," *New York Times,* October 26, 1994, p. A1.

———, "U.S. May Let a Baby Bell Widen Reach," *New York Times,* December 9, 1994, p. C1.

———, "U.S. Seeks Military Airwaves to Make Way for Private Use," *New York Times,* February 10, 1994, p. A1.

———, "Viacom's Cable Sale Threatened," *New York Times,* February 9, 1995, p. C1.

———, "Why G.O.P. Falters on Pro-Business Laws," *New York Times,* December 23, 1995, p. 19.

———, "Wireless Bidders Jostle for Position," *New York Times,* December 5, 1994, p. D1.

Andrews, Edmund L., and Geraldine Fabrikant, "The Black Entrepreneur at a Firestorm's Center," *New York Times,* February 10, 1995, p. C1.

Arendt, Hannah, *The Human Condition* (Chicago: University of Chicago Press, 1958).

Arnold, Thurman W., *The Folklore of Capitalism* (New Haven: Yale University Press, 1937).

Arthur, W. Brian, "Competing Technologies, Increasing Returns, and Lock-in by Historical Events," *Economic Journal* 99 (1989): 106–131.

———, *Increasing Returns and Path Dependence in the Economy,* with a foreword by Kenneth Arrow (Ann Arbor: University of Michigan Press, 1994).

Auletta, Ken, "Annals of Communication," *New Yorker,* May 12, 1997.

Bailey, Joseph, and Lee McKnight, "Internet Economics: What Happens When Constituencies Collide," a paper from an Internet Economics Workshop held at the Massachusetts Institute of Technology, Cambridge, Mass., March 9–10, 1995. Also available at http://rpcp.mit.edu/~bailey/inter_econ.html.

Bajak, Frank, "Hackers Foresee Huge Traffic Jam on the Internet," *Seattle Post-Intelligencer* (Associated Press story), January 3, 1995, p. A1.

Barboza, David, "Another Year of the Bull; Dow Up 22%," *New York Times,* January 1, 1998, p. C1.

Bardarch, Eugene, *The Implementation Game: What Happens After a Bill Becomes a Law* (Cambridge: MIT Press, 1977).

Bardarch, Eugene, and Robert A. Kagan, *Going by the Book: The Problem of Regulatory Unreasonableness* (Philadelphia: Temple University Press, 1982).

Baumgartner, Frank R., and Bryan D. Jones, *Agendas and Instability in American Politics* (Chicago: University of Chicago Press).

Beckman, David, and David Hirsch, "Rules of the Road," *ABA Journal* (September 1996): 86.

Benton Foundation, "Telecommunications Act of 1996: Timeline for Implementation." Available at www.benton.org.

Benveniste, Guy, *The Politics of Expertise*, 2d ed. (San Francisco: Boyd & Fraser Publishing, 1977).

Berkman, Harvey, "Medium Is Message: Courts Say Congress Goofed in CDA Focus on Smut, Not the Internet," *National Law Journal,* August 19, 1996, p. A1.

Blakeley, Craig J., "No Bliss Yet for Online Calls," *National Law Journal,* February 3, 1997, p. C1.

Blumenthal, Sidney, *The Rise of the Counter-Establishment: From Conservative Ideology to Political Power* (New York: Times Books, 1986).

Bradsher, Keith, "US to Aid Industry in Computer Battle with the Japanese," *New York Times,* April 27, 1994, p. A1.

Brady, Henry E., Sidney Verba, and Kay Lehman Schlozman, "Beyond SES: A Resource Model of Political Participation," *American Political Science Review* 89, no. 2 (June 1995): 271–294.
Brady, Robert A., *Business as a System of Power* (New York: Columbia University Press, 1943).
Brock, Gerald W., *The Telecommunications Industry: The Dynamics of Market Structure* (Cambridge: Harvard University Press, 1981).
Brooks, John, *Telephone: The First Hundred Years* (New York: Harper & Row, 1975).
Bryant, Adam, "Along Digital Path, Dead-End Jobs," *New York Times,* February 15, 1994, p. C1.
Cairncross, Frances, "A Connected World: A Survey of Telecommunications," *The Economist,* September 13, 1997.
———, *The Death of Distance* (Cambridge: Harvard Business School Press, 1997).
Cantelon, Philip L., *The History of MCI: 1968–1988, The Early Years* (Dallas: Heritage Press, 1993).
Carlisle, Charles R., "Is the World Ready for Free Trade?" *Foreign Affairs* 75, no. 6 (November/December 1996): 113–126.
Carney, Dan, "Spate of Squabbles Leaves Bill's Fate Still Uncertain," *Congressional Quarterly,* December 23, 1995, pp. 3881–3883.
Cassidy, John, "The Force of an Idea," *New Yorker,* January 12, 1998, pp. 32–37.
Cauley, Leslie, "Baby Bells Challenge FCC with Lawsuit," *Wall Street Journal,* April 28, 1995, p. B4.
———, "Phone Giants Discover the Interactive Path Is Full of Obstacles," *Wall Street Journal,* July 24, 1995, p. A1.
———, "Why Phone Rivals Can't Get into Some Towns," *Wall Street Journal,* August 19, 1996, p. B1.
Cohen, Michael, James March, and Johan Olsen, "A Garbage Can Model of Organizational Choice, *Administrative Science Quarterly* 17 (March 1972): 1–25.
Coll, Steve, *The Deal of the Century: The Breakup of AT&T* (New York: Atheneum, 1986).
Conkin, Paul K., *The New Deal,* 2d ed. (Arlington Heights, Ill.: AHM Publishing, 1975).
Corr, O. Casey, "ads-new@internet.now," *Seattle Times,* September 11, 1994, p. F1.
CQ Almanac 1993, "House Passes Competitiveness Bill" (Washington, D.C.: Congressional Quarterly, 1994), p. 241.
———, "Stumped by Bells' Objections, Senate Kills Overhaul" (Washington, D.C.: Congressional Quarterly, 1994), pp. 203–218.
Crandall, Robert W., *After the Breakup: U.S. Telecommunications in a More Competitive Era* (Washington: Brookings Institution, 1991).
———, "Are We Deregulating Telephone Services? Think Again," *Brookings Policy Brief No. 13* (Washington: Brookings Institution, 1997).
———, "Waves of the Future: Are We Ready to Deregulate Telecommunications?" *Brookings Review* 14, no. 1 (winter 1996): 28.
Croly, Herbert, *Marcus Alonzo Hanna* (New York: MacMillan, 1912).
Dahl, Robert, *Modern Political Analysis* (Englewood Cliffs, N.J.: Prentice Hall, 1998).
Dam, Kenneth, and Herbert Lin, eds., "Cryptography's Role in Securing the Information Society," National Research Council, Computer Science and Telecommunications

Board, Committee to Study National Cryptography Policy, May 30, 1996 (prepublication copy subject to further editorial correction).
Danielian, N. R., *AT&T: The Story of Industrial Conquest* (New York: Vanguard Press, 1939).
Delitte & Touche Consulting Group, "The FCC's Local Competition Rules and the Eighth Circuit Court's Review: View of Key Members of Congress," Copyright LLC 1997.
Derthick, Martha, and Paul J. Quirk, *The Politics of Deregulation* (Washington, D.C.: Brookings Institution, 1985).
Dole, Bob, "Giving Away the Airwaves," *New York Times* (op-ed), March 27, 1997.
Dorrien, Gary, *The Neoconservative Mind: Politics, Culture, and the War of Ideology* (Philadelphia: Temple University Press, 1993).
Drake, Alvin W., Ralph L. Keeney, and Philip M. Morse, eds., *Analysis of Public Systems* (Cambridge: MIT Press, 1972).
Drake, William J., ed., *The New Information Infrastructure: Strategies for US Policy* (New York: Twentieth Century Fund Press, 1995).
———, "The Turning Point," in Drake, *New Information Infrastructure,* pp. 1–27.
Dworkin, Ronald, *Life's Dominion: An Argument About Abortion, Euthanasia, and Individual Freedom* (New York: Alfred A. Knopf, 1993).
———, *A Matter of Principle* (Cambridge: Harvard University Press, 1985).
———, "Only Words," *New York Review of Books* 40 (October 21, 1993): 36–39.
Eads, George C., and Michael Fix, *Relief or Reform? Reagan's Regulatory Dilemma* (Washington, D.C.: Urban Institute Press, 1984).
Elperin, Juliet, "'Informal' Gingrich Adviser Got Congressional ID Card," *Roll Call*, February 24, 1996.
Erickson, Jim, "Internet Poses Real Threat to Microsoft Dominance," *Seattle Post-Intelligencer*, November 14, 1995, p. B5.
———, "U S West Seeks Big Rise in Cost of Local Service," *Seattle Post-Intelligencer,* February 18, 1995, p. A1.
———, "U S West Told to Cut, Not Raise, Its Rates," *Seattle Post-Intelligencer,* April 12, 1996, p. A1.
Fagen, M. D., ed., *A History of Engineering and Science in the Bell System: The Early Years, 1875–1925* (Indianapolis: Bell Telephone Laboratories, 1974).
———, *A History of Engineering and Science in the Bell System: National Service in War and Peace, 1925–1975* (Indianapolis: Bell Telephone Laboratories, 1978).
Fisher, Lawrence M., "Long-Distance Phone Calls on the Internet," *New York Times,* March 14, 1995.
Flamm, Kenneth, "Deciphering the Cryptography Debate," *Brookings Policy Brief No. 21* (Washington, D.C.: Brookings Institution, 1997).
France, Mike, "Are Telecoms Discussing Compliance or Colluding?" *National Law Journal*, January 30, 1995, p. B1.
Galbraith, John Kenneth, *American Capitalism: The Concept of Countervailing Power,* 2d ed. (Boston: Houghton Mifflin, 1956).
Ganley, Oswald H., and Gladys D. Ganley, *To Inform or to Control? The New Communications Networks*, 2d ed. (Norwood, N.J.: Ablex Publishing, 1989).
Gates, Bill, with Nathan Myhrvold and Peter Rinearson, *The Road Ahead* (New York: Viking, 1995).
Gibbs, W. Wayt, "When Cells Divide: Making Space for the Next Wave of Wireless Communications," *Scientific American,* December 1993, pp. 44–45.
———, "Cyber View: Snap, Crunch, or GigaPop?" *Scientific American* (December 1996): 38–40.
Gilpin, Kenneth N., "Market Place," *New York Times,* March 7, 1994, p. C4.

Goldman, Debbie (research economist for the Communications Workers of America), "Telecommunications from Labor's Perspective," Telecommunications Policy Roundtable, Washington D.C., minutes of January 3, 1995.

Gosling, James J., *Budgetary Politics in American Governments,* 2d ed. (New York: Garland Publishing, 1997).

Gotts, Ilene Knable, and Rebecca R. Fry, "Danger May Await Internet Shoppers," *National Law Journal*, March 25, 1996, p. C9.

Goulden, Joseph C., *Monopoly* (New York: G.P. Putnam's Sons, 1968).

Grieder, William, "The Education of David Stockman," *Atlantic Monthly,* December 1981, pp. 17–54.

Gross, Melanie Belman, "Political Poison at the Grass Roots," *New York Times,* May 4, 1996, p. 15.

Gulick, Luther H., and Lyndell Urwick, eds., *Papers on the Science of Administration* (New York: Institute of Public Administration, 1937).

Haber, Samuel, *Efficiency and Uplift: Scientific Management in the Progressive Era, 1890–1920* (Chicago: University of Chicago Press, 1964).

Hafner, Katie, and Matthew Lyon, *Where Wizards Stay Up Late* (New York: Simon & Schuster, 1996).

Hall, Peter A., ed., *The Political Power of Economic Ideas: Keynesianism Across Nations* (Princeton: Princeton University Press, 1989).

Hatry, Harry P., Richard E. Winnie, and Donald M. Fisk, *Practical Program Evaluation for State and Local Governments*, 2d ed. (Washington, D.C.: Urban Institute Press, 1981).

Hayek, Friedrich A., *The Constitution of Liberty* (London: Routledge, 1960).

Held, David, "Democracy, the Nation-State and the Global System," in David Held, ed., *Political Theory Today* (Stanford: Stanford University Press, 1991), pp. 197–235.

Hills, Jill, with Stylianos Papathanassopoulos, *The Democracy Gap: The Politics of Information and Telecommunications Technologies in the United States and Europe* (New York: Greenwood Press, 1991).

Hodgson, Godfrey, *The World Turned Rightside Up: A History of the Conservative Ascendancy in America* (New York: Houghton Mifflin, 1996).

Hofstadter, Richard, *The Age of Reform* (New York: Vintage Books, 1955).

Horwitz, Robert Britt, *The Irony of Regulatory Reform: The Deregulation of American Telecommunications* (New York: Oxford University Press, 1989).

Howell, William, "Point of View: How Social Scientists Can Contribute to the Information Revolution," *Chronicle of Higher Education*, June 8, 1994.

Huber, Peter W., *The Geodesic Network, 1987: Report on Competition in the Telephone Industry* (Washington, D.C.: Department of Justice, 1987).

Hume, David, *A Treatise of Human Nature,* Second edition, edited by L. A. Selby-Bigge (Oxford: Claredon Press, 1978).

Kaason, John, *Civilizing the Machine* (New York: Alfred A. Knopf, 1976).

Karr, Albert R., "Cable Rates Are Up an Average of 10.4% This Year," *Wall Street Journal,* August 29, 1996, p. A2.

———, "FCC's Digital Plan May Be U.S. Bonanza," *Wall Street Journal,* July 26, 1996, p. A3.

Karr, Albert R., and Bryan Gruley, "FCC Rules May Lift Phone Rates for Now," *Wall Street Journal,* August 2, 1996, p. A2.

Katzmann, Robert A., *Regulatory Bureaucracy: The Federal Trade Commission and Antitrust Policy* (Cambridge: MIT Press, 1980).

Keller, John J., "BT-MCI Merger Reshapes Telecom Industry: Even the Giants Will Be Unable to Go It Alone," *Wall Street Journal,* November 5, 1996, p. B1.

Kelman, Steven, *Making Public Policy: A Hopeful View of American Government* (New York: Basic Books, 1987).

———, "Why Public Ideas Matter," in Robert B. Reich, ed., *The Power of Public Ideas* (Cambridge: Ballinger Publishing, 1988), pp. 31–53.

King, Gary, Robert O. Keohane, and Sidney Verba, *Designing Social Inquiry: Scientific Inference in Qualitative Research* (Princeton: Princeton University Press, 1994).

Kingdon, John W., *Agendas, Alternatives, and Public Policies* (Boston: Little, Brown, 1984).

Krugman, Paul, *Peddling Prosperity: Economic Sense and Nonsense in the Age of Diminished Expectations* (New York: W.W. Norton, 1994).

Kuester, Jeffrey R., "Attorney Sites Can Avoid Violations of Ethics Rules," *National Law Journal,* August 12, 1996, p. B11.

Kulikowski, Stan, "File 3—Timeline for a Network History," *Computer Underground Digest,* May 28, 1993 (distributed through BITNET).

Landler, Mark, "F.C.C. Is Urged to Keep Close Eye on Cable Rates," *New York Times,* September 24, 1997, p. C1.

———, "F.C.C. Ready to Establish Phone Rules," *New York Times,* July 31, 1996, p. C1.

———, "Gore Urges Cable Industry to Take On the Bells," *New York Times,* April 30, 1996, p. C1.

———, "New Weapons, New Rivals in Wireless Phone Competition," *New York Times,* November 14, 1996, p. C1.

———, "A Ruling on Satellite Service Limits TCI's Options," *New York Times,* October 30, 1996, p. C1.

———, "Sigh of Relief Greets New Telephone Rules," *New York Times,* August 2, 1996, p. C1.

———, "Time Warner–Turner Deal Said to Face F.T.C. Resistance," *New York Times,* May 8, 1996, p. C1.

Larson, Magali Sarfatti, *The Rise of Professionalism* (Berkeley: University of California Press, 1977).

Latour, Bruno, "*The Prince* for Machines as Well as for Machinations," in Brian Elliott, ed., *Technology and Social Progress* (Edinburgh: Edinburgh University Press,1988), pp. 20–43.

Lavelle, Marianne, "Baby Bells Say: Wrong Number," *National Law Journal,* February 3, 1997, p. A1.

LeLoup, Lance T., and Steven A. Shull, *Congress and the President: The Policy Connection* (San Diego: Harcourt Brace, 1993).

Leuchtenburg, William E., *Franklin D. Roosevelt and the New Deal* (New York: Harper & Row, 1963).

Lewis, Peter H., "'Darkness' to Meet Communications Bill," *New York Times,* February 8, 1996, p. A10.

———, "Doubts Are Raised on Actual Number of Internet's Users," *New York Times,* August 10, 1994, p. A1.

———, "Most Go On Line at Home, Study Finds," *New York Times,* October 23, 1995, p. C6.

———, "Report of High Internet Use Is Challenged," *New York Times,* December 13, 1995, p. C5.

———, "A Traffic Jam on the Data Highway," *New York Times,* February 2, 1994, p. C1.

Lindblom, Charles E., and David K. Cohen, *Usable Knowledge: Social Science and Social Problem-Solving* (New Haven: Yale University Press, 1979).

Loht, Steve, "An Estimated 5.8 Million Log Internet Time in U.S.," *Seattle Post-Intelligencer,* September 27, 1995, p. B7.

Long, Colin D., and Stephen O. Spinks, *International Telecoms Review '97,* © 1997, Coudert Brothers (law firm).

Love, James, "A Primer on the Proposed WIPO Treaty on Database Extraction Rights That Will Be Considered in December 1996," Taxpayers Assets Project, *Info Policy Notes,* October 29, 1996, www.essential.org/cpt/ip/cptdbcom.html.

Lowi, Theodore J., *The End of Liberalism: The Second Republic of the United States,* 2d ed. (New York: W.W. Norton, 1979).

Lubetkin, Wendy (U.S. Information Agency correspondent), "New Treaties Would Update Copyright Law for the Digital Age," USIS Geneva *Daily Bulletin,* December 5, 1996.

Luttwak, Edward, "From Geopolitics to Geo-Economics," *The National Interest* (summer 1990), reprinted in Foreign Affairs Agenda, *The New Shape of World Politics* (New York: W.W. Norton, 1997), pp. 177–186.

McConnell, Grant, *Private Power and American Democracy* (New York: Alfred A. Knopf, 1966).

MacKie-Mason, Jeffrey K., and Hal Varian, "Economic FAQs About the Internet," *Journal of Economic Perspectives* 8, no. 3 (summer 1994): pp. 75–96.

MacKinnon, Catherine, *Only Words* (Cambridge: Harvard University Press, 1993).

McKnight, Lee, and W. Russell Neuman, "Technology Policy and the National Information Infrastructure," in William J. Drake, ed., *The New Information Infrastructure: Strategies for U.S. Policy* (New York: Twentieth Century Fund Press, 1995), pp. 137–154.

MacRae, Duncan, Jr., and James A. Wilde, *Policy Analysis for Public Decisions* (Belmont, Calif.: Duxbury Press, 1979).

Markoff, John, "Bell Companies Assail AT&T's Internet Plan," *New York Times,* February 29, 1996, p. C1.

Meehan, Eugene J., *Ethics for Policymaking: A Methodological Analysis* (New York: Greenwood Press, 1990).

———, *The Quality of Federal Policymaking: Programmed Disaster in Public Housing* (St. Louis: University of Missouri Press, 1979).

———, *Reasoned Argument in Social Science: Linking Research to Policy* (Westport, Conn.: Greenwood Press, 1981).

———, *The Thinking Game* (Chatham, N.J.: Chatham House, 1988).

Miller, Steven E., *Civilizing Cyberspace: Policy, Power, and the Information Superhighway* (New York: ACM Press, 1996).

Millman, S., ed., *A History of Engineering and Science in the Bell System: Communications Sciences, 1925–1980* (Indianapolis: AT&T Bell Laboratories, 1984).

Mills, Joshua, "Great Radio Debate: Can Fewer Owners Mean More Competition?" *New York Times,* July 24, 1995, p. C7.

Mills, Mike, "Baby Bells' Fate Dangling Before Congress, Courts," *CQ* (Congressional Quarterly), February 23, 1991, pp. 458–463.

———, "Bells' Bid to Make Equipment Gains in Both Chambers," *CQ* (Congressional Quarterly), March 23, 1991, p. 741.

———, "Phone Firms Seek Higher Local Rates," *Washington Post,* May 7, 1996, p. A1.

———, "Senate Votes to Eliminate Ban on Bells' Manufacturing," *CQ* (Congressional Quarterly), June 8, 1991, pp. 1490–1491.

———, "Two Powerful Chairmen Duel To Shape the Bells' Future," *CQ* (Congressional Quarterly), June 27, 1992, pp. 1866–1868.

Morrison, Thomas C., and Robert W. Lehrburger, "FTC Targets Deceptive Cyberspace Advertising," *National Law Journal,* August 12, 1996, p. B7.
Mosher, Frederick C., "Professionals in Public Service," *Public Administration Review* 38 (March/April 1978).
Nader, Ralph, *Unsafe at Any Speed: The Designed-in Dangers of the American Automobile* (New York: Grossman, 1965).
Neuman, W. Russell, Lee McKnight, and Richard Jay Solomon, *The Gordian Knot: Political Gridlock on the Information Highway* (Cambridge: MIT Press, 1995).
Noble, David, *America by Design* (New York: Alfred A. Knopf, 1976).
Norris, Pippa, "Does Television Erode Social Capital? A Reply to Putnam," *PS: Political Science and Politics* 29, no. 3 (September 1996): 474–480.
Orren, Gary R., "Beyond Self-Interest," in Robert B. Reich, ed., *The Power of Public Ideas* (Cambridge: Ballinger, 1988), pp. 13–29.
Pagels, Heinz R., *The Dreams of Reason: The Computer and the Rise of the Sciences of Complexity* (New York: Simon & Schuster, 1988).
Paglin, Max D., ed., *A Legislative History of the Communications Act of 1934* (New York: Oxford University Press, 1989).
Parkes, Henry Bamford, *Recent America: A History of the United States Since 1900* (New York: Thomas Y. Crowell, 1941).
Pascall, Glenn, "Depreciation Sound Basis for Rate Hike Sought by U S West," *Seattle Post-Intelligencer,* May 1, 1996, p. A13.
Pearl, Daniel, "'Baby Bells See Better Chance of Gaining Access to New Markets with GOP-Controlled Congress," *Wall Street Journal,* January 20, 1995, p. A14.
———, "Clinton Weighs Backing Changes in Law to Ease Price Rules for Cable Operators," *Wall Street Journal,* January 10, 1995, p. A4.
Persons, Georgia A., *The Making of Energy and Telecommunications Policy* (Westport, Conn.: Praeger, 1995).
Pertschuck, Michael, *Revolt Against Regulation: The Rise and Pause of the Consumer Movement* (Berkeley: University of California Press, 1982).
Peters, Thomas J., and Robert H. Waterman, Jr., *In Search of Excellence: Lessons from America's Best-Run Companies* (New York: Harper & Row, 1982).
Peterson, Paul E., *The Price of Federalism* (Washington, D.C.: Brookings Institution, 1995).
Pitsch, Peter K., "An 'Innovation Age' Perspective on Telecommunications Mergers," Issue Analysis no. 43, November 13, 1996 (Washington, D.C.: Citizens for a Sound Economy Foundation).
Polanyi, Karl, *The Great Transformation: The Political and Economic Origins of Our Time* (Boston: Beacon Press, 1944).
Pool, Ithiel de Sola, *Forecasting the Telephone: A Retrospective Technology Assessment of the Telephone* (Norwood, N.J.: ABLEX Publishing, 1983).
———, *Technologies of Freedom* (Cambridge: Harvard University Press, 1983).
Putnam, Robert D., *Making Democracy Work: Civic Traditions in Modern Italy* (Princeton: Princeton University Press, 1993).
———, "Tuning In, Tuning Out: The Strange Disappearance of Social Capital in America," *PS: Political Science and Politics* 28, no. 4 (December 1995): 664–683.
Quade, E. S., *Analysis for Public Decisions* (New York: North-Holland, 1982).
Reagan, Michael D., *The Managed Economy* (New York: Oxford University Press, 1963).

Rheingold, Howard, *The Virtual Community: Homesteading on the Electronic Frontier* (New York: Addison-Wesley, 1995).

Rhoads, Steven E., *The Economist's View of the World: Government, Markets, and Public Policy* (Cambridge: Cambridge University Press, 1985).

Richards, Bill, "Trojan Horse? In the Race to Wire Your Home, Don't Rule Out the Electric Utilities," *Wall Street Journal,* June 19, 1995, p. R24.

Rivkin, Steven R., "Electric Utilities Will Build Telecom Infrastructure," *New Telecom Quarterly* 2, no. 2 (1994): 15–19.

———, "If Competition Won't Build the NII, Utility Partnerships Will," *New Telecom Quarterly* 4, no. 3 (1996): 19–23.

———, "Positioning the Electric Utility to Build Information Infrastructure," *New Telecom Quarterly* 3, no. 2 (1995): 30–34.

Robichaux, Mark, "Cable Industry Says New Rivals Obviate Rules," *Wall Street Journal,* April 3, 1995.

Robinson, Glen O., "The Federal Communications Act: An Essay on Origins and Regulatory Purpose," in Max D. Paglin, ed., *A Legislative History of the Communications Act of 1934* (New York: Oxford University Press, 1989).

Rohr, John, *To Run a Constitution: The Legitimacy of the Administrative State* (Lawrence: University of Kansas Press, 1986).

Ronfeldt, David, "Cyberocracy Is Coming," *Information Society Journal* 8, no. 4 (1992): 243–296.

Safire, William, "The Greatest Auction Ever," *New York Times,* March 16, 1995, p. A17.

Salamon, Lester M., and Michael S. Lund, *The Reagan Presidency and the Governing of America* (Washington, D.C.: Urban Institute Press, 1984).

Salisbury, Robert H., "Interest Representation: The Dominance of Institutions," *American Political Science Review* 78, no. 1 (March 1984): 64–76.

Schiesel, Seth, "A U.S. Judge Strikes Down Part of '96 Telecommunications Act," *New York Times,* January 1, 1998, p. A1.

Schindler, G., ed., *A History of Engineering and Science in the Bell System: Switching Technology, 1925–1975* (Indianapolis: Bell Telephone Laboratories, 1982).

Schuman, David, and Dick W. Olufs, *Public Administration in the United States,* 2d ed. (Lexington, Mass.: D.C. Heath, 1993).

Schweber, Howard, "Invisible Community: Federalism and the First Amendment in Cyberspace," paper delivered at the 1996 annual meeting of the Pacific Northwest Political Science Association, Portland, Ore.

Seidman, Harold, and Robert Gilmour, *Politics, Position, and Power: From the Positive to the Regulatory State,* 4th ed. (New York: Oxford University Press, 1985).

Sharp, Elaine B., *The Dilemma of Drug Policy in the United States* (New York: HarperCollins College Publishers, 1994).

Simpson, Glenn R., and Edward Felsenthal, "Bingaman Will Leave Antitrust Post," *Wall Street Journal,* August 2, 1996, p. A3.

Skocpol, Theda, *Social Policy in the United States: Future Possibilities in Historical Perspective* (Princeton: Princeton University Press, 1995).

Smith, Richard A., "Advocacy, Interpretation, and Influence in the U.S. Congress," *American Political Science Review* 78, no. 1 (March 1984): 44–63.

Sohn, Gigi B., and Andrew Jay Schwartzman, "Pretty Pictures or Pretty Profits: Issues and Options for the Public Interest and Nonprofit Communities in the Digital Broadcasting Debate" (Washington, D.C.: Benton Foundation, October 1995).

Solomon, Robert C., *The Passions: Emotions and the Meaning of Life* (Indianapolis: Hackett Publishing, 1993).

Spence, Larry D., "An Introduction to a Theory of the Politics of Technology," paper presented at the Instituto de Estudios Superiores de Administración, Caracas, Venezuela, March 29, 1976.

Stimson, James A., *Public Opinion in America: Moods, Cycles, and Swings* (Boulder: Westview Press, 1991).

Stokey, Edith, and Richard Zeckhauser, *A Primer for Policy Analysis* (New York: W.W. Norton, 1978).

Stone, Alan, *Wrong Number: The Breakup of AT&T* (New York: Basic Books, 1989).

Temin, Peter, with Louis Galambos, *The Fall of the Bell System: A Study in Prices and Politics* (Cambridge: Cambridge University Press, 1987).

Thimm, Alfred L., *Business Ideologies in the Reform-Progressive Era, 1880–1914* (University: University of Alabama Press, 1976).

Thorelli, Hans B., *The Federal Antitrust Policy* (Baltimore: Johns Hopkins University Press, 1954).

Tomasko, Robert M., *Rethinking the Corporation: The Architecture of Change* (New York: AMACOM, 1993).

Tribe, Laurence H., *American Constitutional Law*, 2d ed. (Mineola, N.Y.: Foundation Press, 1988).

Tunstall, Jeremy, *Comunications Deregulation: The Unleashing of America's Communications Industry* (London: Basil Blackwell, 1986).

Verba, Sidney, "The Citizen as Respondent: Sample Surveys and American Democracy," *American Political Science Review* 90, no. 1 (March 1996): 1–8.

Verba, Sidney, Kay Lehman Schlozman, Henry Brady, and Norman H. Nie, "Citizen Activity: Who Participates? What Do They Say?" *American Political Science Review* 87, no. 2 (June 1993): 314.

Virgin, Bill, "'Mild Rebuke' for Microsoft in Antitrust Settlement," *Seattle Post-Intelligencer,* July 18, 1994, p. A1.

Viscusi, W. Kip, John M. Vernon, and Joseph E. Harrington, Jr., *Economics of Regulation and Antitrust* (Lexington, Mass.: D.C. Heath, 1992).

von Auw, Alvin, *Heritage and Destiny: Reflections on the Bell System in Transition* (New York: Praeger, 1983).

Waldman, Steven, *The Bill: How Legislation Really Becomes Law: A Case Study of the National Service Bill* (New York: Penguin Books, 1996).

Wanniski, Jude, *The Way the World Works: How Economies Fail—And Succeed* (New York: Basic Books, 1978).

Weaver, Suzanne, *Decision to Prosecute: Organization and Public Policy in the Antitrust Division* (Cambridge: MIT Press, 1977).

WEFA Group, *Economic Impact of Deregulating US Communications Industries* (Burlington, Mass., and Bala Cynwyd, Pa.: WEFA, February 1995).

Weibe, Robert, *Business and Reform: A Study of the Progressive Movement* (Cambridge: Harvard University Press, 1962).

Weinstein, James, *The Corporate Ideal in the Liberal State, 1900–1918* (Boston: Beacon Press, 1968).

Weir, Margaret, *Politics and Jobs: The Boundaries of Employment Policy in the United States* (Princeton: Princeton University Press, 1992).

Wenders, John T., *The Economics of Telecommunications: Theory and Policy* (Cambridge, Mass.: Ballinger Publishing, 1987).

Wenk, Edward, Jr., *Making Waves: Engineering, Politics, and the Social Management of Technology* (Urbana: University of Illinois Press, 1995).

Wiedenbaum, Murray L., *Business and Government in the Global Marketplace* (Englewood Cliffs, N.J.: Prentice-Hall, 1995).
———, "The Shifting Roles of Business and Government in the World Economy," *Challenge,* January/February 1993, pp. 23–29.
Williams, Walter et al., *Studying Implementation: Methodological and Administrative Issues* (Chatham, N.J.: Chatham House, 1982).
Wilson, James Q., ed., *The Politics of Regulation* (New York: Basic Books, 1980).
Warren, Wilson, "24 Million on Net, Survey Says," *Seattle Post-Intelligencer,* October 31, 1995, p. B5.
———, "New Noises for Internet Regulation," *Seattle Post-Intelligencer,* January 8, 1998, p. C1.
Winner, Langdon, *Autonomous Technology: Technics-Out-of-Control as a Theme in Political Thought* (Cambridge: MIT Press, 1977).
Wyatt, Edward, "Stocks Rise with Dow Climbing 39.50 Points," *New York Times,* November 6, 1996, p. C8.
Ziegler, Bart, "Slow Crawl on the Internet," *Wall Street Journal,* August 23, 1996.

Government Documents and Court Cases

Bowers, Attorney General of Georgia v. Hardwick et al., 478 US 186 (1986).
FCC v. Pacifica Foundation, 438 U.S. 726 (1978).
Federal Communications Commission, *Allocation of Frequencies in the Bands Above 890 MC* (27 FCC 359 [1959]).
———, "Answers to Questions Concerning Broadband PCS Auctions," 1996.
———, "Answers to Questions from the June 6, 1994, FCC Bidder's Seminar," part 2, "Designated Entities," June 17, 1994.
———, "Auctions Fact Sheet," January 1996.
———, Report No. DC-2621, Action in Docket Case, June 29, 1994, "Commission Adopts Competitive Bidding Procedures for Broadband PCS" (PP Docket No. 93-253).
———, "Commission Adopts Open Video Systemsorder Enhancing Competition in the Videomarketplace," CS Docket No. 96-46, Report No. DC 96-48.
———, "Draft FCC Implementation Schedule for S 652, The Telecommunications Act of 1996," March 25, 1996.
———, "FCC Adopts Modifications to PCS Band Plan; Creates Significant Benefits for Consumers and Businesses," June 9, 1994.
———, *Investigation of the Telephone Industry in the United States* (Washington, D.C.: Government Printing Office, 1939).
———, 96-182, "Notice of Proposed Rulemaking, Separate Dates for Dialing Parity/Number Administration/Notice of Technical Changes/Access to Rights of Way," released April 19, 1996, CC Docket No. 96-98.
———, "Open Video Systems, Implementation of Section 302 of the Telecommunications Act of 1996, June 3, 1996. By Second Report and Order, CS Docket 96-46, FCC 96-249, adopted May 31, 1996, by the Commission.
———, "Report and Order in the Matter of Federal-State Joint Board on Universal Service," Federal Communications Commission, 97-157, CC Docket No. 96-45.
———, "Second Report and Order on Implementation of Section 302 of the Telecommunications Act of 1996, Open Video Systems," CS Docket No. 96-46, June 3, 1996.
———, *Separations Manual*, October 1947.

Federal Energy Regulatory Commission, "Promoting Wholesale Competition Through Open Access Non-discriminatory Transmission Services by Public Utilities (Docket No. RM95-8-000), Recovery of Stranded Costs by Public Utilities and Transmitting Utilities (Docket No. RM94-7-001), Notice of Proposed Rulemaking and Supplemental Notice of Proposed Rulemaking" (March 29, 1995).

Federal Trade Commission, September 12, 1996, File No. 961-0004, "In The Matter of Time Warner, Inc.; Turner Broadcasting System, Inc.; Tele-Communications, Inc.; and Liberty Media Corporation, Consent Package Including Separate Statement and Dissenting Statements."

Home Box Office, Inc. v. Federal Communications Commission, 567 F.2d 9 (D.C. Circuit 1971).

Iowa Public Utilities Board v. FCC, United States Court of Appeals for the Eighth Circuit, 96-3321 and consolidated cases.

MCI Telecommunications Corporation v. American Telephone & Telegraph Co., Docket 93-356, June 17, 1994.

MCI Telecommunications Corporation v. FCC, 561 F.2d 356 (D.C. Circuit, 1977).

Miller v. California, 413 U.S. 15 (1973).

Munn v. Illinois, 94 U.S. 133 (1877).

NII 200 Steering Committee, Computer Science and Telecommunications Board, Commission on Physical Sciences, Mathematics, and Applications, National Research Council, *The Unpredictable Certainty: Information Infrastructure Through 2000* (Washington, D.C.: National Academy Press, 1996), pp. 9–10.

Reno v. ACLU, 96-511, Supreme Court of the United States.

Sable Communications of California, Inc. v. Federal Communications Commission et al., 492 U.S. 109 S.Ct. 2829, 106 L.Ed.2d 93 (1989).

Smith v. Illinois Bell Tel. Co. (282 U.S. 133, 1930).

Smyth v. Ames, 169 U.S. 466 (1898).

Stanley v. Georgia, 394 US 557 (1969).

U.S. v. American Telephone and Telegraph Co., 552 F. Supp. 131 (D.D.C. 1982), aff'd sub nom., *Maryland v. United States*, 460 U.S. 1001, 103 S. Ct. 1240, 75 L. Ed. 2d 472 (1983).

U.S. v. Thomas, 96 C.D.O.S. 609 (1996).

U.S. Congress, Office of Technology Assessment, *Critical Connections: Communication for the Future*, OTA-CIT-407 (Washington, D.C.: Government Printing Office, January 1990).

———, *Electronic Enterprises: Looking to the Future* (Washington, D.C.: Government Printing Office, May 26, 1994).

U.S. Department of Commerce, Office of the Secretary, "Common Ground: Fundamental Principles for the NII," *NII Advisory Council Report,* December 6, 1994.

Washington Utilities and Transportation Commission, "Alternative Regulation of U S West: Toward A New Paradigm," Olympia, December 1, 1993.

———, U S West Rate Case—970766.

White House, "Administration of Export Control on Encryption Products," signed by President Clinton on November 15, 1996.

———, "Administration White Paper on Communications Act Reforms," January 1994.

———, Executive Order 12864 of September 15, 1993, *United States Advisory Council on the National Information Infrastructure.*

———, "Fact Sheet: Information Infrastructure Task Force (IITF)," January 13, 1995.

———, *Information Infrastructure Task Force Fact Sheet*, March 7, 1995.
———, *The National Information Infrastructure: Agenda for Action*, May 1994.
———, "95 Technology Administration Budget Highlights," February 1994.
———, "Presidential Memorandum on Encryption Export Policy," signed by President Clinton on November 15, 1996.
———, "Technology for Economic Growth: Progress Report," December 1993.
White House, Office of the Vice President, "Background on the Administration's Telecommunications Policy Reform Initiative," January 11, 1994.
———, "Internet II," October 15, 1996.
———, "Remarks by Vice President Gore at the Federal-State-Local Telcom Summit," January 9, 1995.

Index

About the Book

The Making of Telecommunications Policy examines the history, politics, and impact of telecommunications policy.

Beginning with a comparison of several alternate views of the future, Olufs explains how government action makes the widespread use of some new technologies more likely than others. He details the challenges that rapid advances in communications technologies pose for policymaking institutions and considers the ways that government responds to the ideological, economic, and political interests of industry, private advocacy groups, and individuals.

Olufs discussed the recent trend toward deregulation and provides a full analysis of the Telecommunications Act of 1996, including the politics of its enactment and its long-term implications for both industry and the daily lives of citizens.

Dick W. Olufs III is professor of political science at Pacific Lutheran University. He is coauthor (with David Schuman) of *Diversity of Campus*, *Public Administration in the United States*, and *A Preface to Politics*.